William Jackson Brodribb, Alfred John Church, the Younger Pliny

Select Letters - Latin Text, with English Notes

Edited by A.J. Church and W.J. Brodribb

William Jackson Brodribb, Alfred John Church, the Younger Pliny

Select Letters - Latin Text, with English Notes
Edited by A.J. Church and W.J. Brodribb

ISBN/EAN: 9783337142568

Printed in Europe, USA, Canada, Australia, Japan

Cover: Foto ©Andreas Hilbeck / pixelio.de

More available books at **www.hansebooks.com**

SELECT LETTERS

OF

PLINY THE YOUNGER

LATIN TEXT, WITH ENGLISH NOTES

Edited by

A. J. CHURCH, M.A.

PROFESSOR OF LATIN IN UNIVERSITY COLLEGE, LONDON

and

W. J. BRODRIBB, M.A.

LATE FELLOW OF ST. JOHN'S COLLEGE, CAMBRIDGE

NEW EDITION

LONDON

LONGMANS, GREEN, AND CO.

AND NEW YORK : 15 EAST 16th STREET

1888

PRINTED BY
SPOTTISWOODE AND CO., NEW-STREET SQUARE
LONDON

PREFACE

TO

THE SECOND EDITION.

———————

SOME of the faults which disfigured the First Edition
have, we trust, been removed from this. For assistance in this task, as well as for the uniform kindness
with which they have spoken of our work, we have to
thank many critics. We feel bound to make especial
mention of our obligation to Mr. J. R. KING, author
of a review in the *Academy*, and to Mr. J. B. MAYOR
for many valuable suggestions privately made.

A. J. C.
W. J. B.

HENLEY-ON-THAMES:
April 22, 1872.

PREFACE.

We have here made a Selection, amounting to about two-fifths of the whole, from the Epistles of the Younger Pliny. This selection will, we hope, be found useful as a class-book for the upper forms of schools. Pliny, indeed, has been strangely neglected by teachers and students of classical literature. His letters, though somewhat formal, having probably been written with some view to publication, are models in their way. They are in a very elegant style; they are the expression of a highly cultivated mind, and of a singularly refined and affectionate disposition, and their subject-matter is often of the highest interest, especially as showing to us that better side of Roman life under the Empire which indeed it would not be easy to find pourtrayed elsewhere. Difficulties, sometimes considerable, are to be found in them, but they have the advantage of being free from the recondite allusions and the obscurities, often intentional, with which the letters of Cicero are crowded. The only objection that may fairly be made to them—namely, that their Latinity is not always of the purest type, we have endeavoured to obviate by pointing out such words and phrases as seem to differ from the usage of the Augustan writers. On the other hand must be considered the invaluable assistance which the 'modern' tone of Pliny's thoughts will give to the young student in the task of finding Latin equivalents for his own language. The value of his descriptions of scenery, for instance, has long been recognised by masters of the craft of Latin prose writing.

We have divided the Select Letters into five sections, according to the topics of which they treat, and, wherever the subject-matter admitted of it, have arranged them in chronological order.

Our text is, in the main, that of Keil. We have derived great help in putting together our notes from the edition of Doring.

ALFRED J. CHURCH
W. J. BRODRIBB.

HENLEY-ON-THAMES :
Dec. 22, 1870.

INTRODUCTION.

Of the younger Pliny we know really nothing but what he himself tells us in his correspondence, and in the Panegyric addressed by him to Trajan. From these we are able to draw a general outline of his life, and to form an adequate conception of his tastes and character. The few allusions to him which are to be found in the writers of the time are so slight as to add nothing to our acquaintance with him. We have quoted the passages in which these allusions occur at the end of this Introduction.

His full name was Caius Plinius Caecilius Secundus. The second of these names was derived from his uncle and adopting father Plinius, author of the Natural History. The third, the 'nomen gentile,' was that of his father. He was well-born. The 'Caecilia gens' to which he belonged, though originally plebeian, was an ancient and honourable house.

Novum Comum (Como on Lake Como) was the place of his birth. This seems to be a matter of almost absolute certainty. There is only one passage in his letters (VI. 34) which lends the slightest countenance to the belief that Verona was his native town. The expression 'Veronenses nostri,' which he there uses, implies indeed close local ties with Verona, but can hardly be set against the facts that his family had estates at Comum, that he himself had several villas there, that he invariably speaks of the place with

special affection, and that in inscriptions which have
been found on the spot the names of the Plinii frequently occur. A writer of the fifth century, Aurelius
Cassiodorus, assumes him to have been a Novocomensis, following no doubt a trustworthy tradition of
his time.

The year of his birth may be inferred from a statement which he makes in the famous letter describing
the eruption of Vesuvius and the circumstances of his
uncle's death (A. III. 5). He was then, he says, in
his eighteenth year, and the event in question happened in A.D. 79. Consequently A.D. 62, the seventh
year of Nero's reign, was the date of his birth. He
lost his father when he was quite a child, and was then
adopted by his uncle the elder Pliny, from whom he
derived his ' cognomen ' Secundus. It was a pleasure
to him, as we gather from his letters, to dwell on the
recollections of his youth. For his uncle and adopted
father he felt the highest admiration, and under the
influence of his example acquired a sincere love of
letters, and as great industry as weak health would
permit in their pursuit.

His education was conducted under the most favourable auspices. Verginius Rufus, who had twice declined the empire, and who recalled to men's minds the
patriotism of better days, was his guardian, and seems
to have introduced him to public life (A. VIII. 8).
Senecio, Arulenus Rusticus, and Helvidius, names
commemorated by Tacitus, were among his youthful
friends. He studied oratory under the guidance of
the two most fashionable teachers of the time, Quintilian, and Nicetes Sacerdos (VI. 6). Stoic influences
appear to have had a large share in forming his mind.
When a mere lad (B. XX. 5) he attended the lectures

of the eminent Stoic philosopher, Musonius Rufus.
This, we may presume, was his first introduction to
philosophical studies. He also attempted poetry, for
which, he says (VII. 4), he had such a liking that
when a boy of fourteen he wrote a Greek tragedy.
If, however, we may judge from a specimen of his
verses given us in the same letter, his success as a
poet must have been very moderate. In his twentieth
year he had to serve as a 'tribunus' with the Roman
army in Syria. Here he had opportunities, of which
he conscientiously availed himself, of carrying on his
education under the instruction of Euphrates and
Artemidorus, Stoic professors whom he much admired
and esteemed (B. XX. XXI.) He was, it would
appear, from his own account (B. III. 8), at this early
age, a sufficiently accomplished orator to speak in important causes.

On his return from Syria he found Domitian emperor. During this reign he attained the quaestorship
(VII. 16) and the praetorship (B. XX.), the latter
office probably in A.D. 93, the year of the expulsion of
the philosophers and professors from Rome by an imperial edict. He himself appears about the same time
to have temporarily retired from public life and to
have passed the last three years of Domitian's reign
in comparative seclusion. The tyrant took umbrage
at this, and had his life been prolonged, Pliny would
have been added to his other victims. An information
against him by one of the worst of the 'delatores,'
Metius Carus, was actually found among the papers
of the deceased emperor (E. XIV. 14).

Domitian was succeeded by Nerva in A.D. 96. The
new and better age brought with it brilliant prospects
of advancement for Pliny. The retirement of the

last three years had the effect of quickening the energy with which he now entered on his profession as an advocate. His letters imply that he was diligent and successful. Several of the causes in which he was engaged involved the fortunes of some of the wealthiest and most unscrupulous adherents of the late *régime*, and demanded courage as well as ability. We may excuse the self-complacent vanity with which Pliny often dwells on these memorable occasions. Cicero, it would seem, was the model he regularly proposed to himself for imitation. Sometimes he would emulate the eloquence of Demosthenes, and was frequently compared to him by his contemporaries (B. I.). He soon became sufficiently distinguished to number among his friends Tacitus and the best literary men of his time. His success at the bar paved the way to public honours. Trajan recognised his merits and conferred on him a series of distinctions. He became augur, praefect of the agrarium, and attained the consulate in A.D. 100. It was as consul that in conformity with the practice of the time he composed the Panegyricus addressed to Trajan. In A.D. 103 he was appointed pro-praetor of the Asiatic province of Pontica. Why he was styled pro-praetor and not proconsul, as were former governors of that province, has been discussed in Masson's very elaborate life published at Amsterdam in 1709. The difference of the titles appears from one of the letters to Trajan (X. 77) to have implied something more than that Pliny's appointment was conferred by the emperor and not by the senate, although we cannot define in what this consisted. He was pro-praetor with consular power, and is thus described in an extant inscription. Nearly two years were passed by him in his province. It was

here that he had occasion to write the famous letter in
which he records the impressions made on him by his
contact with the Christian Church.   We then lose
sight of him.   Of the time and circumstances of his
death we know nothing.   We may gather from his
letters that he lived to the age of forty-six, but the
various accounts of the year of his death differ widely
and are quite untrustworthy.   They vary, in fact,
between A.D. 107 and 117.

Pliny was twice married, but left no children.   His
second wife, Calpurnia, seems to have been well suited
to his companionship, and he always speaks of her
with great esteem and affection.   She was a graceful
and accomplished woman, and had a genuine sympathy
with her husband's professional life, and with his literary tastes and pursuits.

His extant works consist of ten books of letters, and
of the Panegyricus.   The latter, as has been already
said, is addressed to the emperor Trajan, and as might
be expected from the occasion of its delivery is written
in an adulatory tone, which certainly does not exalt its
amiable author in our estimation.   It would, however,
we think, be utterly unjust to infer from it anything
like a spirit of really base servility.   Pliny, after all,
was only, in all probability, employing the conventional language of the age, and he may well have sin-
cerely regarded Trajan as an eminent benefactor to
the empire and to the world.   The Panegyricus is of
some value to us, from its allusions to himself, and to
the circumstances of the period.   The letters of the
first nine books are addressed to a wide circle of
friends, among whom were some of the best and most
distinguished men of the time.   The tenth book is
made up of his correspondence with Trajan during

the period of his provincial governorship. His letters were probably intended for publication, and they undoubtedly deserved it. They are full of interest and instruction, and, as this volume shows, embrace a great diversity of subjects. Some of the most characteristic features of the age are vividly brought before us, and light is frequently thrown on aspects of Roman life which would otherwise have been hidden in almost total darkness. We are introduced to almost every phase of the best society of Rome. We get glimpses into the life and habits of the Roman aristocracy, and learn how Pliny and his friends passed their leisure when in the retirement of their country houses. But for these letters we should know next to nothing of Tacitus, of Silius Italicus, and indeed generally of the men of letters of the time. We are made acquainted with some of the most famous Greek rhetoricians, a class of men, it would seem, to whom the literary circles of Rome looked up with respectful admiration. We have detailed accounts of great public prosecutions, and allusions to the courts of law and eminent advocates. The character of Regulus, one of the wretched hangers-on of the court of Domitian, is amusingly illustrated by a number of ludicrous anecdotes. The story of the haunted house at Athens reminds us of the conventional ghost story with which we are all familiar. The descriptions of scenery and of rural life, and the evident pleasure with which they are dwelt upon, seem strikingly to anticipate modern tastes and sentiments. In the letters, too, which testify to Pliny's humane considerateness towards his slaves and dependants there is a distinct approach to the modern spirit. We see that there was much that was good and noble in an age which we commonly associate with the ideas of decline and decadence. The very prevalence of suicide, to which the pages of Tacitus and Pliny continually bear witness, though, of course, it had its weak and morbid side, was not simply the offspring of moral degeneracy, but was partially due to feelings and convictions which we are obliged to respect. The higher aspects of the time, both intellectual and moral, are brought before us in these letters with an abundance of valuable illustration.

Pliny's correspondence has been truly said * to give us the fullest and fairest portrait we possess of a Roman gentleman. He was, as we have seen, a gentleman by birth and education, and he had, in an eminent degree, as his letters testify, the tastes and habits of a gentleman. Of the advantages of wealth and position with which he began life, he appears to have made a good use. He was an exceedingly industrious man, although he says that, compared with his uncle, he regarded himself as a mere idler. (B. XI.) The recreations he chiefly allowed himself were of a more or less intellectual kind; and even when he indulged in the pleasures of the chase, he tells us, with something very like a touch of pedantry, that he often had his writing materials with him. For the coarser amusements of the time, the gladiatorial shows, and even the chariot races of the circus, he had a positive distaste. He loathed and despised the vulgar display of wealth which in an age so devoted to material enjoyments was often carried to a ludicrous excess by rich and uncultivated *parvenus*. At the same time he seems to have taken the utmost pains to encourage better and purer tastes, and to inspire others with his own love of learning and refinement. It is pleasant to

* Merivale's *History of the Romans under the Empire*, ch. lxiv.

find a wealthy Roman gentleman endeavouring to dif-
fuse education and culture, and with an enlightened
liberality, worthy of a better time, contributing largely
to the establishment of a school at his native Comum,
and presenting the same town with a library (B. II. ;
D. II.)

The chief blemish in Pliny's character, as in that of
Cicero, whom he emulated in letters, was an anxious
desire of fame which often betrayed him into a petty
vanity occasionally quite exceeding the limits of good
sense and good taste.   There is a marked tone of self-
complacency in the letters which tell us of any generous or noble action.   He does not in the least conceal
his gratification at receiving a complimentary poem
from Martial, even though the poet was enough of a
flatterer to praise a Domitian with extravagant eulogy
(B. XIII.)   He naively confesses (D. XII.) that he
feels a pleasure in the acknowledgment and recognition
of his good actions.   Following the precedent of
Cicero's request to Lucceius, he does not hesitate, in a
letter addressed to Tacitus (A. V.), to express a hope
that his name will find a place in the historian's works,
and he even singles out an incident in his career which
he anxiously desires may be commemorated.   Still
more difficult is it to understand how he could have
seriously persuaded himself that his attempts at poetry,
the feebleness of which must have been apparent to
the least discerning of critics, deserved even so much
as mention.   While, however, we cannot acquit him of
excessive vanity and self-consciousness, we must feel
there is something singularly attractive in his sweetness and amiability, above all, in his genuine sympathy
with cultivated tastes.   To reproach him with a want
of devotion to the old ideal of republican days, is, we

think, to misunderstand the man and his age. We may well suppose that he regarded a true restoration of Roman freedom as hopelessly unattainable, and that with his great contemporary, Tacitus, he had reconciled himself to the imperialism of a Trajan as the most promising combination of liberty and order which the circumstances of the time allowed.

The following passages contain all the extant allusions to Pliny:—

> Nec doctum satis, et parum severum,
> Sed non rusticulum nimis libellum,
> Facundo mea Plinio Thallia
> Ii perfer. MARTIAL, x. 19.

Quattuor sunt genera dicendi; copiosum, in quo Cicero dominatur; breve, in quo Sallustius regnat; siccum, quod Frontoni adscribitur; pingue et floridum, in quo Plinius Secundus quondam et nunc nullo veterum minor Symmachus luxuriatur.—MACROBIUS (*Saturn.*), v. 1.

Epistolas omnes, retractatis exemplaribus enucleatisque, uno volumine includam, Q. Symmachi rotunditatem, C. Plinii disciplinam maturitatemque, vestigiis praesumtuosis insecuturus.—SIDONIUS APOLLINARIS, i. 1.

Si reare quemquam mortalium (cui tamen sermocinari Latialiter cordi est) non pavere, quum in examen aurium tuarum, quippe scriptus, adducitur, tuarum, inquam, aurium, quarum peritiae, si me decursorum ad hoc aevi temporum praerogativa non obruat, nec Frontonianae gravitatis aut ponderis Apuleiani fulmen aequiparem, cui Varrones vel Atacinus vel Terentius, Plinii vel avunculus vel Secundus, compositi impraesentiarum rusticabuntur.—*Idem.* iv. 3.

Ego Plinio, ut discipulus, adsurgo.—*Idem.* iv. 22.

C. Plinius pro Accia Variola plus gloriae de centumvirali suggestu domum retulit, quam quum Marco Ulpio, incomparabili principi, comparabilem panegyricum dixit.—*Idem.* viii. 10.

Celsus et Crispinus. His consulibus Plinius Secundus Novocomensis orator et historicus insignis habetur, cujus ingenii plurima opera exstant.—AURELIUS CASSIODORUS, *in Chronico sub Trajano.*

Section A.

Letters Referring to Matters

of

Historical and Political Interest.

C. PLINI SECUNDI

EPISTOLAE SELECTAE.

—●—

A. I. (iii. 16.)

[Pliny here relates some of the noble sayings and deeds of
Arria, wife of Caecina Paetus, who was put to death by the
Emperor Claudius, A.D. 42, as having been concerned in the revolt of Scribonianus (Sueton. *Claudius*, 13). Arria's daughter
of the same name became the wife of Paetus Thrasea, the
circumstances of whose death under Nero, A.D. 67, are related
by Tacitus (*Ann.* xvi. 34). Fannia, Pliny's informant, was the
daughter of this Thrasea, and the wife of Helvidius Priscus
(E. XII.)]

C. PLINIUS NEPOTI SUO S.

ADNOTASSE videor, facta dictaque virorum femina-
rumque illustrium alia clariora esse, alia maiora. Con- 2
firmata est opinio mea hesterno Fanniae sermone.
Neptis haec Arriae illius, quae marito et solatium mortis et exemplum fuit. Multa referebat aviae suae non
minora hoc, sed obscuriora : quae tibi existimo tam
mirabilia legenti fore, quam mihi audienti fuerunt.
Aegrotabat Caecina Paetus, maritus eius ; aegrotabat 3
et filius, uterque mortifere, ut videbatur : filius decessit, eximia pulchritudine, pari verecundia, et parentibus non minus ob alia carus, quam quod filius erat.
Huic illa ita funus paravit, ita duxit exsequias, ut 4
ignoraret maritus. Quin immo, quoties cubiculum

B 2

eius intraret, vivere filium, atque etiam commodiorem
esse simulabat, ac persaepe interroganti, quid ageret
puer, respondebat, *Bene quievit, libenter cibum sumpsit.*
5 Deinde, cum diu cohibitae lacrymae vincerent pro-
rumperentque, egrediebatur.   Tunc se dolori dabat.
Satiata, siccis oculis, composito vultu redibat, tanquam
6 orbitatem foris reliquisset.   Praeclarum quidem illud
eiusdem, ferrum stringere, perfodere pectus, extrahere
pugionem, porrigere marito, addere vocem immortalem
ac paene divinam, PAETE, NON DOLET.   Sed tamen
ista facienti, ista dicenti gloria et aeternitas ante oculos
erant : quo maius est, sine praemio aeternitatis, sine
praemio gloriae abdere lacrymas, operire luctum,
7 amissoque filio, matrem adhuc agere.   Scribonianus
arma in Illyrico contra Claudium moverat : fuerat
Paetus in partibus ; occiso Scriboniano, Romam trahe-
8 batur.   Erat adscensurus navem : Arria milites orabat,
ut simul imponeretur.   *Nempe enim*, inquit, *daturi
estis consulari viro servulos aliquos, quorum e manu
cibum capiat, a quibus vestiatur, a quibus calcietur:*
9 *omnia sola praestabo.*   Non impetravit.   Conduxit
piscatoriam nauculam, ingensque navigium minimo
secuta est.   Eadem apud Claudium uxori Scribo-
niani, cum illa profiteretur indicium, *Ego*, inquit, *te
audiam, cuius in gremio Scribonianus occisus est,
et vivis ?*   Ex quo manifestum est, ei consilium pul-
10 cherrimae mortis non subitum fuisse.   Quin etiam,
cum Thrasea, gener eius, deprecaretur, ne mori per-
geret, interque alia dixisset, *Vis ergo filiam tuam,
si mihi pereundum fuerit, mori mecum ?* respondit : *Si
tam diu tantaque concordia vixerit tecum, quam ego
11 cum Paeto, volo.*   Auxerat hoc responso curam suorum : attentius custodiebatur : sensit, et, *Nihil agitis,*
inquit : *potestis enim efficere, ut male moriar ; ut non
12 moriar, non potestis.*   Dum haec dicit, exsiluit cathedra,
adversoque parieti caput ingenti impetu impegit, et
corruit.   Focillata, *Dixeram*, inquit, *vobis, inventuram
me, quamlibet duram, ad mortem viam, si vos facilem
13 negassetis.*   Videturne haec tibi maiora illo : *Paete,
non dolet,* ad quod per haec perventum est ?   cum

interim illud quidem ingens fama, haec nulla circumfert. Unde colligitur, quod initio dixi, alia esse
clariora, alia maiora. Vale.

A. II. (vi. 16.)

[In this and the following letter Pliny records, for the information of Tacitus, who was then collecting materials for
his History, his recollections of the great eruption of Vesuvius
(August 24, A.D. 79). Pliny was then in his eighteenth year,
and was residing in the neighbourhood with his mother and
his uncle, the elder Pliny, who was in command of the fleet
off Misenum. The first letter is chiefly occupied with a detailed narrative of the elder Pliny's death, caused as it was by
his philosophic anxiety to investigate the phenomena of the
eruption ; the second gives the writer's own impression of the
scene. No more than a passing allusion is made to the destruction of the two cities, Pompeii and Herculaneum, the chief
event with which we are accustomed to connect the eruption.
For an account of this we have to go to Dion Cassius.

Vesuvius had been inactive from the earliest historical
times. Nothing more than vague traditions testified to its
volcanic character.

These letters are all the more valuable because that portion
of the History in which Tacitus related these events is lost.]

C. PLINIUS TACITO SUO S.

Petis, ut tibi avunculi mei exitum scribam, quo verius tradere posteris possis. Gratias ago ; nam
video, morti eius, si celebretur a te, immortalem
gloriam esse propositam. Quamvis enim pulcherri- 2
marum clade terrarum, ut populi, ut urbes, memorabili
casu, quasi semper victurus, occiderit ; quamvis ipse
plurima opera et mansura condiderit : multum tamen
perpetuitati eius scriptorum tuorum aeternitas addet.
Equidem beatos puto, quibus deorum munere datum 3
est aut facere scribenda, aut scribere legenda ; beatissi-
mos vero, quibus utrumque. Horum in numero avunculus meus et suis libris et tuis erit. Quo libentius
suscipio, deposco etiam, quod iniungis. Erat Miseni, 4

classemque imperio praesens regebat. Nonum Kalend.
Septembres, hora fere septima, mater mea indicat ei,
apparere nubem inusitata et magnitudine et specie.
5 Usus ille sole, mox frigida, gustaverat iacens, stu-
debatque. Poscit soleas, adscendit locum, ex quo
maxime miraculum illud conspici poterat. Nubes
(incertum procul intuentibus, ex quo monte; Vesu-
vium fuisse postea cognitum est) oriebatur, cuius
similitudinem et formam non alia magis arbor, quam
6 pinus, expresserit. Nam longissimo velut trunco
elata in altum, quibusdam ramis diffundebatur: credo,
quia recenti spiritu evecta, deinde senescente eo destituta, aut etiam pondere suo victa, in latitudinem vanescebat: candida interdum, interdum sordida et macu-
7 losa, prout terram cineremve sustulerat. · Magnum
propiusque noscendum, ut eruditissimo viro, visum.
Iubet Liburnicam aptari: mihi, si venire una vellem,
facit copiam. Respondi, studere me malle: et forte
8 ipse, quod scriberem, dederat. Egrediebatur domo:
accipit codicillos Rectinae Caesi Bassi imminenti periculo exterritae: nam villa eius subiacebat, nec ulla
nisi navibus fuga: ut se tanto discrimini eriperet,
9 orabat. Vertit ille consilium, et quod studioso animo
inchoaverat, obit maximo. Deducit quadriremes; adscendit ipse non Rectinae modo, sed multis (erat enim
10 frequens amoenitas orae) laturus auxilium. Properat
illuc, unde alii fugiunt; rectumque cursum, recta
gubernacula in periculum tenet, adeo solutus metu, ut
omnes illius mali motus, omnes figuras, ut deprehende-
11 rat oculis, dictaret enotaretque. Iam navibus cinis
incidebat, quo propius accederent, calidior et densior;
iam pumices etiam, nigrique et ambusti et fracti igne
lapides: iam vadum subitum, ruinaque montis litora
obstantia. Cunctatus paullum, an retro flecteret, mox
gubernatori, ut ita faceret monenti, *Fortes,* inquit,
12 *fortuna iuvat: Pomponianum pete.* Stabiis erat, di-
remtus sinu medio. Nam sensim circumactis cur-
vatisque litoribus mare infunditur. Ibi, quamquam
nondum periculo appropinquante, conspicuo tamen, et,
cum cresceret, proximo, sarcinas contulerat in naves,

certus fugae, si contrarius ventus resedisset: quo tunc
avunculus meus secundissimo invectus complectitur
trepidantem, consolatur, hortatur: utque timorem eius
sua securitate leniret, deferri se in balineum iubet;
lotus accubat, coenat, atque hilaris, aut, quod est aeque
magnum, similis hilari. Interim e Vesuvio monte 13
pluribus locis latissimae flammae altaque incendia re-
lucebant, quorum fulgor et claritas tenebris noctis
excitabatur. Ille, agrestium trepidatione ignes relictos
desertasque villas per solitudinem ardere, in remedium
formidinis dictitabat. Tum se quieti dedit, et quievit
verissimo quidem somno. Nam meatus animae, qui
illi propter amplitudinem corporis gravior et sonantior
erat, ab iis, qui limini obversabantur, audiebatur. Sed 14
area, ex qua diaeta adibatur, ita iam cinere mixtisque
pumicibus oppleta surrexerat, ut, si longior in cubiculo
mora, exitus negaretur. Excitatus procedit, seque
Pomponiano ceterisque, qui pervigilaverant, reddit.
In commune consultant, an intra tecta subsistant, an 15
in aperto vagentur. Nam crebris vastisque tremoribus
tecta nutabant, et quasi emota sedibus suis, nunc
huc nunc illuc abire aut referri videbantur. Sub divo 16
rursus, quamquam levium exesorumque, pumicum
casus metuebatur. Quod tamen periculorum collatio
elegit. Et apud illum quidem ratio rationem, apud
alios timorem timor vicit. Cervicalia capitibus imposita linteis constringunt. Id munimentum adversus
decidentia fuit. Iam dies alibi, illic nox omnibus 17
noctibus nigrior densiorque: quam tamen faces multae
variaque lumina solabantur. Placuit egredi in litus,
et e proximo adspicere, ecquid iam mare admitteret;
quod adhuc vastum et adversum permanebat. Ibi super 18
abiectum linteum recubans, semel atque iterum frigidam
poposcit, hausitque. Deinde flammae flammarumque
praenuntius odor sulfuris alios in fugam vertunt,
excitant illum. Innixus servulis duobus adsurrexit, 19
et statim concidit, ut ego colligo, crassiore caligine
spiritu obstructo, clausoque stomacho, qui illi natura
invalidus et angustus et frequenter aestuans erat. Ubi 20
dies redditus (is ab eo, quem novissime viderat, tertius)

corpus inventum est integrum, illaesum opertumque,
21 ut fuerat indutus: habitus corporis quiescenti, quam
defuncto, similior. Interim Miseni ego et mater. Sed
nihil ad historiam; nec tu aliud, quam de exitu eius,
22 scire voluisti. Finem ergo faciam. Unum adiiciam,
omnia me, quibus interfueram, quaeque statim, cum
maxime vera memorantur, audieram, persecutum. Tu
potissima excerpes. Aliud est enim epistolam, aliud
historiam, aliud amico, aliud omnibus scribere. Vale.

A. III. (vi. 20.)

PLINIUS CORNELIO TACITO SUO S.

Ais, te adductum literis, quas exigenti tibi de morte
avunculi mei scripsi, cupere cognoscere, quos ego
Miseni relictus (id enim ingressus abruperam) non
solum metus, verum etiam casus pertulerim.

*Quamquam animus meminisse horret, — —
incipiam.*

2 Profecto avunculo, ipse reliquum tempus studiis
(ideo enim remanseram) impendi. Mox balineum,
3 coena, somnus inquietus et brevis. Praecesserat per
multos dies tremor terrae, minus formidolosus, quia
Campaniae solitus. Illa vero nocte ita invaluit, ut
4 non moveri omnia, sed verti crederentur. Irrumpit
cubiculum meum mater: surgebam, invicem si qui-
esceret, excitaturus. Resedimus in area domus, quae
5 mare a tectis modico spatio dividebat. Dubito, constantiam vocare an imprudentiam debeam: agebam
enim duodevicesimum annum. Posco librum Titi
Livi, et quasi per otium lego, atque etiam, ut coeperam, excerpo. Ecce, amicus avunculi, qui nuper ad
eum ex Hispania venerat, ut me et matrem sedentes,
me vero etiam legentem videt, illius patientiam, securi-
tatem meam corripit: nihilo segnius ego intentus in
6 librum. Iam hora diei prima, et adhuc dubius et
quasi languidus dies. Iam quassatis circumiacentibus

tectis, quamquam in aperto loco, angusto tamen, magnus
et certus ruinae metus. Tum demum excedere oppido 7
visum. Sequitur vulgus attonitum; quodque in pavore
simile prudentiae, alienum consilium suo praefert, in-
gentique agmine abeuntes premit et impellit. Egressi 8
tecta consistimus. Multa ibi miranda, multas formi-
dines patimur. . Nam vehicula, quae produci iusse-
ramus, quamquam in planissimo campo, in contrarias
partes agebantur, ac ne lapidibus quidem fulta in eodem
vestigio quiescebant. Praeterea mare in se resorberi, 9
et tremore terrae quasi repelli videbamus. Certe pro-
cesserat litus, multaque animalia maris siccis arenis
detinebat. Ab altero latere nubes atra et horrenda,
ignei spiritus tortis vibratisque discursibus rupta, in
longas flammarum figuras dehiscebat: fulguribus illae
et similes et maiores erant. Tum vero ille idem ex 10
Hispania amicus, acrius et instantius, *Si frater*, inquit,
tuus, avunculus vivit, vult esse vos salvos: si periit,
superstites voluit: proinde quid cessatis evadere? Re-
spondimus, non commissuros nos, ut de salute eius
incerti, nostrae consuleremus. Non moratus ultra, 11
proripit se, effusoque cursu periculo aufertur. Nec
multo post illa nubes descendere in terras, operire
maria. Cinxerat Capreas et absconderat: Miseni
quod procurrit, abstulerat. Tum mater orare, hortari, 12
iubere, quoquo modo fugerem; posse enim iuvenem:
se et annis et corpore gravem bene morituram, si mihi
causa mortis non fuisset. Ego contra, salvum me,
nisi una, non futurum: dein manum eius amplexus,
addere gradum cogo. Paret aegre, incusatque se,
quod me moretur. Iam cinis; adhuc tamen rarus. 13
Respicio; densa caligo tergis imminebat, quae nos,
torrentis modo infusā terrae, sequebatur. *Deflectamus,*
inquam, *dum videmus, ne in via strati comitantium turba*
in tenebris obteramur. Vix consederamus, et nox, non 14
qualis illunis aut nubila, sed qualis in locis clausis
lumine exstincto. Audires ululatus feminarum, infan-
tium quiritatus, clamores virorum. Alii parentes, alii
liberos, alii coniuges vocibus requirebant, vocibus
noscitabant. Ili suum casum, illi suorum miserabantur.

15 Erant qui metu mortis mortem precarentur. Multi ad deos manus tollere: plures, nusquam iam deos ullos, aeternamque illam et novissimam noctem mundo interpretabantur. Nec defuerunt, qui fictis mentitisque terroribus vera pericula augerent. Aderant, qui Miseni, illud ruisse, illud ardere, falso, sed credentibus, 16 nuntiabant. Paullum reluxit; quod non dies nobis, sed adventantis ignis indicium videbatur. Et ignis quidem longius substitit: tenebrae rursus, cinis rursus multus et gravis. Hunc identidem adsurgentes excutiebamus; operti alioqui atque etiam oblisi pondere 17 essemus. Possem gloriari, non gemitum mihi, non vocem parum fortem in tantis periculis excidisse, nisi me cum omnibus, omnia mecum perire, misero, magno 18 tamen mortalitatis solatio credidissem. Tandem illa caligo tenuata quasi in fumum nebulamve decessit: mox dies verus, sol etiam effulsit, luridus tamen, qualis esse, quum deficit, solet. Occursabant trepidantibus adhuc oculis mutata omnia, altoque cinere, tanquam 19 nive, obducta. Regressi Misenum, curatis utcunque corporibus, suspensam dubiamque noctem spe ac metu exegimus. Metus praevalebat: nam et tremor terrae perseverabat, et plerique lymphati terrificis vaticina-20 tionibus et sua et aliena mala ludificabantur. Nobis tamen ne tunc quidem, quamquam et expertis periculum, et exspectantibus, abeundi consilium, donec de avunculo nuntius. Haec, nequaquam historia digna, non scripturus leges, et tibi scilicet, qui requisisti, imputabis, si digna ne epistola quidem videbuntur. Vale.

A. IV. (iv. 11.)

[The incident which is the subject of this letter is noticed by Suetonius in his life of Domitian, ch. viii. Domitian had thought fit to revive the ancient punishment of unchaste vestals, and Cornelia, the chief of that college, who, it seems, had been accused of unchastity more than once and acquitted, was finally convicted and buried alive. Her guilt, however, at least in this particular case, was a matter of doubt. It was

believed on the strength of the confession of Licinianus, a
senator, who, being suspected by the Emperor of having in-
trigued with her, admitted, from the fear of worse consequences, that such was the case. It appears from Suetonius
and the present letter that her other alleged paramours had
been flogged to death in the *comitium.* The circumstances of
Cornelia's horrible death are told in detail in this letter.

Licinianus was allowed to retire into exile, and by the
clemency of Nerva was permitted to live in Sicily, where he
maintained himself by the profession of rhetoric.]

C. PLINIUS MINICIANO SUO S.

Audistine Valerium Licinianum in Sicilia profiteri?
Nondum te puto audisse; est enim recens nuntius.
Praetorius hic modo inter eloquentissimos causarum
actores habebatur: nunc eo decidit, ut exul de sena-
tore, rhetor de oratore fieret. Itaque ipse in praefa- 2
tione dixit dolenter et graviter: *Quos tibi, Fortuna,
ludos facis? Facis enim ex professoribus senatores, ex
senatoribus professores.* Cui sententiae tantum bilis,
tantum amaritudinis inest, ut mihi videatur ideo pro-
fessus, ut hoc diceret. Idem, cum Graeco pallio 3
amictus intrasset, (carent enim togae iure, quibus aqua
et igni interdictum est) postquam se composuit, circumspexitque habitum suum: *Latine,* inquit, *declama-
turus sum.* Dices, *tristia et miseranda* : dignum tamen 4
illum, quia haec ipsa studia incesti scelere maculaverit.
Confessus est quidem incestum: sed incertum, utrum 5
quia verum erat, an quia graviora metuebat, si negasset.
Fremebat enim Domitianus, aestuabatque ingenti invidia destitutus. Nam cum Corneliam, vestalium maxi- 6
mam, defodere vivam cupisset, ut qui illustrari seculum
suum eiusmodi exemplis arbitraretur, Pontificis Maximi
iure, seu potius immanitate tyranni, licentia domini,
reliquos pontifices non in Regiam, sed in Albanam
villam convocavit. Nec minore scelere, quam quod
ulcisci videbatur, absentem inauditamque damnavit
incesti, cum ipse fratris filiam incesto non pollu-
isset solum, verum etiam occidisset: nam vidua ab-
ortu periit. Missi statim pontifices, qui defodiendam 7

necandamque curarent.   Illa nunc ad Vestam, nunc ad
ceteros deos manus tendens, multa, sed hoc frequentissime, clamitabat: *Me Caesar incestum putat, qua sacra*
8 *faciente vicit, triumphavit.*   Blandiens haec, an irridens; ex fiducia sui, an ex contemptu Principis dixerit, dubium est.   Dixit, donec ad supplicium, nescio
9 an innocens, certe tanquam innocens, ducta est.   Quin
etiam, cum in illud subterraneum cubiculum demit-
teretur, haesissetque descendenti stola, vertit se ac
recollegit; cumque ei carnifex manum daret, aversata
est, et resiluit, foedumque contagium, quasi plane a
casto puroque corpore, novissima sanctitate reiecit,
omnibusque numeris pudoris πολλὴν πρόνοιαν εἶχεν
10 εὐσχήμως πεσεῖν.   Praeterea Celer, eques Romanus,
cui Cornelia obiiciebatur, cum in comitio virgis caede-
retur, in hac voce perstiterat: *Quid feci? Nihil feci.*
11 Ardebat ergo Domitianus et crudelitatis et iniquitatis
infamia.   Arripit Licinianum, quod in agris suis oc-
cultasset Corneliae libertam.   Ille ab iis, quibus erat
curae, praemonetur, si comitium et virgas pati nollet,
ad confessionem confugeret, quasi ad veniam; fecit.
12 Locutus est pro absente Herennius Senecio tale
quiddam, quale est illud, Κεῖται Πάτροκλος.   Ait
enim: *Ex advocato nuntius factus sum.   Recessit*
13 *Licinianus.*   Gratum hoc Domitiano, adeo quidem, ut
gaudio proderetur, diceretque, *Absolvit nos Licinianus.*
Adiecit etiam, non esse verecundiae eius instandum:
ipsi vero permisit, si qua posset, ex rebus suis raperet,
antequam bona publicarentur; exsilium molle, velut
14 praemium, dedit.   Ex quo tamen postea clementia
divi Nervae translatus est in Siciliam, ubi nunc pro-
15 fitetur, seque de fortuna praefationibus vindicat.   Vides,
quam obsequenter parcam tibi, qui non solum res
urbanas, verum etiam peregrinas tam sedulo scribo, ut
altius repetam.   Et sane putabam te, quia tunc abfuisti,
nihil aliud de Liciniano audisse, quam relegatum ob
incestum.   Summam enim rerum nuntiat fama, non
16 ordinem.   Mercor, ut vicissim, quid in oppido tuo,
quid in finitimis agatur (solent enim notabilia quaedam
incidere) perscribas: denique quidquid voles, dum-

modo non minus longa epistola nuntia. Ego non paginas tantum, sed etiam versus syllabasque numerabo. Vale.

A. V. (vii. 33.)

[Pliny hopes that Tacitus, who was then engaged on the composition of his History, which he is sure was destined to be an immortal work, would not fail to mention him. He proceeds to relate an incident which had occurred in Domitian's reign, on his connection with which the Emperor Nerva had paid him a very high compliment. Pliny had been appointed by the Senate with Herennius Senecio to plead the cause of the province of Baetica against its governor, Baebius Massa. The incident in question, which Pliny hopes that Tacitus will record, arose out of this trial. There is a very singular letter of Cicero's (*Epp. ad Fam.* v. 12), which bears a striking resemblance to this epistle. In it he asks his old friend and neighbour, the historian Lucceius, to devote a separate work to the achievements of his consulate, and even to magnify them at the expense of truth. Pliny seems to allude to this strange display of vanity at the close of this letter.]

C. PLINIUS TACITO SUO S.

Auguror, nec me fallit augurium, historias tuas immortales futuras : quo magis illis (ingenue fatebor) inseri cupio. Nam si esse nobis curæ solet, ut facies 2 nostra ab optimo quoque artifice exprimatur, nonne debemus optare, ut operibus similis tui scriptor praedicatorque contingat ? Demonstro ergo, quamquam 3 diligentiam tuam fugere non possit, cum sit in publicis actis, demonstro tamen, quo magis credas, iucundum mihi futurum, si factum meum, cuius gratia periculo crevit, tuo ingenio, tuo testimonio ornaveris. Dederat 4 me senatus cum Herennio Senecione advocatum provinciae Baeticae contra Baebium Massam, damnatoque Massa, censuerat, ut bona eius publice custodirentur. Senecio, cum explorasset, consules postulationibus vacaturos, convenit me, et, *Qua concordia*, inquit, *iniunctam nobis accusationem exsecuti sumus, hac*

adeamus consules, petamusque, ne bona dissipari sinant,
5 *quorum esse in custodia debent.* Respondi, *Quum simus
advocati a senatu dati, dispice num peractas putes
partes nostras, senatus cognitione finita.* Et ille, *Tu,
quem voles, tibi terminum statues, cui nulla cum provincia necessitudo, nisi ex beneficio tuo, et hoc recenti:*
6 *ipse et natus ibi, et quaestor in ea fui.* Tum ego, *Si
fixum tibi istud ac deliberatum, sequar te, ut, si qua*
7 *ex hoc invidia erit, non tantum tua.* Venimus ad
consules, dicit Senecio, quae res ferebat: aliqua sub-
iungo. Vixdum conticueramus, et Massa questus, *Sene-
cionem non advocati fidem, sed inimici amaritudinem*
8 *implesse,* impietatis reum postulat. Horror omnium:
ego autem, *Vereor,* inquam, *clarissimi consules, ne mihi
Massa silentio suo praevaricationem obiecerit, quod
non et me reum postulavit.* Quae vox et statim ex-
9 cepta, et postea multo sermone celebrata est. Divus
quidem Nerva (nam privatus quoque attendebat his,
quae recte in publico fierent) missis ad me gravissimis
literis, non mihi solum, verum etiam seculo est gratula-
tus, cui exemplum (sic enim scripsit) simile antiquis
10 contigisset. Haec, utcunque se habent, notiora, clariora,
maiora tu facies: quamquam non exigo, ut excedas
actae rei modum. Nam nec historia debet egredi
veritatem, et honeste factis veritas sufficit. Vale.

A. VI. (ix. 13.)

[This long letter gives us a detailed account of a memorable
proceeding which Pliny looked back upon with peculiar
pleasure, and which, it appears, he had made the subject of
one of his works. Among the victims of Domitian's capricious cruelty was Helvidius, the son of the famous Helvidius
Priscus, son-in law of Thrasea, and continually mentioned by
Tacitus. The father was put to death by Vespasian, the son
by Domitian, on the accusation of Publicius Certus, who, as
well as Helvidius, was a senator. Pliny, on the death of
Domitian, resolved to avenge him, chiefly, as he says, on
public grounds. Accordingly, on the accession of Nerva, A.D.

99, he impeached Publicius before the senate. It seems to have been a hazardous experiment. Pliny represents that he was at first assailed with angry questions and remarks. The accused was *praefectus aerarii* and was soon to be consul ; he had besides a host of influential friends. For his counsel he had Veiento, notorious for his informations under Domitian, still powerful for evil, and the intimate friend of the Emperor Nerva, as we may infer from A. VII. But the senate would not hear the defence. The case was at an end, and the accused, though he escaped actual punishment, was superseded in his office, and the consulship, to which he must have shortly risen, was refused him. Pliny considers that he gained his point. He subsequently published his speech, with many additions. Soon after its publication Certus died, and Pliny mentions the popular rumour, which represented him as imagining from that time that the image of his accuser, sword in hand, was continually before him.]

C. PLINIUS QUADRATO SUO S.

Quanto studiosius intentiusque legisti libros, quos de Helvidii ultione composui, tanto impensius postulas, ut perscribam tibi quaeque extra libros, quaeque circa libros, totum denique ordinem rei, cui per aetatem non interfuisti. Occiso Domitiano statui 2 mecum ac deliberavi, esse magnam pulchramque materiam insectandi nocentes, miseros vindicandi, se proferendi. Porro, inter multa scelera multorum, nullum atrocius videbatur, quam quod in senatu senator senatori, praetorius consulari, reo index manus intulisset. Fuerat alioqui mihi cum Helvidio amicitia, quanta potuerat esse cum eo, qui metu temporum nomen ingens paresque virtutes secessu tegebat. Fuerat cum Arria et Fannia : quarum altera Helvidii 3 noverca, altera mater novercae. Sed non ita me iura privata, ut publicum fas et indignitas facti et exempli ratio incitabat. Ac primis quidem diebus redditae 4 libertatis pro se quisque inimicos suos, dumtaxat minores, incondito turbidoque clamore postulaverant simul et oppresserant. Ego et modestius et constantius arbitratus immanissimum reum non communi temporum invidia, sed proprio crimine urgere, cum iam satis

ille primus impetus defremuisset, et languidior in dica
ira ad iustitiam redisset, quamquam tum maxime
tristis, amissa nuper uxore, mitto ad Anteiam, (nupta
haec Helvidio fuerat,) rogo ut veniat, quia me recens
5 adhuc luctus limine contineret. Ut venit, *Destinatum
est,* inquam *mihi, maritum tuum non inultum pati.
Nuntia Arriae et Fanniae;* (ab exsilio redierant :) *consule te, consule illas, an velitis adscribi facto, in quo ego
comite non egeo : sed non ita gloriae meae faverim, ut
6 vobis societate eius invideam.* Perfert Anteia mandata ;
nec illae morantur. Opportune senatus intra diem
tertium. Omnia ego semper ad Corellium retuli,
quem providentissimum aetatis nostrae sapientissi-
mumque cognovi : in hoc tamen contentus consilio
meo fui, veritus, ne vetaret : erat enim cunctantior
cautiorque. Sed non sustinui inducere in animum,
quo minus illi eodem die facturum me indicarem,
quod an facerem, non deliberabam, expertus usu, de
eo, quod destinaveris, non esse consulendos, quibus
7 consultis obsequi debeas. Venio in senatum : ius
dicendi peto : dico paullisper maximo adsensu. Ubi
coepi crimen attingere, reum destinare, (adhuc tamen
sine nomine) undique mihi reclamari. Alius : *Sciamus,
quis sit, de quo extra ordinem referas ;* alius : *Quis
est ante relationem reus ?* alius : *Salvi simus, qui su-
8 persumus.* Audio imperturbatus, interritus : tantum
susceptae rei honestas valet, tantum ad fiduciam vel
metum differt, nolint homines, quod facias, an non
probent. Longum est omnia, quae tunc hinc inde
9 iacta sunt, recensere. Novissime consul : *Secunde,
sententiae loco dices, si quid volueris. Permiseris,* inquam, *quod usque adhuc omnibus permisisti.* Resido :
10 aguntur alia. Interea me quidam ex consularibus
amicis secreto curatoque sermone, quasi nimis fortiter
incauteque progressum, corripit, revocat, monet, ut
desistam, adicit etiam *notabilem me futuris principibus.*
11 *Esto,* inquam, *dum malis.* Vix ille discesserat, rursus
alter : *Quid audes ? cur ruis ? quibus te periculis ob-
icis ? Quid praesentibus confidis, incertus futurorum ?
Lacessis hominem iam praefectum aerarii, et brevi*

consulem: praeterea qua gratia, quibus amicitiis fultum! Nominat quendam, qui tunc ad orientem amplissimum exercitum, non sine magnis dubiisque rumoribus, obtinebat. Ad haec ego: *Omnia praecepi,* [12] *atque animo mecum ante peregi: nec recuso, si ita casus attulerit, luere poenas ob honestissimum factum, dum flagitiosissimum ulciscor.* Iam censendi tempus. Dicit Domitius Apollinaris, consul designatus, dicit [13] Fabricius Veiento, Fabius Maximinus, Vettius Proculus, collega Publicii Certi, de quo agebatur, uxoris autem meae, quam amiseram, vitricus: post hos Ammius Flaccus. Omnes Certum, nondum a me nominatum, ut nominatum defendunt: crimenque quasi in medio relictum defensione suscipiunt. Quae praeterea [14] dixerint, non est necesse narrare; in libris habes. Sum enim cuncta ipsorum verbis persecutus. Dicunt contra Avidius Quietus, Cornutus Tertullus. Quietus: [15] *Iniquissimum esse, querelas dolentium excludi: ideoque Arriae et Fanniae ius querendi non auferendum: nec interesse, cuius ordinis quis sit, sed quam caussam habeat.* Cornutus: *Datum se a consulibus tutorem* [16] *Helvidi filiae, petentibus matre eius et vitrico: nunc quoque non sustinere deserere officii sui partes, in quo tamen, et suo dolori modum imponere, et optimarum feminarum perferre modestissimum adfectum: quas contentas esse, admonere senatum Publici Certi cruentae adulationis, et petere, si poena flagitii manifestissimi remittatur, nota certe quasi censoria inuratur.* Tum [17] Satrius Rufus medio ambiguoque sermone: *Puto,* inquit, *iniuriam factam Publicio Certo, si non absolvitur: nominatus est ab amicis Arriae et Fanniae, nominatus ab amicis suis. Nec debemus soliciti esse. Idem enim nos, qui bene sentimus de homine, indicaturi sumus: si innocens est, sicuti et spero et malo, donec aliquid probetur, credo, poteritis absolvere.* Haec illi, quo quis- [18] que ordine citabantur. Venitur ad me: consurgo, utor initio, quod in libro est, respondeo singulis. Mirum qua intentione, quibus clamoribus omnia exceperint, qui modo reclamabant. Tanta conversio vel negotii dignitatem, vel proventum orationis, vel actoris con-

C

19 stantiam subsecuta est. Finio. Incipit respondere Veiento : nemo patitur : obturbatur, obstrepitur: adeo quidem, ut diceret: *Rogo, Patres C., ne me cogatis implorare auxilium tribunorum.* Et statim Murena tribunus : *Permitto tibi, vir clarissime Veiento, dicere.* 20 Tunc quoque reclamatur. Inter moras consul citatis nominibus et peracta discessione, mittit senatum ; ac paene adhuc stantem tentantemque dicere Veientonem relinquit. Multum ille de hac (ita vocabat) contumelia questus est Homerico versu :

ὦ γέρον, ἦ μάλα δή σε νέοι τείρουσι μαχηταί.

Non fere quisquam in senatu fuit, qui non me com
21 plecteretur, exoscularetur, certatimque laude cumularet, quod intermissum tamdiu morem in publicum consulendi, susceptis propriis simultatibus, reduxissem : quod denique senatum invidia liberassem, qua flagrabat apud ordines alios, quod severus in ceteros, senatoribus solis, dissimulatione quasi mutua, parceret. Haec acta sunt
22 absente Certo. Abfuit enim, seu tale aliquid suspicatus, sive, ut excusabatur, infirmus. Et relationem quidem de eo Caesar ad senatum non remisit ; obtinui tamen, quod intenderam. Nam collega Certi consula-
23 tum, successorem Certus accepit : planeque factum est, quod dixeram in fine : *Reddat praemium sub optimo principe, quod a pessimo accepit.* Postea actionem meam, utcunque potui, recollegi : addidi multa. Accidit
24 fortuitum (sed non tanquam fortuitum) quod, editis libris, Certus intra paucissimos dies implicitus morbo decessit. Audivi referentes, hanc imaginem menti eius,
25 hanc oculis oberrasse, tanquam videret me sibi cum ferro imminere. Verane haec, adfirmare non ausim : interest tamen exempli, ut vera videantur. Habes
26 epistolam, si modum epistolae cogitas, libris, quos legisti, non minorem. Sed imputabis tibi, qui contentus libris non fuisti. Vale.

A. VII. (iv. 22.)

[Pliny in this letter illustrates by two interesting anecdotes the independent spirit of his friend Junius Mauricus, to whom *Epp.* i. 14, ii. 18, vi. 14 are addressed. His name first occurs in Tacitus (*Hist.* iv. 40) in connection with a singularly courageous act. He ventured to ask Domitian, who was at the time prætor of the city and had just taken his seat in the senate (this was A.D. 70), that access to the imperial registers might be given to members of the house, so that they might know on the best authority whom the various *delatores* had proposed to impeach. The question was evaded, but it had the good effect of leading to a general attack on some of the most infamous of these men. Mauricus, as we might have expected, was in exile during Domitian's reign. (See B. XX.) He was, as we gather from E. XVI., recalled by Nerva. He is again mentioned by Tacitus (*Agr.* 45), with his brother Arulenus Rusticus. It is evident from the tone of the letters addressed to him that he was one of Pliny's intimate friends.]

C. PLINIUS SEMPRONIO RUFO SUO S.

Interfui principis optimi cognitioni, in consilium adsumptus. Gymnicus agon apud Viennenses ex cuiusdam testamento celebrabatur. Hunc Trebonius Rufinus, vir egregius nobisque amicus, in duumviratu suo tollendum abolendumque curavit. Negabatur ex auctoritate publica fecisse. Egit ipse causam non minus feliciter quam diserte. Commendabat actionem, 2 quod tanquam homo Romanus et bonus civis in negotio suo mature et graviter loquebatur. Cum sententiae 3 perrogarentur, dixit Iunius Mauricus (quo viro nihil firmius, nihil verius) non esse restituendum Viennensibus agona : adiecit, *Vellem etiam Romae tolli posset.* Constanter, inquis, et fortiter. Quidni? Sed hoc Maurico novum non est. Idem apud Nervam impera- 4 torem non minus fortiter. Coenabat Nervacum paucis. Veiento proximus, atque etiam in sinu recumbebat. Dixi omnia, cum hominem nominavi. Incidit sermo 5 de Catullo Messalino, qui, luminibus orbatus, ingenio saevo mala caecitatis addiderat : non verebatur, non cru-

besecbat, non miserebatur : quo saepius a Domitiano non
6 secus ac tela, quae et ipsa caeca et improvida feruntur,
in optimum quemque contorquebatur. De huius nequitia sanguinariisque sententiis in commune omnes
super coenam loquebantur, cum ipse imperator, *Quid*
7 *putamus passurum fuisse, si viveret?* et Mauricus,
Nobiscum coenaret. Longius abii, libens tamen. Placuit agona tolli, qui mores Viennensium infecerat. ut
noster hic omnium. Nam Viennensium vitia intra
ipsos resident, nostra late vagantur, utque in corporibus, sic in imperio, gravissimus est morbus, qui a capite
diffunditur. Vale.

A. VIII. (ii. 1.)

[This letter contains an account of the circumstances of the
death of Verginius Rufus, one of the most eminent men of
his time. Pliny, it seems, had special reasons for speaking well
of him. Verginius had, by the wish of the elder Pliny, been his
guardian, had treated him as a son, and had done much for
his advancement in life. Our knowledge about the facts of
his life is drawn chiefly from Tacitus. He was consul for the
first time under Nero, A.D. 63 (*Ann.* xv. 23); he was 'legatus'
of Lower Germany, where he had crushed the revolt of Julius
Vindex, at the time of that emperor's death ; the imperial
power was twice offered to him by the army of that province,
and twice declined by him : first, after the suppression of the
above-mentioned revolt ; secondly, after the death of Otho
(*Hist.* i. 8 ; ii. 51). His death, on this latter occasion, was demanded by the angry and disappointed soldiery, who charged
him with attempting the life of Vitellius (*Hist.* ii. 68). Having
escaped this peril, he lived, in honour and prosperity, as we learn
from the present letter, to the age of eighty-three, and was holding
his third consulate (which was conferred on him by the Emperor Nerva, A.D. 97) at the time of his death. Pliny speaks
of him as a writer of playful verses (v. 3), and compares the
two following letters.

Romanus, to whom this and *Epp.* B. XXIII., E. III., E.
V., are addressed, was, we should suppose, the same person as Voconius Romanus, who is spoken of in ii. 13 as (n:

of Pliny's most intimate and accomplished friends, and who
is recommended by him to Trajan, in *Epp. ad Traj.* iv., as
worthy of senatorial rank. If so, he was Pliny's fellow-student,
and by his friend's account was an agreeable talker, a clever
lawyer, and a charming writer of letters.]

C. PLINIUS ROMANO SUO S.

Post aliquot annos insigne, atque etiam memorabile
populi Romani oculis spectaculum exhibuit publicum
funus Vergini Rufi, maximi et clarissimi civis, perinde
felicis. Triginta annis gloriae suae supervixit. Legit 2
scripta de se carmina, legit historias, et posteritati suae
interfuit. Perfunctus est tertio consulatu, ut summum
fastigium privati hominis impleret, cum principis
noluisset. Caesares, quibus suspectus atque etiam 3
invisus virtutibus fuerat, evasit: reliquit incolumem
optimum atque amicissimum, tanquam ad hunc ipsum
honorem publici funeris reservatus. Annum tertium 4
et octogesimum excessit in altissima tranquillitate, pari
veneratione. Usus est firma valetudine: nisi quod
solebant ei manus tremere, citra dolorem tamen.
Aditus tantum mortis durior longiorque, sed hic ipse
laudabilis. Nam cum vocem praepararet, acturus in 5
consulatu principi gratias, liber, quem forte acceperat
grandiorem, et seni et stanti ipso pondere elapsus est.
Hunc dum sequitur colligitque, per leve et lubricum
pavimentum, fallente vestigio, cecidit, coxamque fregit,
quae parum apte collocata, reluctante aetate, male coiit.
Huius viri exsequiae magnum ornamentum principi, 6
magnum seculo, magnum etiam foro et rostris attulerunt.
Laudatus est a consule Cornelio Tacito: nam hic supre-
mus felicitati eius cumulus accessit, laudator eloquen-
tissimus. Et ille quidem plenus annis abiit, plenus 7
honoribus, illis etiam quos recusavit: nobis tamen
quaerendus ac desiderandus est, ut exemplar aevi
prioris, mihi vero praecipue, qui illum non solum
publice, sed etiam privatim, quantum admirabar, tantum
diligebam; primum quod utrique eadem regio, mu- 8
nicipia finitima, agri etiam possessionesque coniunc-
tae: praeterea quod ille mihi tutor relictus, adfectum

parentis exhibuit. Sic candidatum me suffragio ornavit:
sic ad omnes honores meos ex secessibus adcucurrit,
cum iam pridem eiusmodi officiis renuntiasset : sic illo
die, quo sacerdotes solent nominare, quos dignissimos
9 sacerdotio iudicant, me semper nominabat. Quin etiam
in hac novissima valetudine veritus, ne forte inter quinqueviros crearetur, qui minuendis publicis sumptibus
iudicio senatus constituebantur, cum illi tot amici senes
consularesque superessent, me huius aetatis, per quem
excusaretur, elegit, his quidem verbis : *etiam si filium*
10 *haberem, tibi mandarem.* Quibus ex causis necesse est,
tanquam immaturam mortem eius in sinu tuo defleam :
si tamen fas est aut fleri, aut omnino mortem vocari,
qua tanti viri mortalitas magis finita quam vita est.
11 Vivit enim vivetque semper, atque etiam latius memoria
hominum et sermone versabitur, postquam ab oculis re-
12 cessit. Volui tibi multa alia scribere, sed totus animus
in hac una contemplatione defixus est. Verginium
cogito, Verginium video, Verginium iam vanis imagi-
nibus, recentibus tamen, audio, adloquor, teneo : cui
fortasse cives aliquos virtutibus pares et habemus et habebimus, gloria neminem. Vale.

A. IX. (vi. 10.)

[A monument which was in the course of erection to the
memory of the illustrious Verginius Rufus was, it appears,
unfinished ten years after his death. This, Pliny says, was
attributable to the indifference of the person to whom the
matter had been intrusted. He expresses his indignation
at this neglect, which was aggravated by the circumstance
that Verginius had given special directions that an epitaph
composed by himself should be inscribed on his tomb.]

C. PLINIUS ALBINO SUO S.

Cum venissem in socrus meae villam Alsiensem,
quae aliquando Rufi Vergini fuit, ipse mihi locus
optimi illius et maximi viri desiderium non sine dolore
renovavit. Hunc enim colere secessum, atque etiam

senectutis suae nidulum vocare consueverat. Quocun- 2
que me contulissem, illum animus, illum oculi requirebant. Libuit etiam monimentum eius videre, et
vidisse poenituit. Est enim adhuc imperfectum : nec 3
difficultas operis in caussa, modici, ac potius exigui ;
sed inertia eius, cui cura mandata est. Subit indignatio
cum miseratione, post decimum mortis annum reliqui-
as neglectumque cinerem sine titulo, sine nomine iacere, cuius memoria orbem terrarum gloria pervagetur.
At ille mandaverat caveratque, ut divinum illud et 4
immortale factum versibus inscriberetur :

HIC SITUS EST RUFUS, PULSO QUI VINDICE QUONDAM
IMPERIUM ADSERUIT NON SIBI, SED PATRIAE.

Tam rara in amicitiis fides, tam parata oblivio mortuo- 5
rum, ut ipsi nobis debeamus etiam conditoria exstruere,
omniaque heredum officia praesumere. Nam cui non 6
est verendum, quod videmus accidisse Verginio? cuius
iniuriam ut indigniorem, sic etiam notiorem ipsius
claritas facit. Vale.

A. X. (ix. 19.)

[This letter continues the subject of that which precedes it.
A friend, Ruso by name (a promising young advocate, as we
learn from vi. 23), had intimated to Pliny that he thought
the epitaph which Verginius Rufus had ordered to be inscribed
on his tomb savoured of vanity, and that Frontinus, who had
forbidden all such memorials of himself, had acted more wisely.
Pliny defends Verginius. He had known, he says, and esteemed
both these men, and felt that, if any preference was to be
made, it was due to Verginius, a man of singular modesty,
with which this epitaph was not really inconsistent.]

C. PLINIUS RUSONI SUO S.

Significas, legisse te in quadam epistola mea, iussisse
Verginium Rufum inscribi sepulcro suo :

Hic situs est Rufus, pulso qui Vindice quondam
imperium adseruit non sibi, sed patriae.

Reprehendis, quod iusserit; addis etiam, melius rectiusque Frontinum, quod vetuerit omnino monumentum sibi fieri; meque ad extremum, quid de utroque sentiam, consulis. Utrumque dilexi; miratus sum magis, quem tu reprehendis, atque ita miratus, ut non putarem satis umquam laudari posse, cuius nunc mihi subcunda defensio est. Omnes ego, qui magnum aliquod memorandumque fecerunt, non modo venia, verum etiam laude dignissimos iudico, si immortalitatem quam meruere sectantur, victurique nominis famam supremis etiam titulis prorogare nituntur. Nec facile quemquam nisi Verginium invenio, cuius tanta in praedicando verecundia, quanta gloria ex facto. Ipse sum testis, familiariter ab eo dilectus probatusque, semel omnino, me audiente, provectum, ut de rebus suis hoc unum referret, ita secum aliquando Cluvium locutum : *Scis, Vergini, quae historiae fides debeatur : proinde, si quid in historiis meis legis aliter ac velles, rogo ignoscas.* Ad hoc ille ; *Tune ignoras, Cluvi, ideo me fecisse, quod feci, ut esset liberum vobis scribere, quae libuisset?* Agedum, hunc ipsum Frontinum in hoc ipso, in quo tibi parcior videtur et pressior, comparemus. Vetuit exstrui monumentum : sed quibus verbis? *Impensa monumenti supervacua est : memoria nostri durabit, si vita meruimus.* An restrictius arbitraris per orbem terrarum legendum dare, duraturam memoriam sui, quam uno in loco duobus versiculis signare, quod feceris? Quamquam non habeo propositum illum reprehendendi, sed hunc tuendi : cuius quae potest apud te iustior esse defensio, quam ex collatione eius, quem praetulisti? Meo quidem iudicio neuter culpandus, quorum uterque ad gloriam pari cupiditate, diverso itinere, contendit : alter, dum expetit debitos titulos : alter, dum mavult videri contempsisse. Vale.

A. XI. (ii. 11.)

[We have in this letter the particulars of a *cause célèbre*, twice alluded to by Juvenal as a flagrant illustration of one of the many abuses of his time. According to the Satirist, the criminal, though condemned, often practically escaped with impunity.

> Exsul ab octava Marius bibit et fruitur Dis
> Iratis: at tu, victrix provincia, ploras.—i. 49.

The second allusion is in the following passage :

> Quanta autem inde feres tam dirae praemia culpae,
> Cum tenues nuper Marius discinxerit Afros?—viii. 119.

The case, as we here gather from Pliny, was not one of mere ordinary oppression of a province by plunder and extortion. Marius Priscus, proconsul of Africa, was charged with having received bribes to condemn and put to death innocent persons. The question arose in the senate, and was discussed with great warmth, whether under these circumstances he could be tried by a select commission of *judices* in the praetor's court. When the worst charges against him were clearly understood to be true, the trial was adjourned to the next meeting of the senate, and was heard before an unusually full house, the Emperor presiding. Pliny was counsel for the province. It was an era in his life. He was, he says, nervous and anxious when he rose to speak in so great a cause before that august assembly. The accused was himself a man of high position ; he had been consul, and a member of one of the great religious colleges. He was defended by Salvius Liberalis, an able advocate, who was again opposed to Pliny in a similar case (A. XIII.), and who, according to Suetonius (*Vesp.* xiii.), said when he was pleading the cause of some rich person, 'What is it to the Emperor if the accused has a hundred million sesterces ? ' Salvius, Pliny tells us, put forth all his strength on this occasion. He was answered by Tacitus in a speech exhibiting the best qualities of the historian's eloquence. The trial lasted three days. Marius was condemned, and sentenced to banishment from Rome and Italy. He was also ordered to refund to the *aerarium* the moneys which he had unlawfully received.

The trial of Marius took place A.D. 100, in Trajan's reign.]

C. PLINIUS ARRIANO SUO S.

Solet esse gaudio tibi, si quid actum est in senatu dignum ordine illo. Quamvis enim quietis amore secesseris, insidet tamen animo tuo maiestatis publicae cura. Accipe ergo, quod per hos dies actum est, per-
2 sonae claritate famosum, severitate exempli salubre, rei magnitudine aeternum. Marius Priscus, accusantibus Afris, quibus pro consule praefuit, omissa defensione, iudices petiit. Ego et Cornelius Tacitus, adesse provincialibus iussi, existimavimus fidei nostrae convenire, notum senatui facere, excessisse Priscum immanitate et saevitia crimina, quibus dari iudices possent, cum ob
3 innocentes condemnandos, interficiendos etiam, pecunias accepisset. Respondit Fronto Catius, deprecatusque est, ne quid ultra repetundarum legem quaereretur, omniaque actionis suae vela vir movendarum lacry-
4 marum peritissimus, quodam velut vento miserationis implevit. Magna contentio, magni utrinque clamores, aliis cognitionem senatus lege conclusam, aliis liberam
5 solutamque dicentibus, quantumque admisisset reus, tantum vindicandum. Novissime consul designatus Iulius Ferox, vir rectus et sanctus, Mario quidem
6 iudices interim censuit dandos, evocandos autem, quibus diceretur innocentium poenas vendidisse. Quae sententia non praevaluit modo, sed omnino post tantas dissensiones fuit sola frequens : adnotatumque experimentis, quod favor et misericordia acres et vehementes
7 primos impetus habent, paullatim, consilio et ratione quasi restincta, considunt. Unde evenit, ut, quod multi clamore permixto tuentur, nemo tacentibus ceteris dicere velit : patescit enim, cum separaris a
8 turba, contemplatio rerum, quae turba teguntur. Venerunt, qui adesse erant iussi, Vitellius Honoratus et Flavius Martianus, ex quibus Honoratus trecentis millibus exsilium equitis Romani, septemque amicorum eius ultimam poenam, Martianus unius equitis Romani septingentis millibus plura supplicia arguebatur emisse : erat enim fustibus caesus, damnatus in

metallum, strangulatus in carcere. Sed Honoratum 9 cognitioni senatus mors opportuna subtraxit, Martianus inductus est absente Prisco. Itaque Tuccius Cerialis consularis iure senatorio postulavit, ut Priscus certior fieret, sive quia miserabiliorem, sive quia invidiosiorem fore arbitrabatur, si praesens fuisset, sive (quod maxime credo) quia aequissimum erat, commune crimen ab utroque defendi, et si dilui non potuisset, in utroque puniri. Dilata res est in proxi- 10 mum senatum, cuius ipse conspectus augustissimus fuit. Princeps praesidebat; erat enim consul: ad hoc Ianuarius mensis cum cetera, tum praecipue senatorum frequentia celeberrimus: praeterea causae amplitudo, auctaque dilatione expectatio et fama, insitumque mortalibus studium magna et inusitata noscendi, omnes undique exciverat. Imaginare, quae solicitudo nobis, 11 qui metus, quibus super tanta re, in illo coetu, praesente Caesare, dicendum erat. Equidem in senatu non semel egi: quin immo nusquam audiri benignius soleo: tunc me tamen, ut nova omnia novo metu permovebant. Obversabatur praeter illa, quae supra dixi, causae 12 difficultas: stabat modo Consularis, modo Septemvir Epulonum, iam neutrum. Erat igitur perquam one- 13 rosum, accusare damnatum: quem ut premebat atrocitas criminis, ita quasi peractae damnationis miseratio tuebatur. Utcunque tamen animum cogitationemque 14 collegi, coepi dicere non minore audientium adsensu, quam solicitudine mea: dixi horis paene quinque. Nam XII clepsydris quas spatiosissimas acceperam, sunt additae quatuor. Adeo illa ipsa, quae dura et adversa dicturo videbantur, secunda dicenti fuerunt. Caesar quidem 15 mihi tantum studium, tantum etiam curam (nimium est enim dicere solicitudinem) praestitit, ut libertum meum post me stantem saepius admoneret, voci laterique consulerem, cum me vehementius putaret intendi, quam gracilitas mea perpeti posset. Respondit mihi pro Martiano Claudius Marcellinus. Missus deinde senatus, et revo- 16 catus in posterum. Neque enim iam inchoari poterat actio, nisi ut noctis interventu scinderetur. Postero 17 die dixit pro Mario Salvius Liberalis, vir subtilis, dis-

positus, acer, disertus : in illa vero causa omnes artes
suas protulit. Respondit Cornelius Tacitus eloquen-
18 tissime, et, quod eximium orationi inest, σεμνῶς. Dixit
pro Mario rursus Fronto Catius insigniter: utque iam
locus ille poscebat, plus in precibus temporis, quam in
defensione consumpsit. Huius actionem vespera inclu-
sit, non tamen sic, ut abrumperet. Itaque in tertium
diem probationes exierunt. Iam hoc ipsum pulchrum
et antiquum, senatum nocte dimitti, triduo vocari,
19 triduo contineri. Cornutus Tertullus, Consul designatus, vir egregius, et pro veritate firmissimus, censuit
*septingenta millia, quae acceperat Marius, aerario infer-
enda, Mario urbe Italiaque interdicendum ; Martiano
hoc amplius, Africa.* In fine sententiae adiecit, *Quod
ego et Tacitus iniuncta advocatione diligenter forti-
terque functi essemus, arbitrari senatum, ita nos fecisse,
20 ut dignum mandatis partibus fuerit.* Adsenserunt consules designati, omnes etiam consulares usque ad Pompeium Collegam : ille et *septingenta millia, aerario in-
ferenda, et Martianum in quinquennium relegandum :
Marium repetundarum poenae, quam iam passus esset,
21 censuit relinquendum.* Erant in utraque sententia
multi, fortasse etiam plures in hac vel solutiore vel
molliore. Nam quidam ex iliis quoque, qui Cornuto
videbantur adsensi, hunc, qui post ipsos censuerat. se-
22 quebantur. Sed cum fieret discessio, qui sellis consulum
adstiterant, in Cornuti sententiam ire coeperunt. Tum
illi, qui se Collegae adnumerari patiebantur, in diver-
sum transierunt : Collega cum paucis relictus. Multum
postea de impulsoribus suis, praecipue de Regulo,
questus est, qui se in sent ntia, quam ipse dictaverat.
deseruisset. Est alioqui Regulo tam mobile ingenium,
23 ut plurimum audeat. plurimum timeat. Hic finis cognitionis amplissimae. Superest tamen λειτούργιον non
leve, Hostilius Firminus, legatus Mari Prisci, qui per-
mixtus caussae graviter vehementerque vexatus est.
Nam et rationibus Martiani, et sermone, quem ille
habuerat in ordine Leptitanorum, operam suam Prisco
ad turpissimum ministerium commodasse, stipulatusque
de Martiano quinquaginta millia denariorum probabatur,

ipse praeterea accepisse sestertiûm decem millia, foedissimo quidem titulo, nomine unguentarii, qui titulus a vita hominis compti semper et pumicati non abhorrebat. Placuit, censente Cornuto, referri de eo proximo 24 senatu, tunc enim, casu incertum, an conscientia, abfuerat. Habes res urbanas. Invicem rusticas scribe, 25 quid, arbusculae tuae, quid vineae, quid segetes agant, quid oves delicatissimae. In summa, nisi aeque longam epistolam reddes, non est quod postea, nisi brevissimam, expectes. Vale.

A. XII. (ii. 12.)

[The subject of this letter is in close connection with that of the preceding. The 'legatus' of Marius Priscus was found to be involved in the guilt of his chief, for whom he had undertaken some disgraceful business. The money he had received on this account had been entered in the accounts under a false description. The case was heard before the senate; and it was decided after some discussion, that he should not be deprived of his senatorial rank, but that, in the assignment of the provincial governorships, his name should be passed over. The sentence, Pliny says, though accepted as being less harsh than degradation from the senatorial order, was in fact painfully humiliating, while at the same time it was inconsistent with the public interests.]

C. PLINIUS ARRIANO SUO S.

Λειτούργιον illud, quod superesse Mari Prisci causae proxime scripseram, nescio an satis circumcisum, tamen et adrasum est. Firminus inductus in senatum re- 2 spondit crimini noto. Secutae sunt diversae sententiae consulum designatorum. Cornutus Tertullus censuit ordine movendum : Acutius Nerva, in sortitione provinciae rationem eius non habendam. Quae sententia, tanquam mitior, vicit, cum sit alioqui durior tristiorque. Quid enim miserius, quam exsectum et exemtum hon- 3 oribus senatoriis, labore et molestia non carere ? quid gravius, quam tanta ignominia adfectum, non in solitu

dine latere, sed in hac altissima specula conspiciendum
4 se monstrandumque praebere? Praeterea quid publice
minus aut congruens aut decorum? notatum a senatu in
senatu sedere? ipsisque illis, a quibus sit notatus, ae-
quari? submotum a proconsulatu, quia se in legatione
turpiter gesserat, de proconsulibus iudicare? damna-
5 tumque sordium, vel damnare alios vel absolvere? Sed
hoc pluribus visum est. Numerantur enim sententiae, non
ponderantur: nec aliud in publico consilio potest fieri, in
quo nihil est tam inaequale, quam aequalitas ipsa. Nam
6 cum sit impar prudentia, par omnium ius est. Implevi
promissum, priorisque epistolae fidem exsolvi, quam ex
spatio temporis iam recepisse te colligo. Nam et fes-
tinanti et diligenti tabellario dedi: nisi quid impedi-
7 menti in via passus est. Tuae nunc partes, ut primum
illam, deinde hanc remuncreris literis, quales isthinc
redire uberrimae possunt. Vale.

A. XIII. (iii. 9.)

[This letter is on a kindred subject to the two preceding. The
province of Baetica (one of the divisions of Hispania Ulterior,
and taking its name from the river Baetis, the Guadalquiver)
had been grievously wronged by its proconsul Caecilius
Classicus, the year of whose government coincided with that
of the notorious Marius Priscus in Africa. It was a singular
fact that Classicus came from Africa, and Priscus from Baetica.
The misdoings of Classicus, however, were on a wider scale
than those of Priscus, and his guilt was so transparent that
his death, which occurred just before his impeachment, was
possibly, as Pliny hints, his own act. But the province would
not let the matter drop, and pressed the case against a number
of persons who had lent themselves to the iniquities of the
proconsul. In all these various proceedings Pliny was counsel
for the provincials. The proof of the proconsul's guilt was
sufficiently easy; it was indeed amply furnished by his own
letters. It was much more difficult, Pliny says, to convict
his accomplices; so that the entire cause was exceedingly
laborious and intricate. Pliny's efforts on behalf of the province were on the whole successful, though it would appear

that some of the accused were men with very powerful friends.

The different trials were held before a bench of *judices*, who, we may suppose, had been specially selected for the occasion. Classicus, had he lived, would have been impeached, as Priscus was, before the senate.

Cornelius Minicianus, to whom this and A. IV. are addressed, is mentioned also in vii. 22. He is recommended by Pliny for a military tribunate, and is described as a man of illustrious birth, great wealth, and a zealous love of letters. He had distinguished himself as an upright judge, and as a courageous advocate.

The ' Minician gens' (derived originally from Brixia, now Brescia) appears only under the Empire.]

C. PLINIUS MINICIANO SUO S.

Possum iam perscribere tibi, quantum in publica provinciae Baeticae causa laboris exhauserim. Nam fuit 2 multiplex, actaque est saepius cum magna varietate. Unde varietas? unde plures actiones? Caecilius Classicus, homo foedus et aperte malus, proconsulatum in ea non minus violenter quam sordide gesserat, eodem anno, quo in Africa Marius Priscus. Erat autem Priscus 3 ex Baetica, ex Africa Classicus. Inde dictum Baeticorum (ut plerumque dolor etiam venustos facit) non illepidum ferebatur: *Dedi malum et accepi.* Sed 4 Marium una civitas publice, multique privati reum peregerunt; in Classicum tota provincia incubuit. Ille 5 accusationem vel fortuita vel voluntaria morte praevertit. Nam fuit mors eius infamis, ambigua tamen : ut enim credibile videbatur, voluisse exire de vita, quum defendi non posset, ita mirum, pudorem damnationis morte fugisse, quem non puduisset damnanda committere. Nihilominus Baetica etiam in defuncti accusatione perstabat. Provisum hoc legibus, intermissum tamen, et post longam intercapedinem tunc reductum. Addiderunt Baetici, quod simul socios ministrosque Classici detulerunt: nominatimque in eos inquisitionem postulaverunt. Aderam Baeticis, mecumque Lucceius 7 Albinus, vir in dicendo copiosus, ornatus : quem ego cum olim mutuo diligerem, ex hac officii societate amare

8 ardentius coepi. Habet quidem gloria, in studiis praesertim, quiddam ἀκοινώνητον: nobis tamen nullum certamen, nulla contentio: cum uterque pari iugo non pro se, sed pro causa niteretur. Cuius et magnitudo et 9 utilitas visa est postulare, ne tantum oneris singulis actionibus subiremus. Verebamur, ne nos dies, ne vox, ne latera deficerent, si tot crimina, tot reos uno velut fasce complecteremur: deinde, ne iudicum intentio multis nominibus multisque causis non lassaretur modo, verum etiam confunderetur: mox, ne gratia singulorum collata atque permista, pro singulis quoque vires omnium 10 acciperet: postremo, ne potentissimi, vilissimo quoque quasi piaculari dato, alienis poenis elaberentur. Et- 11 enim tum maxime favor et ambitio dominatur, cum sub aliqua specie severitatis delitescere potest. Erat in consilio Sertorianum illud exemplum, qui robustissimum et infirmissimum militem iussit caudam equi . . . reliqua nosti. Nam nos quoque tam numerosum agmen 12 reorum ita demum videbamus posse superari, si per singulos carperetur. Placuit in primis ipsum Classicum ostendere nocentem: hic aptissimus ad socios eius et ministros transitus erat, quia socii ministrique probari, nisi illo nocente, non poterant. Ex quibus duos statim Classico iunximus, Baebium Probum, et Fabium His- 13 panum, utrumque gratia, Hispanum etiam facundia, validum. Et circa Classicum quidem brevis et expeditus labor. Sua manu reliquerat scriptum, quid ex quaque re, quid ex quaque causa accepisset. Miserat etiam epistolas Romam ad amiculam quandam, iactantes et gloriosas, his quidem verbis: *Io io, liber ad te venio:* 14 *iam sestertium quadragies redegi, parte vendita Baeticorum.* Circa Hispanum et Probum multum sudoris. Horum antequam crimina ingrederer, necessarium credidi elaborare, ut constaret, ministerium crimen esse: 15 quod nisi effecissem, frustra ministros probassem. Neque enim ita defendebantur, ut negarent, sed ut necessitati veniam precarentur: esse enim se provinci- 16 ales, et ad omne proconsulum imperium metu cogi. Solet dicere Claudius Restitutus, qui mihi respondit, vir exercitatus et vigilans, et quamlibet subitis paratus, nunquam sibi tantum caliginis, tantum perturbationis

offusum, quam cum ea praerepta et extorta defensioni
suae cerneret, in quibus omnem fiduciam reponebat. Con- 17
silii nostri exitus fuit: bona Classici, quae habuisset
ante provinciam, placuit senatui a reliquis separari, illa
filiae, haec spoliatis relinqui. Additum est, ut pecuniae,
quas creditoribus solverat, revocarentur. Hispanus et
Probus in quinquennium relegati. Adeo grave visum est,
quod initio dubitabatur, an omnino crimen esset. Post 18
paucos dies Clavium Fuscum, Classici generum, et Stil-
lonium Priscum, qui tribunus cohortis sub Classico fuerat, accusavimus, dispari eventu. Prisco in biennium
Italia interdictum: absolutus est Fuscus. Actione 19
tertia commodissimum putavimus plures congregare,
ne, si longius esset extracta cognitio, satietate et taedio
quodam iustitia cognoscentium severitasque languesce-
ret: et alioqui supererant minores rei, data opera hunc
in locum reservati, excepta tamen Classici uxore, quae
sicut implicita suspicionibus, ita non satis convinci probationibus visa est. Nam Classici filia, (quae et ipsa 20
inter reos erat) ne suspicionibus quidem haerebat. Itaque cum ad nomen eius in extrema actione venissem,
(neque enim, ut initio, sic etiam in fine verendum erat,
ne per hoc totius accusationis auctoritas minueretur)
honestissimum credidi, non premere immerentem, idque ipsum dixi libere et varie. Nam modo legatos 21
interrogabam, docuissentne me aliquid, quod re probari posse confiderent? modo consilium a senatu petebam,
putaretne debere me, si quam haberem in dicendo facultatem, in iugulum innocentis, quasi telum aliquod, intendere? postremo totum locum in hoc fine conclusi,
*Dicet aliquis, Iudicas ergo? Ego vero non iudico:
memini tamen, me advocatum ex iudicibus datum.* Hic 22
numerosissimae causae terminus fuit, quibusdam abso-
lutis, pluribus damnatis, atque etiam relegatis, aliis in
tempus, aliis in perpetuum. Eodem senatusconsulto 23
industria, fides, constantia nostra plenissimo testimonio comprobata est dignum solumque par pretium
tanti laboris. Concipere animo potes, quam simus 24
fatigati, quibus toties agendum, toties altercandum, tam
multi testes interrogandi, sublevandi, refutandi. Iam 25

D

illa quam ardua, quam molesta, tot reorum amicis secreto rogantibus negare, adversantibus palam obsistere?
Referam unum aliquid ex iis, quae dixi. Cum mihi
quidam e iudicibus ipsis pro reo gratiosissimo reclama-
rent, *Non minus*, inquam, *hic innocens erit, si ego omnia*
26 *dixero.* Coniectabis ex hoc, quantas contentiones,
quantas etiam offensas subierimus, dumtaxat ad breve
tempus. Nam fides in praesentia eos, quibus resistit,
offendit, deinde ab illis ipsis suspicitur laudaturque.
Non potui magis te in rem praesentem perducere.
27 Dices, *Non fuit tanti.* *Quid enim mihi cum tam longa*
epistola? Nolito ergo identidem quaerere, quid Romae
geratur. Et tamen memento esse non epistolam longam,
quae tot dies, tot cognitiones, tot denique reos cau-
28 sasque complexa sit. Quae omnia videor mihi non minus breviter, quam diligenter, persecutus. Temere dixi
diligenter: succurrit quod praeterieram, et quidem sero:
sed, quamquam praepostere, reddetur. Facit hoc Homerus, multique illius exemplo. Est alioqui perdecorum;
29 a me tamen non ideo fiet. Ex testibus quidam, sive
iratus, quod evocatus esset invitus, sive subornatus ab
aliquo reorum, ut accusationem exarmaret, Norbanum
Licinianum, legatum et inquisitorem, reum postulavit,
tanquam in causa Castae (uxor haec Classici) praevari-
30 caretur. Est lege cautum, ut reus ante peragatur,
tunc de praevaricatore quaeratur, videlicet quia optime
31 ex accusatione ipsa accusatoris fides aestimatur. Norbano tamen non ordo legis, non legati nomen, non
inquisitionis officium praesidio fuit: tanta conflagravit
invidia homo alioqui flagitiosus, et Domitiani temporibus usus, ut multi: electusque tunc a provincia ad
inquirendum, non tamquam bonus et fidelis, sed
32 tanquam Classici inimicus. Erat ab illo relegatus.
Dari sibi diem et edi crimina postulavit. Neutrum
impetravit: coactus est statim respondere: respondit:
malum pravumque ingenium hominis facit, ut dubi-
33 tem, confidenter an constanter, certe paratissime. Ob-
iecta sunt multa, quae magis, quam praevaricatio, no-
cuerunt. Quin etiam duo consulares, Pomponius Rufus
et Libo Frugi, laeserunt eum testimonio, tanquam apud

iudicem, sub Domitiano, Salvii Liberalis accusatoribus adfuisset. Damnatus et in insulam relegatus est. Itaque 34 cum Castam accusarem, nihil magis pressi, quam quod accusator eius praevaricationis crimine corruisset. Pressi tamen frustra : accidit enim res contraria et nova, ut, accusatore praevaricationis damnato, rea absolveretur. Quaeris, quid nos, dum haec aguntur? Indicavimus 35 senatui, ex Norbano didicisse nos publicam causam, rursusque debere ex integro discere, si ille praevaricator probaretur; atque ita, dum ille peragitur reus, sedimus : postea Norbanus omnibus diebus cognitionis interfuit, eandemque usque ad extremum vel constantiam vel audaciam pertulit. Interrogo ipse me, an 36 aliquid omiserim rursus : et rursus paene omisi. Summo die Salvius Liberalis reliquos legatos graviter increpuit, tanquam non omnes, quos mandasset provincia, reos peregissent, atque, ut est vehemens et disertus, in discrimen adduxit. Protexi viros optimos, eosdemque gratissimos ; mihi certe debere se praedicant, quod illum turbinem evaserint. Hic erit epistolae finis, re 37 vera finis : literam non addam ; etiamsi adhuc aliquid praeterisse me sensero. Vale.

- - - - - - - -

A. XIV. (iv. 9.)

[The subject of this letter is the impeachment of Julius Bassus and his defence by Pliny. Bassus is described as a man whom misfortunes had made famous. After long delays, he had been acquitted of charges brought against him in the reign of Vespasian; he was, however, subsequently banished by Domitian, but recalled by Nerva, under whom he became governor of Bithynia. Here his ill-fortune pursued him, and he was charged by the province with various corrupt practices. His accusers, it appears, were determined to press the case against him, and Bassus, fearing the worst, instructed Pliny to conduct the principal part of his defence. If we may trust Pliny, Bassus had been guilty of no graver offence than receiving presents from some of the provincials with whom he had been on friendly terms during his quaestorship in the

province. He had, however, as Pliny admits, clearly trans-
gressed the letter of the law, so that his defence was a difficult
matter, and required great tact. The case was argued before
the senate, and lasted four days, the speech of the principal
accuser being prolonged into the night of the third day, so
that, contrary to the usual practice, the Senate House was
lighted up. It was ultimately decided that the accused might,
without any loss of dignity, have his cause tried before an
inferior court composed of a commission of *judices*. Pliny
professes himself to have been satisfied with the result. Popular
feeling seems, on the whole, to have been with Bassus. As he
left the house, he was saluted with the acclamations of a
crowd of citizens, who sympathised with the troubles of his
old age.

We know nothing of Cornelius Ursus, to whom this and
Epp. v. 20; vi. 5, 13; viii. 9 (the three first of which are
connected in their subject-matter with the present letter) are
addressed.]

C. PLINIUS CORNELIO URSO SUO S.

Causam per hos dies dixit Iulius Bassus, homo
laboriosus et adversis suis clarus. Accusatus est sub
Vespasiano a privatis duobus: ad senatum remissus,
diu pependit, tandemque absolutus vindicatusque est.
2 Titum timuit, ut Domitiani amicus; a Domitiano relegatus est. Revocatus a Nerva, sortitusque Bithyniam,
rediit reus, accusatus non minus acriter, quam fideliter
defensus. Varias sententias habuit, plures tamen quasi
3 mitiores. Egit contra eum Pomponius Rufus, vir paratus
et vehemens; Rufo successit Theophanes, unus ex le-
4 gatis, fax accusationis et origo. Respondi ego. Nam
mihi Bassus iniunxerat, ut totius defensionis funda-
menta iacerem, dicerem de ornamentis suis, quae illi
et ex generis claritate et ex periculis ipsis magna
5 erant, dicerem de conspiratione delatorum, quam in
quaestu habebant, dicerem causas, quibus factiosissi-
mum quemque, ut illum ipsum Theophanem, offendisset.
Eundem me voluerat occurrere crimini, quo maxime
premebatur. In aliis enim, quamvis auditu gravioribus,
non absolutionem modo, verum etiam laudem mere-
6 batur: hoc illum onerabat, quod homo simplex et
incautus quaedam a provincialibus, ut amicis, acceperat.

Nam fuerat in provincia eadem quaestor. Haec accu-
satores furta ac rapinas, ipse munera vocabat; sed lex
munera quoque accipi vetat. Hic ego quid agerem? 7
quod iter defensionis ingrederer? Negarem? Verebar,
ne plane furtum videretur, quod confiteri timerem.
Praeterea rem manifestam infitiari, augentis erat crimen,
non diluentis; praesertim cum reus ipse nihil integrum
advocatis reliquisset. Multis enim, atque etiam Principi,
dixerat, sola se munuscula, dumtaxat natali suo aut
Saturnalibus, accepisse, et plerisque misisse. Veniam 8
ergo peterem? Iugularem reum, quem ita deliquisse
concederem, ut servari, nisi venia, non posset. Tanquam
recte factum tuerer? Non illi profuissem, sed ipse im-
pudens extitissem. In hac difficultate placuit medium 9
quiddam tenere. Videor tenuisse. Actionem meam,
ut praelia solet, nox diremit. Egeram horis tribus et
dimidia; supererat sesquihora. Nam cum e lege accusator sex horas, novem reus accepisset; ita diviserat
tempus reus inter me et eum, qui dicturus post erat,
ut ego quinque horis, ille reliquis uteretur. Mihi 10
successus actionis silentium finemque suadebat. Temerarium est enim, secundis non esse contentum. Ad hoc
verebar, ne me corporis vires iterato labore desererent;
quem difficilius est repetere, quam iungere. Erat etiam 11
periculum, ne reliqua actio mea et frigus ut deposita,
et taedium ut resumpta pateretur. Ut enim faces ignem
assidua concussione custodiunt, dimissum aegerrime
reparant; sic et dicentis calor et audientis intentio
continuatione servatur, intercapedine et quasi remissione languescit. Sed Bassus multis precibus, paene 12
etiam lacrymis, obsecrabat, implerem meum tempus.
Parui, utilitatemque eius praetuli meae. Bene cessit:
inveni ita erectos animos senatus, ita recentes, ut
priore actione incitati magis, quam satiati viderentur.
Successit mihi Luccius Albinus, tam apte ut orationes 13
nostrae varietatem duarum, contextum unius habuisse
credantur. Respondit Herennius Pollio instanter et 14
graviter, deinde Theophanes rursus. Fecit enim hoc
quoque, ut cetera, impudentissime, quod post duos, et
consulares et disertos, tempus sibi, et quidem laxius,

vindicavit. Dixit in noctem, atque etiam nocte inlatis
15 lucernis. Postero die egerunt pro Basso Homullus et
Fronto, mirifice: quartum diem probationes occupa-
16 verunt. Censuit Baebius Macer, consul designatus,
lege repetundarum Bassum teneri: Caepio Hispo,
17 salva dignitate iudices dandos. Uterque recte. Qui
fieri potest, inquis, cum tam diversa censuerint? Quia
scilicet et Macro, legem intuenti, consentaneum fuit
damnare eum, qui contra legem munera acceperat, et
Caepio, cum putaret licere senatui, sicut licet, et
mitigare leges et intendere, non sine ratione veniam
18 dedit facto, vetito quidem, non tamen inusitato. Praevaluit sententia Caepionis: quin immo consurgenti
ei ad censendum acclamatum est, quod solet residentibus. Ex quo potes aestimare, quanto consensu sit
exceptum, cum diceret, quod tam favorabile fuit, cum
19 dicturus videretur. Sunt tamen, ut in senatu, ita in
civitate, in duas partes hominum iudicia divisa. Nam
quibus sententia Caepionis placuit, sententiam Macri,
ut rigidam duramque, reprehendunt: quibus Macri,
illam alteram dissolutam atque etiam incongruentem
vocant; negant enim congruens esse, retinere in
20 senatu, cui iudices dederis. Fuit et tertia sententia.
Valerius Paullinus adsensus Caepioni, hoc amplius
censuit, referendum de Theophane, cum legationem
renuntiasset. Arguebatur enim multa in accusatione
fecisse, quae illa ipsa lege, qua Bassum accusaverat,
21 tenerentur. Sed hanc sententiam consules, quamquam
maximae parti senatus mire probabatur, non sunt per-
secuti. Paullinus tamen et iustitiae famam et constan-
22 tiae tulit. Misso senatu, Bassus magna hominum
frequentia, magno clamore, magno gaudio exceptus
est. Fecerat eum favorabilem renovata discriminum
vetus fama, notumque periculis nomen, et in procero
23 corpore moesta et squalida senectus. Habebis hanc
interim epistolam ut πρόδρομον: exspectabis orationem
plenam onustamque: exspectabis diu: neque enim
leviter et cursim, ut de re tanta, retractanda est. Vale.

A. XV. (ii. 7.)

[On the motion of the Emperor Trajan a statue had been decreed by the senate to Vestricius Spurinna, who had been, as we learn from Tacitus (*Hist.* ii. 11, 18, 36), one of Otho's generals, and who was one of Pliny's most intimate friends. The honour was paid to him in consideration of his having completely overawed, without actual hostilities, the German tribe of the Bructeri. A statue had been also voted to his son Cottius, who had died in his father's absence. The distinction, Pliny says, was well deserved, and would have a good moral effect.

Spurinna, as we may infer from v. 17, was an accomplished man, and liked to encourage literary merit. *Epp.* iii. 10 and v. 17 are addressed to him. We have a pleasant picture of his old age in E. XV.

Of Macrinus, to whom this and *Epp.* iii. 4; vii. 6, 10; viii. 17; ix. 4 are addressed, we know nothing, except what we are told in *Ep.* viii. 5, that he had a singularly excellent wife, with whom he had lived in uninterrupted harmony for thirty-nine years.]

C. PLINIUS MACRINO SUO S.

Heri a senatu Vestricio Spurinnae, Principe auctore, triumphalis statua decreta est, non ita, ut multis, qui nunquam in acie steterunt, nunquam castra viderunt, nunquam denique tubarum sonum, nisi in spectaculis, audierunt, verum ut illis, qui decus istud sudore et sanguine et factis adsequebantur. Nam Spurinna Bructerum regem vi et armis 2 induxit in regnum: ostentatoque bello, ferocissimam gentem (quod est pulcherrimum victoriae genus) terrore perdomuit. Et hoc quidem virtutis prae- 3 mium; illud solatium doloris accepit, quod filio eius Cottio, quem amisit absens, habitus est honor statuae. Rarum id in iuvene: sed pater hoc quoque merebatur, cuius gravissimo vulneri magno aliquo fomento medendum fuit. Praeterea Cottius ipse 4 tam clarum specimen indolis dederat, ut vita eius brevis et angusta debuerit hac veluti immortalitate proferri. Nam tanta ei sanctitas, gravitas auctoritas

etiam, ut posset senes illos provocare virtute, quibus
5 nunc honore adaequatus est. Quo quidem honore,
quantum ego interpretor, non modo defuncti memoriæ,
dolori patris, verum etiam exemplo prospectum est.
Acuent ad bonas artes iuventutem adolescentibus
quoque (digni sint modo) tanta praemia constituta;
acuent principes viros ad liberos suscipiendos et gaudia
ex superstitibus, et ex amissis tam gloriosa solatia.
6 Ilis ex causis statua Cotti publice laetor, nec privatim minus. Amavi consummatissimum iuvenem
tam ardenter, quam nunc impatienter requiro. Erit
ergo pergratum mihi hanc effigiem eius subinde intueri,
subinde respicere, sub hac consistere, praeter hanc
7 commeare. Etenim si defunctorum imagines domi
positae dolorem nostrum levant, quanto magis eae,
quibus in celeberrimo loco non modo species et vultus
illorum, sed honor etiam et gloria refertur? Vale.

A. XVI. (iii. 20.)

[It appears from this letter that vote by ballot had been
lately introduced into the senate as a remedy for the unseemly
disorder and confusion which had commonly attended the
election of magistrates. Pliny thinks the new system will
work well for a time, but he says that he is afraid that it may
lead to the evils which opponents of the ballot in the present
day hold to be inseparable from it. In iv. 25 (addressed
to Messius Maximus) he alludes to an evil which had sprung
from it. Vote by ballot, as we learn from Cicero (*De Leg.*
iii. 15, 16), had been introduced into the *comitia* by four suc-
cessive laws (*leges tabellariae*). The ultimate result was, that
magistrates were elected, laws passed or repealed, judicial proceedings decided on this system, the principle of which had
thus been fully recognised. All this business was, in the
time of Tiberius, transferred from the comitia to the senate
(as we are told by Tacitus, *Ann.* i. 15), but was for a time
transacted by open voting.]

C. PLINIUS MAXIMO SUO S.

Meministine, te saepe legisse, quantas contentiones excitarit lex tabellaria, quantumque ipsi latori vel gloriae vel reprehensionis adtulerit? At nunc in 2 senatu sine ulla dissensione hoc idem, ut optimum, placuit; omnes comitiorum die tabellas postulaverunt. Excesseramus sane manifestis illis apertisque suffragiis 3 licentiam concionum. Non tempus loquendi, non tacendi modestia, non denique sedendi dignitas custodiebatur. Magni undique dissonique clamores; pro- 4 currebant omnes cum suis candidatis; multa agmina in medio, multique circuli et indecora confusio: adeo desciveramus a consuetudine parentum, apud quos omnia disposita, moderata, tranquilla, maiestatem loci pudoremque retinebant. Supersunt senes, ex quibus 5 audire soleo hunc ordinem comitiorum. Citato nomine candidati, silentium summum. Dicebat ipse pro se, explicabat vitam suam, testes et laudatores dabat, vel eum, sub quo militaverat vel eum, cui quaestor fuerat, vel utrumque, si poterat; addebat quosdam ex suffragatoribus; illi graviter et paucis loquebantur. Plus hoc quam preces proderat. Nonnunquam candi- 6 datus aut natales competitoris aut annos aut etiam mores arguebat. Audiebat senatus gravitate censoria. Ita saepius digni quam gratiosi praevalebant. Quae 7 nunc immodico favore corrupta ad tacita suffragia, velut ad remedium decucurrerunt; quod interim plane remedium fuit: erat enim novum et subitum. Sed 8 vereor, ne procedente tempore ex ipso remedio vitia nascantur. Est enim periculum, ne tacitis suffragiis impudentia irrepat. Nam quotocuique eadem honestatis cura secreto, quae palam? Multi famam, conscientiam pauci verentur. Sed nimis cito de futuris: 9 interim beneficio tabellarum habebimus magistratus, qui maxime fieri debuerunt. Nam ut in recuperatoriis iudiciis, sic nos in his comitiis, quasi repente apprehensi, sinceri iudices fuimus. Haec tibi scripsi, primum, ut 10 aliquid novi scriberem, deinde ut nonnunquam de

republica loquerer, cuius materiae nobis quanto rarior.
quam veteribus, occasio, tanto minus omittenda est.
11 Et Hercule quousque illa vulgaria?   *Quid agis?*
Ecquid commode vales?   Habeant nostrae quoque
literae aliquid non humile, nec sordidum, nec privatis
12 rebus inclusum.   Sunt quidem cuncta sub unius
arbitrio, qui pro utilitate communi solus omnium curas
laboresque suscepit: quidam tamen salubri tempera-
mento ad nos quoque, velut rivi ex illo benignissimo
fonte, decurrunt, quos et haurire ipsi, et absentibus
amicis quasi ministrare epistolis possumus.   Vale.

A. XVII. (vi. 19.)

[This letter refers to an attempt made by the Emperor
Trajan to stop the corrupt practices of candidates for office.
Such persons had been in the habit of entertaining, giving
presents, and depositing money in the hands of agents for the
purpose of bribery. For these abuses the Emperor was asked
to find a remedy. This he did by at once fixing a limit to
the legal expenses of candidates, and also by compelling them
to invest a third part of their property in the soil of Italy.
The keen competition for land to which this enactment gave
rise enormously enhanced its price; and, as Pliny tells his
friend Nepos, now was the time for selling Italian estates and
purchasing others in the provinces. Trajan, of course, designed
this singular measure in the interest of Rome and Italy,
for the security and prosperity of which he was peculiarly
anxious.]

C. PLINIUS NEPOTI SUO S.

Scis tu accessisse pretium agris praecipue suburbanis?
Causa subitae caritatis res multis agitata sermonibus.
Proximis comitiis honestissimas voces senatus expressit:
candidati ne convirentur, ne mittant munera, ne pec-
2 *unias deponant.*   Ex quibus duo priora tam aperte
quam immodice fiebant, hoc tertium, quanquam occul-
3 taretur, pro comperto habebatur. Homullus deinde
noster vigilanter usus hoc consensu senatus, sententiae
loco postulavit, ut consules desiderium universorum

notum Principi facerent, peterentque, sicut aliis vitiis huic quoque providentia sua occurreret. Occurrit: 4 nam sumptus candidatorum, foedos illos et infames, ambitus lege restrinxit; eosdem patrimonii tertiam partem conferre jussit in ea quae solo continerentur, deforme arbitratus, ut erat, honorem petituros urbem Italiam, non pro patria, sed pro hospitio aut stabulo quasi peregrinantes habere. Concursant ergo candi- 5 dati; certatim, quidquid venale audiunt, emptitant, quoque sint plura venalia efficiunt. Proinde si poenitet te Italicorum praediorum, hoc vendendi tempus tam Hercule quam in provinciis comparandi, dum idem candidati illic vendunt, ut his emant. Vale.

A. XVIII. (viii. 24.)

[This is a pleasant and interesting letter, showing, as it does, Pliny's good sense and good feeling. It is a specimen of his liberal and enlightened views as to the government of a conquered country, which had peculiarly strong claims on the indulgence of the conqueror. Pliny's friend Maximus, who had been Quaestor in Bithynia, and had brought back thence a singularly good name, was to be governor of the more important province of Achaia, where he would have the regulation of such cities as Corinth, Athens, and Lacedaemon. Pliny exhorts him to remember what Greece had been, how much Rome owed to her, and to look upon the old age of a country as being as venerable as that of a man. It would, he says, be a brutal and barbarous act to rob such a land of the little liberty which yet remained to her. There can be hardly a doubt that Pliny, when he wrote this letter, had in his mind the famous and elaborate epistle addressed by Cicero to his brother Quintus, in which the duties and qualifications of a provincial governor are pointed out in detail.—*Epp. ad Quint.* i. 1.]

C. PLINIUS MAXIMO SUO S.

Amor in te meus cogit, non ut praecipiam, (neque enim praeceptore eges) admoneam tamen, ut, quae scis, teneas et observes, aut scias melius. Cogita, te 2 missum in provinciam Achaiam, illam veram et meram

Graeciam, ubi humanitas, literae, etiam fruges, inventae esse creduntur; missum ad ordinandum statum liberarum civitatum, id est, ad homines maxime homines, ad liberos maxime liberos, qui ius a natura datum virtute, meritis, amicitia, foedere denique et religione tenuerunt.
3 Reverere conditores deos et nomina deorum. Reverere gloriam veterem, et hanc ipsam senectutem, quae in homine venerabilis, in urbibus sacra. Sit apud te honor antiquitati, sit ingentibus factis, sit fabulis quoque. Nihil ex cuiusquam dignitate, nihil ex libertate, nihil
4 etiam ex iactatione decerpseris. Habe ante oculos, hanc esse terram, quae nobis miserit iura, quae leges non victis sed petentibus dederit; Athenas esse, quas adeas, Lacedaemonem esse, quam regas, quibus reliquam umbram, et residuum libertatis nomen eripere,
5 durum, ferum, barbarumque est. Vides a medicis, quamquam in adversa valetudine nihil servi ac liberi differant, mollius tamen liberos clementiusque tractari. Recordare, quid quaeque civitas fuerit, non, ut despicias, quod esse desierit. Absit superbia, asperitas.
6 Nec timueris contemptum. An contemnitur, qui imperium, qui fasces habet, nisi qui humilis, et sordidus, et qui se primus ipse contemnit? Male vim suam potestas aliorum contumeliis experitur, male terrore veneratio adquiritur, longeque valentior amor ad obtinendum, quod velis, quam timor. Nam timor abit, si recedas; manet amor: ac sicut ille in odium, hic in
7 reverentiam vertitur. Te vero etiam atque etiam (repetam enim) meminisse oportet officii tui titulum, ac tibi ipsum interpretari, quale quantumque sit ordinare statum liberarum civitatum. Nam quid ordina-
8 tione civilius? quid libertate pretiosius? Porro quam turpe, si ordinatio eversione, libertas servitute mutetur? Accedit, quod tibi certamen est tecum: onerat te quaesturae tuae fama, quam ex Bithynia optimam revexisti: onerat testimonium Principis: onerat tribunatus, praetura, atque haec ipsa legatio, quasi
9 praemium data. Quo magis nitendum est, ne in longinqua provincia, quam suburbana, ne inter servientes, quam liberos, ne sorte, quam iudicio missus,

ne rudis et incognitus, quam exploratus probatusque,
humanior, melior, peritior fuisse videaris : cum sit
alioqui, ut saepe audisti, saepe legisti, multo deformius
amittere, quam non adsequi laudem. Haec velim ic
credas (quod initio dixi) scripsisse me admonentem,
non praecipientem ; quamquam praecipientem quoque.
Quippe non vereor, in amore ne modum excesserim.
Neque enim periculum est, ne sit nimium, quod esse
n aximum debet. Vale.

A. XIX. (ix. 5.)

[Pliny here commends his friend Calestrius Tiro, the
governor of Baetica, for seeking, by kindness and courtesy in
his administration, to win the esteem of the provincials, but
warns him against forgetting the distinction of classes.]

C. PLINIUS TIRONI SUO S.

Egregie facis (inquiro enim) et persevera quod iustitiam tuam provincialibus multa humanitate commen-
das : cuius praecipua pars est, honestissimum quemque
complecti, atque ita a minoribus amari, ut simul a
principibus diligare. Plerique autem, dum verentur, 2
ne gratiae potentium nimium impertire videantur,
sinisteritatis atque etiam malignitatis famam consequuntur. A quo vitio tu longe recessisti ; scio, sed
temperare mihi non possum quominus laudem similis
monenti, quod eum modum tenes, ut discrimina ordinum dignitatumque custodias ; quae si confusa, turbata,
permixta sunt, nihil est ipsa aequalitate inaequalius.
Vale.

A. XX. (Epp. ad Traj. xcvi.)

[In this famous letter, which gives us the earliest information that we possess from external sources about primitive Christianity, Pliny puts before the Emperor a grave difficulty which had occurred in his province. Persons belonging to the sect known as *Christiani* had been brought before him. He had had no hesitation in punishing with severity those who confessed the fact and gloried in it. But this was not all. An anonymous accusation had involved great numbers of all ages and ranks. Some of these persons he had examined. He had not discovered anything criminal in the superstition, but he is alarmed at its wide spread, and seeks advice. The Emperor's letter, which is appended, directs Pliny to punish such *Christiani* as might be brought before him, but not to make search for them. Anonymous accusations were to be disregarded]

C. PLINIUS TRAIANO IMP.

Sollemne est mihi, Domine, omnia, de quibus dubito, ad te referre. Quis enim potest melius vel cunctationem meam regere, vel ignorantiam instruere? Cognitionibus de Christianis interfui nunquam : ideo nescio, quid et quatenus aut puniri soleat, aut quaeri. 2 Nec mediocriter haesitavi, sitne aliquod discrimen aetatum, an quamlibet teneri nihil a robustioribus differant, deturne poenitentiae venia, an ei, qui omnino Christianus fuit, desisse non prosit, nomen ipsum, etiamsi flagitiis careat, an flagitia cohaerentia nomini puniantur. Interim in iis, qui ad me tanquam Christiani 3 deferebantur, hunc sum secutus modum. Interrogavi ipsos, *an essent Christiani?* Confitentes iterum ac tertio interrogavi, supplicium minatus: perseverantes duci iussi. Neque enim dubitabam, qualecunque esset, quod faterentur, pervicaciam certe, et inflexibilem obstinationem debere puniri. Fuerunt alii similis amen4 tiae : quos, quia cives Romani erant, annotavi in urbem remittendos. Mox ipso tractatu, ut fieri solet, diffun-

dente se crimine, plures species inciderunt. Propositus 5
est libellus sine auctore, multorum nomina continens.
Qui negarent se esse Christianos, aut fuisse, cum, praeeunte me, deos appellarent, et imagini tuae, quam propter hoc iusseram cum simulacris numinum afferri,
thure ac vino supplicarent, praeterea male dicerent
Christo, quorum nihil cogi posse dicuntur, qui sunt
revera Christiani, ego dimittendos putavi.   Alii ab 6
indice nominati, esse se Christianos dixerunt, et mox
negaverunt : fuisse quidem, sed desiisse, quidam ante
triennium, quidam ante plures annos, non nemo etiam
ante viginti quoque.   Omnes et imaginem tuam, deo-
rumque simulacra venerati sunt et Christo male dixerunt.   Affirmabant autem, hanc fuisse summam vel 7
culpae suae, vel erroris, quod essent soliti stato die ante
lucem convenire, carmenque Christo, quasi deo, dicere
secum invicem, seque sacramento non in scelus aliquod
obstringere, sed ne furta, ne latrocinia, ne adulteria
committerent, ne fidem fallerent, ne depositum appellati
abnegarent : quibus peractis morem sibi discedendi
fuisse, rursusque coeundi ad capiendum cibum, promiscuum tamen, et innoxium : quod ipsum facere desiisse post edictum meum, quo secundum mandata tua
hetaerias esse vetueram.   Quo magis necessarium cre- 8
didi, ex duabus ancillis, quae ministrae dicebantur,
quid esset veri et per tormenta quaerere.   Sed nihil
aliud inveni, quam superstitionem pravam et immodi-
cam, ideoque, dilata cognitione, ad consulendum te
decurri.   Visa est enim mihi res digna consultatione, 9
maxime propter periclitantium numerum.   Multi enim
omnis aetatis, omnis ordinis, utriusque sexus etiam,
vocantur in periculum, et vocabuntur.   Neque enim
civitates tantum, sed vicos etiam atque agros super-
stitionis istius contagio pervagata est : quae videtur
sisti et corrigi posse.   Certe satis constat, prope iam 10
desolata templa coepisse celebrari, et sacra sollemnia
diu intermissa repeti : passimque venire victimas,
quarum adhuc rarissimus emptor inveniebatur. Ex quo
facile est opinari, quae turba hominum emendari possit,
si sit poenitentiae locus.

TRAIANUS PLINIO S.

Actum, quem debuisti, mi Secunde, in excutiendis causis eorum, qui Christiani ad te delati fuerant, secutus es. Neque enim in universum aliquid, quod quasi 2 certam formam habeat, constitui potest. Conquirendi non sunt: si deferantur et arguantur, puniendi sunt, ita tamen, ut, qui negaverit se Christianum esse, idque re ipsa manifestum fecerit, id est, supplicando diis nostris, quamvis suspectus in praeteritum fuerit, veniam ex poenitentia impetret. Sine auctore vero propositi libelli, nullo crimine locum habere debent. Nam et pessimi exempli, nec nostri saeculi est.

Section B.

LETTERS ON SUBJECTS OF LITERARY INTEREST.

B. I. (i. 2.)

[Pliny sends to his friend a volume of speeches which he was revising, and on which he wishes to have a candid opinion. He had taken, he says, not without some hesitation, Demosthenes for his model, and the subject (see note on *desidia*) had lent itself to the style. He hopes that his friend will express himself freely, as he is thinking of publishing—a course to which he is inclined by the favourable reports which the booksellers give him of the sale of his former works.

Several letters (A. XI. XII., B. XXIV., &c.) are addressed to Arrianus. Pliny in *Ep.* iii. 2, speaks of him as a valued friend whose judgment both in ordinary matters of business and in literary questions he greatly respected.]

C. PLINIUS ARRIANO SUO S.

Quia tardiorem adventum tuum prospicio, librum quem prioribus epistolis promiseram, exhibeo. Hunc rogo, ex consuetudine tua et legas et emendes, eo magis, quod nihil ante peraeque eodem ζήλῳ scripsisse 2 videor. Tentavi enim imitari Demosthenem semper tuum, Calvum nuper meum, dumtaxat figuris orationis : nam vim tantorum virorum, *pauci, quos aequus amavit*, adsequi possunt. Nec materia ipsa huic (vereor, ne 3 improbe dicam) aemulationi repugnavit : erat enim prope tota in contentione dicendi, quod me longae desidiae indormientem excitavit, si modo is sum ego, qui excitari possim. Non tamen omnino Marci nostri 4 ληκύθους fugimus, quoties paullulum itinere decedere non intempestivis amoenitatibus admonebamur : acres enim esse, non tristes, volebamus. Nec est quod 5 putes, me sub hac exceptione veniam postulare. Nam, quo magis intendam limam tuam, confitebor et ipsum me et contubernales ab editione non abhorrere, si modo tu fortasse errori nostro album calculum adieceris. Est enim plane aliquid edendum, atque utinam hoc 6 potissimum, quod paratum est ! (audis desidiae votum) edendum autem ex pluribus causis : maxime quod libelli, quos emisimus, dicuntur in manibus esse, quamvis iam gratiam novitatis exuerint; nisi tamen auribus nostris bibliopolae blandiuntur. Sed sane blandiantur, dum per hoc mendacium nobis studia nostra commendent. Vale.

B. II. (i. 8.)

[It appears from this letter that Pliny had presented a library to the inhabitants of his native ' municipium,' and had promised an annual sum of money for the maintenance of the children of its poorer freeborn citizens. He had made a speech on the occasion in the local ' curia ' before the ' decuriones,' a body which seems to have corresponded to our mayor and corporation. He now gives his reasons for wishing to publish this speech, and he asks his friend, who had already seen it and made a few general remarks on it, to read it through carefully and criticise it in detail. He may seem, he says, to be extolling his own merits, but he feels that on the whole the publication will have a good effect, both on himself and on others. His liberality had not taken a vulgar and popular form, and it was consequently all the more expedient to set forth its usefulness, and encourage his fellow-citizens to take advantage of it.

Pompeius Saturninus is spoken of at length in B. XIX. He seems to have been remarkable for the variety of his accomplishments.]

C. PLINIUS POMPEIO SATURNINO SUO S.

Peropportune mihi redditae sunt literae tuae, quibus flagitabas, ut tibi aliquid ex scriptis meis mitterem, cum ego id ipsum destinassem. Addidisti ergo calcaria sponte currenti, pariterque et tibi veniam recusandi 2 laboris, et mihi exigendi verecundiam sustulisti. Nam nec me timide uti decet eo, quod oblatum est : nec te gravari, quod depoposcisti. Non est tamen, quod ab homine desidioso aliquid novi operis exspectes. Petiturus sum enim, ut rursus vaces sermoni, quem apud 3 municipes meos habui bibliothecam dedicaturus. Memini quidem, te iam quaedam adnotasse, sed generaliter : ideo nunc rogo, ut non tantum universitati

eius attendas, verum etiam particulas, qua soles lima,
persequaris. Erit enim et post emendationem liberum
nobis vel publicare vel continere. Quin immo fortasse 4
hanc ipsam cunctationem nostram in alterutram sententiam emendationis ratio deducet, quae aut indignum
editione, dum saepius retractat, inveniet, aut dignum,
dum id ipsum experitur, efficiet. Quamquam huius 5
cunctationis meae causae non tam in scriptis, quam in
ipso materiae genere consistunt. Est enim paullo quasi
gloriosius et elatius. Onerabit hoc modestiam nostram,
etiamsi stilus ipse fuerit pressus demissusque, propterea
quod cogimur cum de munificentia parentum nostrorum, tum de nostra disputare. Anceps hic et lubri- 6
cus locus est, etiam cum illi necessitas lenocinatur.
Etenim si alienae quoque laudes parum aequis auribus
accipi solent, quam difficile est obtinere, ne molesta
videatur oratio de se aut de suis disserentis? Nam cum
ipsi honestati, tum aliquanto magis gloriae eius praedi-
cationique invidemus, atque ea demum recte facta minus detorquemus et carpimus, quae in obscuritate et
silentio reponuntur. Qua ex causa saepe ipse mecum, 7
nobisne tantum, quidquid est istud, composuisse, an et
aliis debeamus? Ut nobis, admonet illud, quod pleraque,
que, quae sunt agendae rei necessaria, eadem peracta
nec utilitatem parem nec gratiam retinent. Ac, ne 8
longius exempla repetamus, quid utilius fuit, quam
munificentiae rationem etiam stilo prosequi? Per hoc
enim adsequebamur, primum ut honestis cogitationibus
immoraremur; deinde ut pulchritudinem illarum longiore tractatu pervideremus; postremo, ut subitae largitionis comitem poenitentiam caveremus. Nascebatur
ex his exercitatio quaedam contemnendae pecuniae.
Nam cum homines ad custodiam eius natura restrinx- 9
erit, nos contra multum ac diu pensitatus amor li-
beralitatis communibus avaritiae vinculis eximebat:
tantoque laudabilior munificentia nostra fore videbatur, quod ad illam non impetu quodam, sed consilio
trahebamur. Accedebat his causis, quod non ludos 10
aut gladiatores, sed annuos sumptus in alimenta ingenuorum pollicebamur. Oculorum porro et aurium

voluptates adeo non egent commendatione, ut non tam
11 incitari debeant oratione, quam reprimi : ut vero aliquis libenter educationis taedium laboremque suscipiat,
non praemiis modo, verum etiam exquisitis adhorta-
12 tionibus impetrandum est. Nam si medici salubres sed
voluptate carentes cibos blandioribus alloquiis prose-
quuntur, quanto magis decuit publice consulentem
utilissimum munus, sed non perinde populare, comitate
orationis inducere ? praesertim cum enitendum haberemus, ut, quod parentibus dabatur, et orbis probaretur ;
honoremque paucorum ceteri patienter et exspectarent
13 et mererentur. Sed ut tunc communibus magis com-
modis quam privatae iactantiae studebamus, eum intentionem effectumque muneris nostri vellemus intelligi,
ita nunc in ratione edendi veremur, ne forte non aliorum utilitatibus, sed propriae laudi servisse videamur.
14 Praeterea meminimus, quanto maiore animo honestatis
fructus in conscientia, quam in fama, reponatur. Sequi
enim gloria, non appeti, debet ; nec, si casu aliquo non
sequatur, idcirco quod gloriam non meruit, minus pul-
15 chrum est. Ii vero, qui benefacta sua verbis adornant,
non ideo praedicare, quia fecerint, sed ut praedicarent,
fecisse creduntur. Sic, quod magnificum referente alio
fuisset, ipso qui gesserat recensente, vanescit. Homines
enim, cum rem destruere non possunt, iactationem
eius incessunt. Ita si silenda feceris, factum ipsum,
16 si laudanda, quod non sileas, ipse culparis. Me vero
peculiaris quaedam impedit ratio. Etenim hunc ipsum
sermonem non apud populum, sed apud decuriones
17 habui, nec in propatulo, sed in curia. Vereor ergo, ut
sit satis congruens, cum in dicendo adsentationem vulgi
acclamationemque defugerim, nunc eadem illa editione
sectari : cumque plebem ipsam, cui consulebatur, limine curiae parietibusque discreverim, ne quam in
speciem ambitionis inciderem, nunc eos etiam, ad quos
ex munere nostro nihil pertinet praeter exemplum,
18 velut obvia ostentatione conquirere. Habes cunctationis meae causas : obsequar tamen consilio tuo, cuius
mihi auctoritas pro ratione sufficiet. Vale.

B. III. (v. 8.)

[The friend to whom this letter is addressed had, with
other friends, urged Pliny to undertake some historical work.
Pliny replies that his own wishes and the example of his
uncle pointed in the same direction, but that there were many
reasons which made him hesitate. He admits indeed that it
is easier on the whole to succeed as a historian than as a poet
or as an orator, and he explains his grounds for so thinking;
but he says that, as he had the intention of re-writing some
of his more important speeches, and of thus handing down to
posterity the result of his forensic labours, he could not for
the present enter on a new field of literary work. He also
points out that the selection of a suitable period for historical
writing is beset with difficulty, and he hopes that when he is
prepared to begin, his friend will choose for him the subject-
matter of his work.

Titinius Capito is mentioned in B. XXV. as a constant and
liberal patron of literature, in which he was also himself pro-
ficient. From i. 17 it appears that he was a lover of the
memories of the Republic, having in his house the statues of
Brutus and Cassius.]

C. PLINIUS CAPITONI SUO S.

Suades, ut historiam scribam, et suades non solus:
multi hoc me saepe monuerunt, et ego volo, non quia
commode facturum esse confido (id enim temere credas, nisi expertus), sed quia mihi pulchrum in primis
videtur, non pati occidere, quibus aeternitas debeatur,
aliorumque famam cum sua extendere. Me autem 2
nihil aeque ac diuturnitatis amor et cupido solicitat,
res homine dignissima, praesertim qui nullius sibi con-
scius culpae posteritatis memoriam non reformidet.
Itaque diebus ac noctibus cogito, si *qua me quoque* 3
possim Tollere humo (id enim voto meo sufficit: illud
supra votum) *victorque virum volitare per ora*. *Quamquam o!* Sed hoc satis est, quod prope sola historia
polliceri videtur. Orationi enim et carmini parva gra- 4
tia, nisi eloquentia est summa: historia quoquo modo
scripta delectat. Sunt enim homines natura curiosi, et
quamlibet nuda rerum cognitione capiuntur, ut qui

sermunculis etiam fabellisque ducantur. Me vero ad
hoc studium impellit domesticum quoque exemplum.
5 Avunculus meus, idemque per adoptionem pater, historias, et quidem religiosissime, scripsit. Invenio autem
apud sapientes, honestissimum esse maiorum vestigia
sequi, si modo recto itinere praecesserint. Cur ergo
6 cunctor? Egi magnas et graves causas. Has (etiamsi
mihi tenuis ex eis spes) destino retractare, ne tantus
ille labor meus, nisi hoc, quod reliquum est studii, ad-
7 didero, mecum pariter intercidat. Nam si rationem
posteritatis habeas, quidquid non est peractum, pro
non inchoato est. Dices, *Potes simul et rescribere actiones, et componere historiam.* Utinam! sed utrumque
8 tam magnum est, ut abunde sit alterum efficere. Un-
devicesimo aetatis anno dicere in foro coepi, et nunc
demum, quid praestare debeat orator, adhuc tamen
per caliginem, video. Quid, si huic oneri novum ac-
9 cesserit? Habet quidem oratio et historia multa communia, sed plura diversa in his ipsis, quae communia
videntur. Narrat illa, narrat haec: sed aliter. Huic
pleraque humilia et sordida et ex medio petita, illi
10 omnia recondita, splendida, excelsa conveniunt. Hanc
saepius ossa, musculi, nervi; illam tori quidam et
quasi iubae decent. Haec vel maxime vi, amaritudine,
instantia; illa tractu et suavitate atque etiam dulce-
dine placet. Postremo alia verba, alius sonus, alia
11 constructio. Nam plurimum refert, ut Thucydides
ait, κτῆμα sit, an ἀγώνισμα: quorum alterum oratio,
alterum historia est. His ex causis non adducor, ut
duo dissimilia, et hoc ipso diversa, quod maxima, con-
fundam misceamque, ne tanta quasi colluvione turbatus ibi faciam, quod hic debeo: ideoque interim
veniam (ne a meis verbis recedam) advocandi peto.
12 Tu tamen iam nunc cogita, quae potissimum tempora
adgrediar. Vetera et scripta aliis? parata inquisitio,
sed onerosa collatio: intacta et nova? graves offensae,
13 levis gratia. Nam praeter id, quod in tantis vitiis
hominum plura culpanda sunt, quam laudanda: tum si
laudaveris, parcus; si culpaveris, nimius fuisse dicaris,
quamvis illud plenissime, hoc restrictissime feceris.

Sed haec me non retardant: est enim mihi pro fide 14
satis animi. Illud peto, praesternas ad quod hortaris,
eligasque materiam, ne mihi, iam scribere parato, alia
rursus cunctationis et morae iusta ratio nascatur. Vale.

B. IV. (vii. 9.)

[This is a letter of literary advice to a friend. Fuscus
wished to know how he might most profitably pursue his
studies with the view of becoming a good speaker. Pliny
recommends him to turn Greek into Latin and Latin into
Greek, and points out the special advantages of the practice,
the very laboriousness of which, as he says, renders it peculiarly useful. He tells him not to confine himself to one kind
of composition, but to practise himself from time to time in
the writing of history, of letters, and of poetry, each of which
has its distinct use in the cultivation of a good style.

Fuscus, to whom E. I. is addressed, was, as we gather
from *Epp.* vi. 11, 26, an accomplished and learned man of
senatorian family, whom Pliny highly esteemed. He was
living in A.D. 118, in which year he was consul with the
Emperor Hadrian.]

C. PLINIUS FUSCO SUO S.

Quaeris, quemadmodum in secessu, quo iamdiu
frueris, putem te studere oportere. Utile in primis, 2
et multi praecipiunt, vel ex Graeco in Latinum, vel ex
Latino vertere in Graecum: quo genere exercitationis
proprietas splendorque verborum, copia figurarum, vis
explicandi, praeterea imitatione optimorum similia in-
veniendi facultas paratur: simul quae legentem fefel-
lissent, transferentem fugere non possunt. Intelligentia
ex hoc et iudicium adquiritur. Nihil obfuerit, quae 3
legeris hactenus, ut rem argumentumque teneas, quasi
aemulum scribere, lectisque conferre, ac sedulo pen-
sitare, quid tu, quid ille commodius. Magna gratulatio, si non nulla tu; magnus pudor, si cuncta ille
melius. Licebit interdum et notissima eligere, et certare
cum electis. Audax haec, non tamen improba, quia 4

secreta, contentio: quamquam multos videmus eiusmodi certamina sibi cum multa laude sumpsisse, quosque
subsequi satis habebant, dum non desperant, anteces-
5 sisse. Poteris et, quae dixeris, post oblivionem retrac
tare, multa retinere, plura transire, alia interscribere,
6 alia rescribere. Laboriosum istud et taedio plenum,
sed difficultate ipsa fructuosum, recalescere ex integro,
et resumere impetum fractum omissumque, postremo,
nova velut membra peracto corpori intexere, nec tamen
7 priora turbare. Scio, nunc tibi esse praecipuum studium orandi · sed non ideo semper pugnacem hunc et
quasi bellatorium stilum suaserim. Ut enim terrae variis
mutatisque seminibus, ita ingenia nostra nunc hac,
8 nunc illa meditatione recoluntur. Volo interdum aliquem ex historia locum apprehendas, volo epistolam
diligentius scribas. Nam saepe in orationes quoque
non historicae modo, sed prope poëticae descriptionis
necessitas incidit; et pressus sermo purusque ex epis-
9 tolis petitur. Fas est et carmine remitti: non dico
continuo et longo (id enim perfici nisi in otio non
potest), sed hoc arguto et brevi, quod apte quan-
10 taslibet occupationes curasque distinguit. Lusus vocantur, sed hi lusus non minorem interdum gloriam,
quam seria consequuntur: atque adeo (cur enim te ad
versus non versibus adhorter?)

11   Ut laus est cerae, mollis cedensque sequatur
       si doctos digitos, iussaque fiat opus,
     et nunc informet Martem castamque Minervam,
       nunc Venerem effingat, nunc Veneris puerum
     utque sacri fontes non sola incendia sistunt,
       saepe etiam flores vernaque prata iuvant:
     sic hominum ingenium flecti ducique per artes
       non rigidas docta mobilitate decet.

12   Itaque summi oratores, summi etiam viri sic se aut
exercebant aut delectabant, immo delectabant exer-
13 cebantque. Nam mirum est, ut his opusculis animus intendatur, remittatur. Recipiunt enim amores,
odia, iras, misericordiam, urbanitatem, omnia denique,
quae in vita atque etiam in foro caussisque ver-

santur. Inest his quoque eadem, quae aliis carmi- 14
nibus utilitas, quod metri necessitate devincti, soluta
oratione laetamur, et quod facilius esse comparatio
ostendit, libentius scribimus. Habes plura etiam for- 15
tasse, quam requirebas; unum tamen omisi; non enim
dixi, quae legenda arbitrarer: quamquam dixi, cum
dicerem, quae scribenda. Tu memineris sui cuiusque
generis auctores diligenter eligere. Aiunt enim, multum legendum esse, non multa. Qui sint hi, adeo notum 16
provulgatumque est, ut demonstratione non egeat: et
alioqui tam immodice epistolam extendi, ut, dum tibi,
quemadmodum studere debeas, suadeo, studendi tempus abstulerim. Quin ergo pugillares resumis, et aliquid ex his, vel istud ipsum quod coeperas, scribis?
Vale.

B. V. (viii. 19.)

[Pliny, having at the time of writing many causes of
sorrow, dwells on the solace which he found in literature.
At the same time he begs his friend's opinion on a book
which accompanied his letter.]

C. PLINIUS MAXIMO SUO S.

Et gaudium mihi et solatium in literis; nihilque
tam laetum, quod his laetius, tam triste, quod non
per has sit minus triste. Itaque et infirmitate uxoris,
et meorum periculo, quorundam vero etiam morte
turbatus, ad unicum doloris levamentum studia con-
fugio; quae praestant, ut adversa magis intelligam, sed
patientius feram. Est autem mihi moris, quod sum 2
daturus in manus hominum, ante amicorum iudicio
examinare, in primis tuo. Proinde, si quando, nunc
intende libro, quem cum hac epistola accipies, quia
vereor, ne ipse, ut tristis, parum intenderim. Imperare enim dolori, ut scriberem, potui; ut vacuo animo
laetoque, non potui. Porro, ut ex studiis gaudium, sic
studia hilaritate proveniunt. Vale.

B. VI. (ix. 11.)

[Pliny expresses his surprise at hearing that there were booksellers at Lugdunum (Lyons), and his pleasure at learning that his own works were held in esteem in the provinces.]

C. PLINIUS GEMINO SUO S.

Epistolam tuam iucundissimam recepi, eo maxime, quod aliquid ad te scribi volebas, quod libris inseri posset. Obveniet materia, vel haec ipsa quam monstras, vel potior alia. Sunt enim in hac offendicula nonnulla : 2 circumfer oculos, et occurrent. Bibliopolas Lugduni esse non putabam, ac tanto libentius ex literis tuis cognovi venditari libellos meos, quibus peregre manere gratiam, quam in urbe collegerint, delector. Incipio enim satis absolutum existimare, de q io tanta diversitate regionum discreta hominum iudicia consentiunt. Vale.

B. VII. (vii. 20.)

[Pliny and Tacitus had recently been interchanging works with each other for the sake of mutual criticism. Pliny delights in the thought of being conjoined in public estimation with a man whom he had always greatly admired, and had set before himself as a literary model. The passage relating to the age of the two friends is worthy of notice.]

C. PLINIUS TACITO SUO S.

Librum tuum legi, et quam diligentissime potui, adnotavi, quae commutanda, quae eximenda arbitrarer. Nam et ego verum dicere adsuevi, et tu libenter audire. Neque enim ulli patientius reprehenduntur, quam qui 2 maxime laudari merentur. Nunc a te librum meum cum adnotationibus tuis exspecto. O iucundas, o pulchras vices ! Quam me delectat, quod, si qua posteris cura nostri, usquequaque narrabitur, qua concordia, 3 simplicitate, fide, vixerimus ! Erit rarum et insigne, duos homines, aetate, dignitate propemodum aequales, nonnullius in literis nominis (cogor enim de te quoque parcius dicere, quia de me simul dico) alterum alterius studia fovisse. Equidem adolescentulus, cum iam tu 4 fama gloriaque floreres, te sequi, tibi *longo, sed proximus, intervallo* et esse et haberi concupiscebam. Et erant multa clarissima ingenia : sed tu mihi (ita similitudo naturae ferebat) maxime imitabilis, maxime imitandus videbaris. Quo magis gaudeo, quod, si quis 5 de studiis sermo, una nominamur ; quod de te loquentibus statim occurro. Nec desunt, qui utrique nostrum praeferantur. Sed nihil interest mea, quo loco iun- 6 gimur ; nam mihi primus, qui a te proximus. Quin etiam in testamentis debes adnotasse : nisi quis forte alterutri nostrum amicissimus, eadem legata, et quidem pariter, accipimus. Quae omnia huc spectant, ut in- 7 vicem ardentius diligamus, cum tot vinculis nos studia, mores, fama, suprema denique hominum iudicia constringant. Vale.

B. VIII. (viii. 7.)

[Pliny, modestly confessing his inferiority to his friend Tacitus, acknowledges a book which he had sent to him, and promises to criticise it.]

C. PLINIUS TACITO SUO S.

Neque ut magistro magister, neque ut discipulo discipulus (sic enim scribis), sed ut discipulo magister, (nam tu magister, ego contra : atque adeo tu in scholam revocas, ego adhuc Saturnalia extendo) librum misisti. Num potui longius hyperbaton facere, atque hoc ipso 2 probare, eum me esse, qui non modo magister tuus, sed ne discipulus quidem debeam dici ? Sumam tamen personam magistri, exseramque in librum tuum ius, quod dedisti, eo liberius, quo nihil ex meis interim missurus sum tibi, in quo te ulciscaris. Vale.

B. IX. (ix. 14.)

[This, like the preceding, is a letter of friendly compliment to his friend Tacitus.]

C. PLINIUS TACITO SUO S.

Nec ipse tibi plaudis, et ego nihil magis ex fide,
quam de te scribo. Posteris an aliqua cura nostri,
nescio: nos certe meremur, ut sit aliqua, non dico ingenio (id enim superbum), sed studio, et labore, et reverentia posterorum. Pergamus modo itinere instituto,
quod ut paucos in lucem famamque provexit, ita multos
e tenebris et silentio protulit. Vale.

B. X. (ix. 23.)

[Pliny tells his friend Maximus of two incidents which had
greatly gratified him; the former as showing that he was
coupled with Tacitus as a representative of Roman letters,
the latter as proving that his name was not unknown in the
provinces. He defends what might have been thought vanity
by the example of Demosthenes.]

C. PLINIUS MAXIMO SUO S.

Frequenter agenti mihi evenit, ut centumviri, cum
diu se intra iudicum auctoritatem gravitatemque tenu-
issent, omnes repente quasi victi coactique consur-
2 gerent laudarentque. Frequenter e senatu famam,
qualem maxime optaveram, rettuli: nunquam tamen
maiorem cepi voluptatem, quam nuper ex sermone
Corneli Taciti. Narrabat, sedisse se cum quodam
Circensibus proximis: hunc post varios eruditos-
que sermones requisisse, *Italicus es, an provincialis?*
3 se respondisse, *Nosti me, et quidem ex studiis.* Ad
hoc illum, *Tacitus es, an Plinius?* Exprimere non possum, quam sit iucundum mihi, quod nomina nostra,
quasi literarum propria, non hominum, literis reddun-

tur; quod uterque nostrum his etiam ex studiis notus, quibus aliter ignotus est. Accidit aliud ante pauculos [4] dies simile. Recumbebat mecum vir egregius, Fabius Rufinus: super eum municeps ipsius, qui illo die primum venerat in urbem; cui Rufinus, demonstrans me, *Vides hunc?* Multa deinde de studiis nostris. Et ille, *Plinius est,* inquit. Verum fatebor, capio magnum [5] laboris mei fructum. An, si Demosthenes iure laetatus est, quod illum anus Attica ita noscitavit, Οὗτός ἐστι Δημοσθένης, ego celebritate nominis mei gaudere non debeo? Ego vero et gaudeo, et gaudere me dico. Neque enim vereor, ne iactantior videar, cum de me [6] aliorum iudicium, non meum, profero: praesertim apud te, qui nec ullius invides laudibus, et faves nostris. Vale.

B. XI. (iii. 5.)

[In this letter we have a complete list of the works of the elder Pliny. His way of life, too, is described in detail. So unwearied was his industry that absolute recreation appears to have been a thing unknown to him. The results of these incessant literary labours, which were on a prodigious scale, are now, with the exception of a few fragments, solely represented by the 'Natural History,' a much more comprehensive treatise than its name would suggest to a modern reader. It embraced the study both of organic and inorganic nature, and thus included a multitude of subjects which have no connection with 'natural history' in our sense. As the most trustworthy account we possess of this remarkable man, who was not merely distinguished by such varied attainments, but who had served as an officer in Germany and had been procurator in Spain, the present letter is especially interesting.

Baebius Macer, to whom this letter is addressed, is mentioned in A. XIV. as consul elect at the time when Pliny was engaged in the defence of Julius Bassus, who was impeached by the province of Bithynia.]

C. PLINIUS MACRO SUO S.

Pergratum est mihi, quod tam diligenter libros

avunculi mei lectitas, ut habere omnes velis, quaeras-
2 que, qui sint omnes. Fungar indicis partibus, atque
etiam, quo sint ordine scripti, notum tibi faciam. Est
enim haec quoque studiosis non iniucunda cognitio.
3 De iaculatione eqestri unus. Hunc, cum praefectus alae militaret, pari ingenio curaque composuit.
De vita Pomponii Secundi duo, a quo singulariter amatus, hoc memoriae amici quasi debitum munus
4 exsolvit.   Bellorum Germaniae viginti, quibus
omnia quae cum Germanis gessimus bella collegit.
Inchoavit, cum in Germania militaret, somnio monitus.
Adstitit ei quiescenti Drusi Neronis effigies, qui Germaniae latissime victor ibi periit: commendabat memoriam suam, orabatque, ut se ab iniuria oblivionis
5 adsereret.   Studiosi tres, in sex volumina propter
amplitudinem divisi: quibus oratorem ab incunabulis
instituit et perficit.   Dubii sermonis octo: scripsit
sub Nerone, novissimis annis, quum omne studiorum
genus paullo liberius et erectius periculosum servitus
6 fecisset.   A fine Aufidii Bassi triginta unus.
Naturae historiarum triginta septem, opus dif-
fusum, eruditum, nec minus varium quam ipsa natura.
7 Miraris, quod tot volumina, multaque in his tam scrupulosa, homo occupatus absolverit? Magis miraberis,
si scieris, illum aliquamdiu causas actitasse, decessisse
anno sexto et quinquagesimo, medium tempus dis-
tentum impeditumque qua officiis maximis, qua amicitia
8 principum egisse.   Sed erat acre ingenium, incredibile
studium, summa vigilantia.   Lucubrare Vulcanalibus
incipiebat, non auspicandi causa, sed studendi, statim a
nocte multa: hieme vero, ab hora septima, vel quum
tardissime, octava, saepe sexta. Erat sane somni paratissimi, nonnunquam etiam inter ipsa studia instantis
9 et deserentis.   Ante lucem ibat ad Vespasianum impe-
ratorem, nam ille quoque noctibus utebatur: inde ad
delegatum sibi officium. Reversus domum, quod re-
10 licum temporis, studiis reddebat.   Post cibum saepe
(quem interdiu levem et facilem veterum more sume-
bat) aestate, si quid otii, iacebat in sole: liber legebatur: adnotabat excerpebatque.   Nihil enim legit,

quod non excerperet. Dicere etiam solebat, nullum
esse librum tam malum, ut non aliqua parte prodesset.
Post solem plerumque frigida lavabatur. Deinde 11
gustabat, dormiebatque minimum. Mox, quasi alio
die, studebat in coenae tempus. Super hanc liber
legebatur, adnotabatur, et quidem cursim. Memini 12
quendam ex amicis, cum lector quaedam perperam pro-
nuntiasset, revocasse et repeti coëgisse : huic avuncu-
lum meum dixisse : *Intellexeras nempe?* quum ille
aduuisset, *Cur ergo revocabas? decem amplius versus
hac tua interpellatione perdidimus.* Tanta erat parsi- 13
monia temporis. Surgebat aestate a coena luce ; hieme
intra primam noctis, et tanquam aliqua lege cogente.
Haec inter medios labores urbisque fremitum. In 14
secessu solum balinei tempus studiis eximebatur. Cum
dico balinei, de interioribus loquor. Nam dum destringitur tergiturque, audiebat aliquid aut dictabat. In 15
itinere, quasi solutus ceteris curis, huic uni vacabat.
Ad latus notarius cum libro et pugillaribus, cuius manus
hieme manicis muniebantur, ut ne caeli quidem asperitas ullum studiis tempus eriperet : qua ex causa
Romae quoque sella vehebatur. Repeto, me correptum 16
ab eo, cur ambularem. *Poteras,* inquit, *has horas non
perdere.* Nam perire omne tempus arbitrabatur, quod
studiis non impertiretur. Hac intentione tot ista vo- 17
lumina peregit, Electorumque commentarios centum
sexaginta mihi reliquit, opisthographos quidem et minu-
tissime scriptos : qua ratione multiplicatur hic numerus. Referebat ipse, potuisse se, cum procuraret
in Hispania, vendere hos commentarios Largio Licinio
quadringentis millibus nummum: et tunc aliquanto pauciores erant. Nonne videtur tibi, recordanti quantum 18
legerit, quantum scripserit, nec in officiis ullis, nec in amicitia principum fuisse? rursus, cum audis, quid officiis
laboris impenderit, nec scripsisse, nec legisse? Quid est
enim, quod non aut illae occupationes impedire, aut haec
instantia non possit efficere? Itaque soleo ridere, 19
cum me quidam studiosum vocant, qui, si comparer
illi, sum desidiosissimus. Ego autem tantum, quem
partim publica, partim amicorum officia distringunt?

F

Quis ex istis, qui tota vita literis adsident, collatus illi,
20 non quasi somno et inertiae deditus erubescat? Extendi epistolam, cum hoc solum, quod requirebas,
scribere destinassem, quos libros reliquisset. Confido
tamen, haec quoque tibi non minus grata, quam ipsos
libros, futura: quae te non tantum ad legendos eos,
verum etiam ad simile aliquid elaborandum, possunt
aemulationis stimulis excitare. Vale.

B. XII. (iii. 7.)

[Pliny tells his friend of the death of Silius Italicus, who
under the pressure of an incurable disease had terminated his
life. He reviews the political character of the deceased,
makes a brief allusion to his poetry, and speaks more at
length of his tastes as a connoisseur. Readers of the *De Bello
Punico* will notice the special veneration which he is said to
have paid to the statue of Virgil. Silius had survived all his
contemporaries, and Pliny takes occasion from this circumstance to moralise on the brevity of life, and the necessity of
our leaving behind us some permanent memorial of ourselves.]

Modo nuntiatus est Silius Italicus in Neapolitano
2 suo inedia finisse vitam. Causa mortis valetudo. Erat
illi natus insanabilis clavus, cujus taedio ad mortem
irrevocabili constantia decucurrit, usque ad supremum
diem beatus et felix, nisi quod minorem ex liberis
duobus amisit, sed majorem melioremque florentem
3 atque etiam consularem reliquit. Laeserat famam
suam sub Nerone; credebatur sponte accusasse: sed
in Vitelli amicitia sapienter se et comiter gesserat: ex
proconsulatu Asiae gloriam reportaverat: maculam
4 veteris industriae laudabili otio abluerat. Fuit inter
principes civitatis sine potentia, sine invidia. Saluta-
batur, colebatur, multumque in lectulo iacens, cubiculo
semper non ex fortuna frequenti, doctissimis sermoni-
5 bus dies transigebat, cum a scribendo vacaret. Scribebat carmina maiore cura quam ingenio; nonnunquam
6 iudicia hominum recitationibus experiebatur. Novis-

sime, ita suadentibus annis, ab urbe secessit, seque in
Campania tenuit, ac ne adventu quidem novi principis
inde commotus est. Magna Caesaris laus, sub quo 7
hoc liberum fuit: magna illius, qui hac libertate ausus
est uti. Erat φιλόκαλος usque ad emacitatis reprehensionem. Plures isdem in locis villas possidebat, ada- 8
matisque novis, priores negligebat. Multum ubique
librorum, multum statuarum, multum imaginum, quas
non habebat modo, verum etiam venerabatur, Vergili
ante omnes, cuius natalem religiosius, quam suum, ce-
lebrabat, Neapoli maxime, ubi monimentum eius adire,
ut templum, solebat. In hac tranquillitate annum 9
quintum et septuagesimum excessit, delicato magis
corpore, quam infirmo. Utque novissimus a Nerone
factus est consul, ita postremus ex omnibus, quos Nero
consules fecerat, decessit. Illud etiam notabile: ulti- 10
mus ex Neronianis consularibus obiit, quo consule Nero
periit. Quod me recordantem, fragilitatis humanae
miseratio subit. Quid enim tam circumcisum, tam 11
breve, quam hominis vita longissima? An non videtur
tibi Nero modo fuisse, cum interim ex iis, qui sub illo
gesserant consulatum, nemo iam superest? Quamquam 12
quid hoc miror? Nuper Lucius Piso, pater Pisonis
illius, qui a Valerio Festo per summum facinus in
Africa occisus est, dicere solebat, *Neminem se videre in*
senatu, quem consul ipse sententiam rogavisset. Tam 13
angustis terminis tantae multitudinis vivacitas ipsa
concluditur: ut mihi non venia solum dignae, verum
etiam laude videantur illae regiae lacrymae. Nam
ferunt, Xerxem, cum immensum exercitum oculis ob-
isset, illacrimasse, quod tot millibus tam brevis immi-
neret occasus. Sed tanto magis hoc, quidquid est 14
temporis, futilis et caduci, si non datur factis (nam
horum materia in aliena manu), certe studiis proferamus,
et quatenus nobis denegatur diu vivere, relinquamus
aliquid, quo nos vixisse testemur. Scio te stimulis non 15
egere; me tamen tui caritas evocat, ut currentem quoque instigem, sicut tu soles me. Ἀγαθὴ δ' ἔρις, cum
invicem se mutuis exhortationibus amici ad amorem
immortalitatis exacuunt. Vale.

F 2

B. XIII. (iii. 21.)

[This letter is an obituary notice of the poet Martial.
Pliny expresses a high opinion of his talents, and speaks of
the help which he had given him. This help was in fact
an acknowledgment of some high compliments which the poet
had paid him in an epigram, part of which is here quoted,
and which may be found in x. 19.

Cornelius Priscus, to whom this and letters ii. 13, vi. 8,
vii. 8, &c. are addressed, is mentioned in v. 20 as a Consularis.
Probably he was the Priscus who was consul A.D. 93, the
year of Agricola's death (v. Tac. *Agr.* 44).]

C. PLINIUS PRISCO SUO S.

Audio Valerium Martialem decessisse, et moleste
fero. Erat homo ingeniosus, acutus, acer, et qui plurimum in scribendo et salis haberet et fellis, nec can-
2 doris minus. Prosecutus eram viatico secedentem.
Dederam hoc amicitiae, dederam etiam versiculis, quos
3 de me composuit. Fuit moris antiqui, eos, qui vel
singulorum laudes, vel urbium scripserant, aut honoribus aut pecunia ornare : nostris vero temporibus, ut
alia speciosa et egregia, ita hoc in primis exolevit. Nam
postquam desimus facere laudanda, laudari quoque
4 ineptum putamus. Quaeris, qui sint versiculi, quibus
gratiam rettuli? Remitterem te ad ipsum volumen,
nisi quosdam tenerem : tu, si placuerint hi, ceteros in
5 libro requires. Adloquitur Musam, mandat, ut domum
meam Esquilis quaerat, adeat reverenter :

> Sed, ne tempore non tuo disertam
> pulses ebria ianuam, videto.
> Totos dat tetricae dies Minervae,
> dum centum studet auribus virorum
> hoc, quod secula posterique possint
> Arpinis quoque comparare chartis.
> Seras tutior ibis ad lucernas.
> Haec hora est tua, cum furit Lyaeus,
> cum regnat rosa, cum madent capilli.
> Tunc me vel rigidi legant Catones.

Meritone eum, qui haec de me scripsit, et tunc dimisi 6
amicissime, et nunc, ut amicissimum, defunctum esse
doleo? Dedit enim mihi, quantum maximum potuit,
daturus amplius, si potuisset. Tametsi quid homini
potest dari maius, quam gloria, et laus, et aeternitas?
At non erunt aeterna quae scripsit. Non erunt fortasse : ille tamen scripsit tanquam essent futura. Vale.

B. XIV. (ii. 3.)

[This letter is an eulogium of Isaeus, a rhetorician of whom
Juvenal speaks (iii. 74) as a singularly powerful speaker, and
who is noticed at some length by Philostratus in his *Lives
of the Sophists*. Isaeus did not practise as an advocate, but
delivered extempore declamations with wonderful correctness
and fluency, Pliny tells us, though on this point Philostratus
contradicts him.

Three letters beside this are addressed to Nepos. He is not
to be identified with the praetor Licinius Nepos (iv. 29, &c.),
but is the Varisidius Nepos of iv. 4, for whom Pliny asks
from Sosius Senecio a military tribuneship. Nepos was a
warm admirer of Pliny. He afterwards obtained the governorship of a province.]

C. PLINIUS NEPOTI SUO S.

Magna Isaeum fama praecesserat : maior inventus
est. Summa est facultas, copia, ubertas : dicit semper
ex tempore, sed tamquam diu scripserit. Sermo Grac-
cus, immo Atticus : praefationes tersae, graciles, dul-
ces ; graves interdum et erectae. Ponit controversias 2
plures, electionem auditoribus permittit, saepe etiam
imparatus : surgit, amicitur, incipit. Statim omnia ac
paene pariter ad manum : sensus reconditi occursant,
verba, sed qualia! quaesita et exculta. Multa lectio in
subitis, multa scriptio elucet. Prooemiatur apte, narrat 3
aperte, pugnat acriter, colligit fortiter, ornat excelse :
postremo docet, delectat, adficit ; quid maxime, dubites.
Crebra νοήματα, crebri syllogismi, circumscripti et

effeci: quod stilo quoque adsequi magnum est. In-
credibilis memoria: repetit altius, quae dixit ex tem-
4 pore, ne verbo quidem labitur. Ad tantam ἕξιν studio
et exercitatione pervenit: nam diebus et noctibus nihil
5 aliud agit, nihil audit, nihil loquitur. Annum sexagesimum excessit, et adhuc scholasticus tantum est:
quo genere hominum nihil aut simplicius, aut sincerius,
aut melius. Nos enim, qui in foro verisque litibus
terimur, multum malitiae, quamvis nolimus, addiscimus.
6 Schola, et auditorium, et ficta causa, res inermis, in-
noxia est, nec minus felix, senibus praesertim. Nam
quid in senectute felicius, quam quod dulcissimum est
7 in iuventa? Quare ego Isaeum non disertissimum
tantum, verum etiam beatissimum iudico, quem tu nisi
8 cognoscere concupiscis, saxeus ferreusque es. Proinde,
si non ob alia nosque ipsos, at certe ut hunc audias,
veni. Numquamne legisti, Gaditanum quendam, Titi
Livi nomine gloriaque commotum, ad visendum eum
ab ultimo terrarum orbe venisse, statimque, ut viderat,
abisse? Ἀφιλόκαλον, illiteratum, iners, ac paene etiam
turpe est, non putare tanti cognitionem, qua nulla est
iucundior, nulla pulchrior, nulla denique humanior.
9 Dices: *Habeo hic quos legam, non minus disertos.*
Etiam: sed legendi semper occasio est, audiendi non
semper. Multo magis, ut vulgo dicitur, viva vox adficit. Nam licet acriora sint, quae legas, altius tamen
in animo sedent, quae pronuntiatio, vultus, habitus,
10 gestus etiam dicentis adfigit; nisi vero falsum putamus
illud Aeschinis, qui cum legisset Rhodiis orationem
Demosthenis, admirantibus cunctis, adiecisse fertur:
Τί δέ, εἰ αὐτοῦ τοῦ θηρίου ἠκούσατε; Et erat Aeschines,
si Demostheni credimus, λαμπροφωνότατος. Fatebatur
tamen, longe melius eadem illa pronuntiasse ipsum,
11 qui pepererat. Quae omnia huc tendunt, ut audias
Isaeum: vel ideo tantum, ut audieris. Vale.

B. XV. (v. 5.)

[Pliny here deplores the premature death of Caius Fannius, who, though he was a pleader in large practice, had found time to complete a considerable part of a work on the deaths of those who had been executed or banished by Nero. This book had attracted numerous readers, but Fannius had not lived to finish it. Pliny relates a singular dream which the deceased man had taken to be a warning of his approaching end.]

C. PLINIUS MAXIMO SUO S.

Nuntiatur mihi C. Fannium decessisse, qui nuntius gravi me dolore confudit: primum, quod amavi hominem elegantem disertum : deinde, quod iudicio eius uti solebam. Erat enim natura acutus, usu exercitatus, veritate promptissimus. Angit me super ista casus 2 ipsius ; decessit veteri testamento : omisit, quos maxime diligebat: prosecutus est, quibus offensior erat. Sed hoc utcunque tolerabile ; gravius illud, quod pulcherrimum opus imperfectum reliquit. Quamvis enim 3 agendis causis distringeretur, scribebat tamen exitus occisorum aut relegatorum a Nerone, et iam tres libros absolverat, subtiles, et diligentes, et Latinos, atque inter sermonem historiamque medios ; ac tanto magis reliquos perficere cupiebat, quanto frequentius hi lectitabantur. Mihi autem videtur acerba semper 4 et immatura mors eorum, qui immortale aliquid parant. Nam qui voluptatibus dediti quasi in diem vivunt, vivendi causas quotidie finiunt : qui vero posteros cogitant, et memoriam sui operibus extendunt, his nulla mors non repentina est, ut quae semper inchoatum aliquid abrumpat. Caius quidem Fannius, quod acci- 5 dit, multo ante praesensit. Visus est sibi per nocturnam quietem iacere in lectulo suo compositus in habitu studentis, habere ante se scrinium (ita solebat): mox imaginatus est venisse Neronem, in toro sedisse, prempsisse primum librum, quem de sceleribus eius ediderat, eumque ad extremum revolvisse ; idem in

6 secundo ac tertio fecisse; tunc abiisse. Expavit; et sic
interpretatus est, tanquam idem sibi futurus esset scri-
7 bendi finis, qui fuisset illi legendi: et fuit idem. Quod
me recordantem miseratio subit, quantum vigiliarum,
quantum laboris exhauserit frustra. Occursant animo
mea mortalitas, mea scripta. Nec dubito, te quoque
eadem cogitatione terreri pro istis, quae inter manus
8 habes. Proinde, dum suppetit vita, enitamur, ut mors
quam paucissima, quae abolere possit, inveniat. Vale.

B. XVI. (vi. 21.)

[Pliny praises one of his literary contemporaries, a writer
of comedies not inferior, in his judgment, to those of Plautus
and Terence. He had lately heard him read one of them to
a select audience, and had been much impressed with his
genius.]

C. PLINIUS CANINIO SUO S.

Sum ex iis, qui mirantur antiquos: non tamen, ut
quidam, temporum nostrorum ingenia despicio. Neque
enim, quasi lassa et effeta, natura nihil iam laudabile
2 parit. Atque adeo nuper audii Vergilium Romanum
paucis legentem comoediam, ad exemplar veteris co-
moediae scriptam tam bene, ut esse quandoque possit
3 exemplar. Nescio, an noris hominem. Quamquam
nosse debes; est enim probitate morum, ingenii ele-
4 gantia, operum varietate monstrabilis. Scripsit mimi-
ambos tenuiter, argute, venuste, atque in hoc genere
eloquentissime. Nullum est enim genus, quod, absolu-
lutum, non possit eloquentissimum dici. Scripsit co-
moedias, Menandrum aliosque aetatis eiusdem aemula-
tus. Licet has inter Plautinas Terentianasque numeres.
5 Nunc primum se in vetere comoedia, sed non tanquam
inciperet, ostendit. Non illi vis, non granditas, non
subtilitas, non amaritudo, non dulcedo, non lepos defuit.
Ornavit virtutes, insectatus est vitia: fictis nominibus
6 decenter, veris usus est apte. Circa me tantum be-

nignitate nimia modum excessit, nisi quod tamen poëtis mentiri licet. In summa, extorquebo ei librum, le- 7 gendumque, immo ediscendum, mittam tibi. Neque enim dubito futurum, ut non deponas, si semel sumpseris. Vale.

B. XVII. (ix. 22.)

[Pliny here recounts the praises of the poet Passennus Paullus, expresses the grief which he had felt when the life of his friend had recently been endangered by sickness, and congratulates himself and literature in general on the fact that the danger was past.]

C. PLINIUS SEVERO SUO S.

Magna me solicitudine adfecit Passenni Paulli valetudo, et quidem plurimis iustissimisque de causis. Vir est optimus, honestissimus, nostri amantissimus; praeterea in literis veteres aemulatur, exprimit, reddit: Propertium in primis, a quo genus ducit, vera soboles, eoque simillima illi, in quo ille praecipuus. Si elegos 2 eius in manum sumpseris, leges opus tersum, molle, iucundum, et plane in Propertii domo scriptum. Nuper ad lyrica deflexit, in quibus ita Horatium, ut in illis illum alterum, effingit. Putes, si quid in studiis cognatio valet, et huius propinquum. Magna varietas, magna mobilitas. Amat, ut qui verissime; dolet, ut qui impatientissime; laudat, ut qui benignissime; ludit, ut qui facetissime: omnia denique tamquam singula absolvit. Pro hoc ego amico, pro hoc ingenio, non minus 3 aeger animo, quam corpore ille, tandem illum, tandem me recepi. Gratulare mihi; gratulare etiam literis ipsis, quae ex periculo eius tantum discrimen adierunt, quantum ex salute gloriae consequentur. Vale.

B. XVIII. (viii. 4.)

[Pliny's friend and fellow-townsman, Caninius Rufus, was
thinking of describing in a poem Trajan's two campaigns in
Dacia. The result of this war, which lasted from A.D. 101 to
106, was two triumphs, the defeat and death of the Thracian
king Decebalus, and the reduction of Dacia to a province.
Such a subject, Pliny says, could not fail to present a wide
scope for poetical genius. Among the difficulties of the work
would be the adaptation to verse of the rude and barbarous
names which would have to be introduced. Pliny, however,
encourages his friend to persist in his design, and expresses a
hope that he shall soon be permitted to see the opening lines
of the poem.]

C. PLINIUS CANINIO SUO S.

Optime facis, quod bellum Dacicum scribere paras.
Nam quae tam recens, tam copiosa, tam lata, quae denique tam poëtica, et (quamquam in verissimis rebus)
2 tam fabulosa materia? Dices immissa terris nova flumina, novos pontes fluminibus iniectos, insessa castris
montium abrupta, pulsum regia, pulsum etiam vita regem nihil desperantem; super haec, actos bis trium-
phos; quorum alter ex invicta gente primus, alter
3 novissimus fuit. Una, sed maxima, difficultas, quod
haec aequare dicendo, arduum, immensum, etiam tuo
ingenio, quamquam altissime adsurgat, et amplissimis
operibus increscat. Nonnullus et in illo labor, ut
barbara et fera nomina, in primis regis ipsius, Graecis
4 versibus non resultent. Sed nihil est, quod non arte
curaque, si non potest vinci, mitigetur. Praeterea, si
datur Homero et mollia vocabula et Graeca ad levitatem
versus contrahere, extendere, inflectere; cur tibi similis
audentia, praesertim non delicata, sed necessaria, ne-
5 getur? Proinde iure vatum, invocatis diis, et inter eos
ipso, cuius res, opera, consilia dicturus es, immitte
rudentes, pande vela, ac, si quando alias, toto ingenio
vehere. Cur enim non ego quoque poëtice cum poëta?
6 Illud iam nunc paciscor : prima quaeque ut absolveris,
mittito immo etiam antequam absolvas; sicut erunt

recentia, et rudia, et adhuc similia nascentibus. Re-7
spondebis, non posse perinde carptim ut contexta,
perinde inchoata placere ut effecta. Scio. Itaque et
a me aestimabuntur ut coepta, spectabuntur ut membra,
extremamque limam tuam opperientur in scrinio nostro.
Patere hoc me super cetera habere amoris tui pignus,
ut ea quoque norim, quae nosse neminem velles. In 8
summa, potero fortasse scripta tua magis probare,
laudare, quanto illa tardius cautiusque; sed ipsum te
magis amabo, magisque laudabo, quanto celerius et
incautius miseris. Vale.

B. XIX. (i. 16.)

[Pliny here descants on the literary accomplishments of his
friend Pompeius Saturninus, who was on a visit to him at the
time, and whose advice we find him asking in B. II. in
reference to the publication of a speech lately delivered by
him.

The Erucius to whom this letter is addressed is mentioned in
ii. 9, where we find that Pliny had been the means of securing
for him senatorial rank and a quaestorship. Aulus Gellius
speaks of him as a man attached to the study of ancient literature, and as having been prefect of the city and twice
consul. He was nephew to the Septicius to whom Pliny
dedicates his letters.]

C. PLINIUS ERUCIO SUO S.

Amabam Pompeium Saturninum, hunc dico nostrum,
laudabamque eius ingenium, etiam antequam scirem,
quam varium, quam flexibile, quam multiplex esset:
nunc vero totum me tenet, habet, possidet. Audivi 2
causas agentem acriter et ardenter, nec minus polite et
ornate, sive meditata sive subita proferret. Adsunt
aptae crebraeque sententiae, gravis et decora constructio, sonantia verba et antiqua. Omnia haec mire
placent, cum impetu quodam et flumine praevehuntur,
placent, si retractentur. Senties, quod ego, cum ora-3
tiones eius in manus sumpseris; quas facile cuilibet

4 veterum, quorum est aemulus, comparabis. Idem tamen in historia magis satisfaciet vel brevitate, vel luce, vel suavitate, vel splendore, etiam sublimitate narrandi. Nam in concionibus eadem, quae in orationibus, vis est: pressior tamen, et circumscriptior, et adductior.

5 Praeterea facit versus, quales Catullus aut Calvus. Quantum illis leporis, dulcedinis, amaritudinis, amoris! Inserit sane, sed data opera, mollibus levibusque duriusculos quosdam; et hoc, quasi Catullus aut Calvus.

6 Legit mihi nuper epistolas: uxoris esse dicebat: Plautum vel Terentium metro solutum legi credidi. Quae sive uxoris sunt, ut adfirmat, sive ipsius, ut negat, pari gloria dignus, qui aut illa componat, aut uxorem, quam virginem accepit, tam doctam politamque reddiderit.

7 Est ergo mecum per diem totum: eundem antequam scribam, eundem cum scripsi, eundem etiam cum remittor, non tanquam eundem, lego. Quod te quoque

8 ut facias, et hortor et moneo. Neque enim debet operibus eius obesse, quod vivit. An, si inter eos, quos nunquam vidimus, floruisset, non solum libros eius, verum etiam imagines conquireremus; eiusdem nunc honor praesentis et gratia, quasi satietate, languescit?

9 At hoc pravum malignumque est, non admirari hominem admiratione dignissimum, quia videre, adloqui, audire, complecti, nec laudare tantum, verum etiam amare contigit. Vale.

B. XX. (iii. 11.)

[Pliny here dwells on the merits of his friend Artemidorus, whose acquaintance he had first made when serving as military tribune in Syria, and whom he had served both by personal support and by the loan of a sum of money when Domitian expelled the philosophers from Rome. To this class Artemidorus belonged, though he was free from the peculiarities which were offensively evident in some of them. He was son-in-law of the famous Stoic philosopher, Musonius Rufus. (Comp. Tacitus, *Ann.* xiv. 59; *Hist.* iii. 81, &c.)]

C. PLINIUS IULIO GENITORI SUO S.

Est omnino Artemidori nostri tam benigna natura, ut officia amicorum in maius extollat : inde etiam meum meritum, ut vera, ita supra meritum praedicatione circumfert. Equidem, cum essent philosophi ab urbe 2 submoti, fui apud illum in suburbano : et quo notabilius hoc et periculosius esset, fui praetor. Pecuniam etiam, qua tunc illi ampliore opus erat, ut aes alienum exsolveret, contractum ex pulcherrimis causis, mussantibus magnis quibusdam et locupletibus amicis, mutuatus ipse, gratuitam dedi. Atque haec feci, cum, 3 septem amicis meis aut occisis aut relegatis (occisis Senecione, Rustico, Helvidio; relegatis Maurico, Gratilla, Arria, Fannia), tot circa me iactis fulminibus quasi ambustus, mihi quoque impendere idem exitium, certis quibusdam notis augurarer. Non ideo tamen 4 eximiam gloriam meruisse me, ut ille praedicat, credo, sed tantum effugisse flagitium. Nam et C. Musonium, 5 socerum eius (quantum licitum est per aetatem), cum admiratione dilexi, et Artemidorum ipsum iam tum, cum in Syria tribunus militarem, arcta familiaritate complexus sum : idque primum nonnullius indolis dedi specimen, quod virum aut sapientem, aut proximum simillimumque sapienti, intelligere sum visus. Nam ex 6 omnibus, qui nunc se philosophos vocant, vix unum aut alterum invenies tanta sinceritate, tanta veritate. Mitto, qua patientia corporis hiemes iuxta et aestates ferat, ut nullis laboribus cedat, ut nihil in cibo, in potu voluptatibus tribuat, ut oculos animumque contineat. Sunt 7 haec magna, sed in alio : in hoc vero minima, si ceteris virtutibus comparentur, quibus meruit, ut a C. Musonio ex omnibus omnium ordinum adsectatoribus gener adsumeretur. Quae mihi recordanti est quidem iucun- 8 dum, quod me cum apud alios, tum apud te, tantis laudibus cumulat : vereor tamen, ne modum excedat, quem benignitas eius (illuc enim, unde coepi, revertor) non solet tenere. Nam in hoc uno interdum, vir 9 alioqui prudentissimus, honesto quidem, sed tamen errore versatur, quod pluris amicos suos, quam sunt, arbitratur. Vale.

B. XXI. (i. 10.)

[This letter is an account of a Stoic philosopher whose acquaintance Pliny had made as a youth when he was on military service in Syria. Pliny speaks of the philosopher in terms of the highest esteem and admiration; he dwells on his remarkable abilities, the excellence and uprightness of his character, and the sweetness of his disposition and manners—a specially noteworthy quality in a Stoic. He concludes with an expression of regret that his legal occupations interfere with his enjoyment of so good a man's society.

Euphrates is the subject of one of Philostratus' *Lives of the Sophists*, and his oratorical powers are spoken of by Arrian, the pupil of Epictetus and the author of Alexander's Expedition into Asia (*Dissert. Epictet.* iii. 15, iv. 8), and by Marcus Aurelius, afterwards Emperor (x. 31).]

C. PLINIUS ATTIO SUO S.

Si quando urbs nostra liberalibus studiis floruit, nunc
2 maxime floret. Multa claraque exempla sunt. Sufficeret unum, Euphrates philosophus. Hunc ego in Syria, cum adolescentulus militarem, penitus et domi inspexi. amarique ab eo laboravi, etsi non erat laboran-
dum. Est enim obvius et expositus, plenusque humani-
3 tate, quam praecipit. Atque utinam sic ipse, quam spem tunc ille de me concepit, impleverim, ut ille multum virtutibus suis addidit! aut ego nunc illas magis miror, quia magis intelligo. Quamquam ne nunc
4 quidem satis intelligo. Ut enim de pictore, sculptore, fictore, nisi artifex, iudicare, ita, nisi sapiens, non potest
5 perspicere sapientem. Quantum mihi tamen cernere datur, multa in Euphrate sic eminent et elucent, ut mediocriter quoque doctos advertant et adficiant. Disputat subtiliter, graviter, ornate: frequenter etiam Platoni-
cam illam sublimitatem et latitudinem effingit. Sermo est copiosus et varius: dulcis in primis, et qui repug-
6 nantes quoque ducat, impellat. Ad hoc, proceritas corporis, decora facies, demissus capillus, ingens et cana barba: quae licet fortuita et inania putentur, illi ta-
7 men plurimum venerationis adquirunt. Nullus horror

in cultu, nulla tristitia, multum severitatis : reverearis
occursum, non reformides. Vitae sanctitas summa,
comitas par. Insectatur vitia, non homines : nec cas-
tigat errantes, sed emendat. Sequaris monentem
attentus et pendens : et persuaderi tibi, etiam cum
persuaserit, cupias. Iam vero liberi tres, duo mares, 8
quos diligentissime instituit. Socer Pompeius Iulianus,
cum cetera vita, tum vel hoc uno magnus et clarus,
quod ipse provinciae princeps, inter altissimas conditiones, generum non honoribus principem, sed sapientia,
elegit. Quamquam quid ego plura de viro, quo mihi 9
frui non licet ? An ut magis angar, quod non licet ?
Nam distringor officio, ut maximo, sic molestissimo.
Sedeo pro tribunali, subnoto libellos, conficio tabulas :
scribo plurimas sed illiteratissimas literas. Soleo non- 10
nunquam (nam id ipsum quando contingit !) de his occupationibus apud Euphratem queri. Ille me consolatur ; adfirmat etiam, esse hanc philosophiae, et quidem
pulcherrimam partem, agere negotium publicum, cognoscere, iudicare, promere et exercere iustitiam, quaeque ipsi doceant, in usu habere. Mihi tamen hoc 11
unum non persuadet, satius esse ista facere, quam cum
illo dies totos audiendo discendoque consumere. Quo
magis te, cui vacat, hortor, cum in urbem proxime
veneris (venias autem ob hoc maturius), illi te expolien-
dum limandumque permittas. Neque enim ego, ut 12
multi, invideo aliis bonum quo ipse careo, sed contra
sensum quendam voluptatemque percipio, si ea, quae
mihi denegantur, amicis video superesse. Vale.

B. XXII. (i. 13.)

[Pliny complains that, though there were many poets of a high order in Rome, the audiences which were gathered at their recitations were careless and indifferent. He himself, he says, set a better example, prolonging his stay in town that he might encourage by his presence these rising men of genius.]

C. PLINIUS SOSIO SENECIONI SUO S.

Magnum proventum poëtarum annus hic attulit. Toto mense Aprili nullus fere dies, quo non recitaret aliquis. Iuvat me, quod vigent studia, proferunt se ingenia hominum et ostentant: tametsi ad audiendum 2 pigre coitur. Plerique in stationibus sedent, tempusque audiendi fabulis conterunt, ac subinde sibi nuntiari iubent, an iam recitator intraverit, an dixerit praefationem, an ex magna parte evolverit librum: tum demum, ac tunc quoque lente cunctanterque, veniunt: nec tamen permanent, sed ante finem recedunt, alii 3 dissimulanter et furtim, alii simpliciter et libere. At Hercule memoria parentum Claudium Caesarem ferunt, cum in palatio spatiaretur, audissetque clamorem, causam requisisse; cumque dictum esset, recitare Nonianum, subitum recitanti inopinatumque venisse. 4 Nunc otiosissimus quisque multo ante rogatus, et identidem admonitus, aut non venit, aut, si venit, queritur 5 se diem, quia non perdiderit, perdidisse. Sed tanto magis laudandi probandique sunt, quos a scribendi recitandique studio haec auditorum vel desidia vel superbia non retardat. Equidem prope nemini defui. Erant sane plerique amici: neque enim est fere quis- 6 quam, qui studia, ut non simul et nos amet. His ex causis longius, quam destinaveram, tempus in urbe consumpsi. Possum iam repetere secessum, et scribere aliquid, quod non recitem; ne videar, quorum recitationibus adfui, non auditor fuisse, sed creditor. Nam ut in ceteris rebus, ita in audiendi officio perit gratia, si reposcatur. Vale.

B. XXIII. (vi. 15.)

[Pliny here relates the amusing incident of a ridiculous interruption which had happened at a recitation of Passennus Paullus. For an account of Passennus see B. XVII.]

C. PLINIUS ROMANO SUO S.

Mirificae rei non interfuisti: ne ego quidem: sed me recens fabula excepit. Passennus Paullus, splendidus eques Romanus et in primis eruditus, scribit elegos. Gentilicium hoc illi: est enim municeps Properti, atque etiam inter maiores suos Propertium numerat. Is cum recitaret, ita coepit dicere, *Prisce*, 2 *iubes.* Ad hoc Iavolenus Priscus (aderat enim, ut Paullo amicissimus), *Ego vero non iubeo.* Cogita, qui risus hominum, qui ioci. Est omnino Priscus dubiae 3 sanitatis: interest tamen officiis, adhibetur consiliis, atque etiam ius civile publice respondet: quo magis, quod tunc fecit, et ridiculum et notabile fuit. Interim 4 Paullo aliena deliratio aliquantum frigoris attulit. Tam sollicite recitaturis providendum est, non solum ut sint ipsi sani, verum etiam ut sanos adhibeant. Vale.

B. XXIV. (viii. 12.)

[Pliny, in reply to a friend who desired his presence on a certain day, excuses himself. He felt himself obliged to attend a recitation given by Titinius Capito, an accomplished author, a patron of letters, and a friend of his own, who had written moreover on a subject in which Pliny felt great interest, *The Deaths of Distinguished Men.*]

C. PLINIUS MINUTIANO SUO S.

Hunc solum diem excuso. Recitaturus est Titinius Capito, quem ego audire, nescio magis debeam, an cupiam. Vir est optimus, et inter praecipua seculi

G

ornamenta numerandus: colit studia, studiosos amat.
fovet, provehit, multorum, qui aliqua componunt, portus, sinus, praemium; omnium exemplum; ipsarum
denique literarum iam senescentium reductor ac refor-
2 mator. Domum suam recitantibus praebet: auditoria,
non apud se tantum, benignitate mira frequentat;
mihi certe, si modo in urbe, defuit nunquam. Porro
tanto turpius gratiam non referre, quanto honestior
3 caussa referendae. An, si litibus tererer, obstrictum
esse me crederem obeunti vadimonia mea; nunc, quia
mihi omne negotium, omnis in studiis cura, minus ob-
ligor tanta sedulitate celebranti, in quo obligari ego,
4 ne dicam solo, certe maxime possum? Quod si illi
nullam vicem, nulla quasi mutua officia deberem, soli-
citarer tamen vel ingenio hominis pulcherrimo et maximo, et in summa severitate dulcissimo, vel honestate
materiae. Scribit exitus illustrium virorum, in his
5 quorundam mihi carissimorum. Videor ergo fungi pio
munere, quorumque exsequias celebrare non licuit,
horum quasi funebribus laudationibus, seris quidem,
sed tanto magis veris, interesse. Vale.

B. XXV. (viii. 21.)

[We have in this letter Pliny's reasons for composing and
reading aloud to his friends various light and playful effusions.
It was his practice to read the entire composition, and not, as
was the habit of most authors, to select a few passages. By
this means he hoped to get the benefit of thorough and candid
criticism.]

C. PLINIUS ARRIANO SUO S.

Ut in vita, sic in studiis, pulcherrimum et humanis-
simum existimo, severitatem comitatemque miscere, ne
2 illa in tristitiam, haec in petulantiam excedat. Qua
ratione ductus, graviora opera lusibus iocisque dis-
tinguo. Ad hos proferendos et tempus et locum op-
portunissimum elegi; utque iam nunc adsuescerent et

ab otiosis et in triclinio audiri, Iulio mense, quo maxime
lites quiescunt, positis ante lectos cathedris, amicos col-
locavi. Forte accidit, ut eo die mane in advocationem 3
subitam rogarer : quod mihi causam praeloquendi dedit.
Sum enim deprecatus, ne quis ut irreverentem operis
argueret, quod recitaturus, quamquam et amicis et
paucis, idem iterum amicis, foro et negotiis non abstinuissem. Addidi, hunc ordinem me et in scribendo
sequi, ut necessitates voluptatibus, seria iucundis ante-
ferrem, ac primum amicis, tum mihi scriberem. Liber 4
fuit et opusculis varius et metris. Ita solemus, qui
ingenio parum fidimus, satietatis periculum fugere.
Recitavi biduo : hoc adsensus audientium exegit : et
tamen ut alii transeunt quaedam, imputantque, quod
transeant ; sic ego nihil praetereo, atque etiam non
praeterire me testor. Lego enim omnia, ut omnia
emendem, quod contingere non potest electa recitantibus. At illud modestius et fortasse reverentius. Sed 5
hoc simplicius et amantius. Amat enim, qui se sic
amari putat, ut taedium non pertimescat ; et alioqui
quid praestant sodales, si conveniunt voluptatis suae
causa ? Delicatus ac similis ignoto est, qui amici librum
bonum mavult audire, quam facere. Non dubito, cupere 6
te, pro cetera mei caritate, quam maturissime legere
hunc adhuc musteum librum. Leges, sed retractatum ;
quae causa recitandi fuit ; et tamen non nulla iam ex
eo nosti. Haec vel emendata postea, vel (quod interdum longiore mora solet) deteriora facta, quasi nova
rursus, et rescripta cognosces. Nam, plerisque mutatis,
ea quoque mutata videntur, quae manent. Vale.

Section C.

LETTERS ON SUBJECTS CONNECTED WITH THE AUTHOR'S PROFESSION AS AN ADVOCATE

C. I. (ii. 14.)

[Pliny describes his growing disgust at the character of the practice in the court of the Centumviri. The causes were, for the most part, insignificant, the advocates young and inexperienced, but full of offensive assurance, the audience actually hired to applaud. He relates an anecdote, which he had heard from his master Quintilian, of the origin of this practice of hiring *claqueurs*.]

C. PLINIUS MAXIMO SUO S.

Verum opinaris: distringor centumviralibus causis, quae me exercent magis, quam delectant. Sunt enim pleraeque parvae et exiles. Raro incidit vel personarum claritate vel negotii magnitudine insignis. Ad 2 hoc, pauci, cum quibus iuvat dicere: ceteri audaces, atque etiam magna ex parte adolescentuli obscuri, ad declamandum huc transeunt, tam irreverenter et temere, ut mihi Attilius noster expresse dixisse videatur, sic in foro pueros a centumviralibus causis auspicari, ut ab Homero in scholis. Nam hic quoque, ut illic, primum coepit esse, quod maximum est. At Hercule 3 ante memoriam meam (ita maiores natu solent dicere), ne nobilissimis quidem adolescentibus locus erat, nisi aliquo consulari producente: tanta veneratione pulcherrimum opus colebatur. Nunc, refractis pudoris et 4 reverentiae claustris, omnia patent omnibus; nec inducuntur, sed irrumpunt. Sequuntur auditores actoribus similes, conducti et redempti: manceps convenitur; in media basilica tam palam sportulae, quam in triclinio, dantur. Ex iudicio in iudicium pari mercede transitur. Inde iam non inurbane Σοφοκλεῖς vocantur [ἀπὸ 5 τοῦ σοφῶς καὶ καλεῖσθαι]: isdem Latinum nomen impositum est laudicoeni. Et tamen crescit in dies foeditas utraque lingua notata. Heri duo nomenclatores 6 mei (habent sane aetatem eorum, qui nuper togas sumpserunt) ternis denariis ad laudandum trahebantur. Tanti constat, ut sis disertissimus. Hoc pretio quamlibet numerosa subsellia implentur: hoc ingens corona

colligitur : hoc infiniti clamores commoventur, cum
: μεσόχορος dedit signum. Opus est enim signo apud
non intelligentes, ne audientes quidem : nam plerique
8 non audiunt, nec ulli magis laudant. Si quando trans-
ibis per basilicam, et voles scire, quomodo quisque
dicat, nihil est, quod tribunal adscendas, nihil, quod
praebeas aurem : facilis divinatio. Scito, eum pessime
9 dicere, qui laudabitur maxime. Primus hunc audiendi
morem induxit Largius Licinus : hactenus tamen, ut
auditores corrogaret. Ita certe ex Quintiliano, prae-
10 ceptore meo, audisse memini. Narrabat ille : *Adsecta-
bar Domitium Afrum. Cum apud centumviros diceret
graviter et lente (hoc enim illi actionis genus erat), audiit ex proximo immodicum insolitumque clamorem.
Admiratus reticuit. Ubi silentium factum est, repetiit
quod abruperat. Iterum clamor, iterum reticuit: et post*
11 *silentium, coepit idem tertio. Novissime, quis diceret,
quaesivit: responsum est, Licinus. Tum intermissa
causa, Centumviri, inquit, hoc artificium periit.*
12 Quod alioqui perire incipiebat, cum periisse Afro videretur ; nunc vero prope funditus exstinctum et eversum
est. Pudet referre, quae, quam fracta pronuntiatione
dicantur ; quibus, quam teneris clamoribus excipiantur.
13 Plausus tantum, ac potius sola cymbala et tympana
illis canticis desunt : ululatus quidem (neque enim alio
vocabulo potest exprimi theatris quoque indecora lau-
14 datio) large supersunt. Nos tamen adhuc et utilitas
amicorum, et ratio aetatis moratur ac retinet. Veremur
enim, ne forte non has indignitates reliquisse, sed
laborem fugisse videamur. Sumus tamen solito rari-
ores : quod initium est gradatim desinendi. Vale.

C. II. (iv. 24.)

[In this letter Pliny dwells on the changes which during
his connection with the court of the Centumviri he had wit-
nessed among his fellow advocates. Some were dead, some
were in exile, some in the enjoyment of a prosperous old age,
others had ceased to be civilians and were even commanding
armies. His own life too had been one of change. The time
measured by years was short, measured by events was an age.
It would seem that the period of which he speaks would com-
prise part of Domitian's reign, the whole of Nerva's, and part
of Trajan's.]

C. PLINIUS VALENTI SUO S.

Proxime cum apud centumviros in quadruplici iudicio dixissem, subiit recordatio, egisse me iuvenem aeque
in quadruplici. Processit animus, ut solet, longius: 2
coepi reputare, quos in hoc iudicio, quos in illo socios
laboris habuissem. Solus eram, qui in utroque dixissem: tantas conversiones aut fragilitas mortalitatis
aut fortunae mobilitas facit. Quidam ex iis, qui tunc 3
egerant, decesserunt; exulant alii; huic actas et valetudo silentium suasit; hic sponte beatissimo otio fruitur;
alius exercitum regit; illum civilibus officiis principis
amicitia exemit. Circa nos ipsos quam multa mutata 4
sunt! Studiis processimus, studiis periclitati sumus,
rursusque processimus. Profuerunt nobis bonorum 5
amicitiae, bonorum obfuerunt, iterum prosunt. Si com-
putes annos, exiguum tempus: si vices rerum, aevum
putes. Quod potest esse documento, nihil desperare, 6
nulli rei fidere, cum videamus tot varietates tam volu-
bili orbe circumagi. Mihi autem familiare est, omnes 7
cogitationes meas tecum communicare, isdemque te
vel praeceptis vel exemplis monere, quibus ipse me
moneo: quae ratio huius epistolae fuit. Vale.

C. III. (vi. 2.)

[In this letter, written on the occasion of Regulus's death.
Pliny notes the prejudicial effect which that event had pro-
duced on the eloquence of pleaders. Regulus, though by no
means a first-rate orator, was so energetic a pleader that
his presence could not but be missed in the law courts. Even
his peculiarities and affectations, which are here dwelt on,
proceeded, in Pliny's opinion, from a genuine esteem for the
pursuit of oratory. Hence his death, though it could hardly
be regarded as a misfortune, led to the decline of the eloquence
of the bar. Advocates were now expected to confine their
speaking within narrower limits, and cases were more promptly
decided. All this Pliny seems to have considered an evil, and
consequently, whenever he had to hear a cause, he says that
he invariably allowed the lawyers to speak as long as they
pleased, and never refused to listen to what might appear at
the outset to be irrelevant and superfluous matter. This, he
observes, was the practice of their ancestors, who were at least
as wise as their descendants.]

C. PLINIUS ARRIANO SUO S.

Soleo nonnunquam in iudiciis quaerere Marcum Regulum, nolo enim dicere, desiderare. Cur ergo quaero?
2 Habebat studiis honorem, timebat, pallebat, scribebat:
quamvis non posset ediscere. Illud ipsum, quod oculum
modo dextrum, modo sinistrum circumlinebat; dextrum, si a petitore, alterum, si a possessore esset
acturus: quod candidum splenium in hoc aut illud
supercilium transferebat: quod semper aruspices consulebat de actionis eventu, a nimia superstitione, sed
3 tamen et a magno studiorum honore veniebat. Iam
illa perquam iucunda una dicentibus, quod libera tempora petebat, quod audituros corrogabat. Quid enim
iucundius, quam sub alterius invidia, quamdiu velis, et
in alieno auditorio quasi deprehensum commode dicere?
4 Sed utcunque se habent ista, bene fecit Regulus, quod
est mortuus; melius, si ante. Nunc enim sane poterat
sine malo publico vivere sub eo principe, sub quo nocere non poterat. Ideo fas est, nonnunquam eum

quaerere. Nam postquam obiit ille, increbuit passim 5
et invaluit consuetudo, binas vel singulas clepsydras,
interdum et dimidias, et dandi et petendi. Nam et qui
dicunt, egisse malunt, quam agere: et qui audiunt,
finire, quam iudicare. Tanta negligentia, tanta desidia,
tanta denique irreverentia studiorum periculorumque
est. An nos sapientiores maioribus nostris? nos legi- 6
bus ipsis iustiores, quae tot horas, tot dies, tot comperendinationes largiuntur? hebetes illi et supra modum
tardi? nos apertius dicimus, celerius intelligimus, religiosius iudicamus, quia paucioribus clepsydris praecipit-
amus causas, quam diebus explicari solebant? O 7
Regule, qui iam ambitione ab omnibus obtinebas, quod
fidei paucissimi praestant! Equidem quoties iudico,
quod vel saepius facio quam dico, quantum quis plurimum postulat aquae, do. Etenim temerarium ex- 8
istimo divinare, quam spatiosa sit causa inaudita, tempusque negotio finire, cuius modum ignores: praesertim
cum primam religioni suae iudex patientiam debeat,
quae pars magna iustitiae est. At quaedam supervacua, dicuntur. Etiam: sed satius est et haec dici,
quam non dici necessaria. Praeterea, an sint super- 9
vacua, nisi cum audieris, scire non possis. Sed de
his melius coram, ut de pluribus vitiis civitatis. Nam
tu quoque amore communium soles emendari cupere,
quae iam corrigere difficile est. Nunc respiciamus 10
domos nostras. Ecquid omnia in tua recte? In mea
novi nihil. Mihi autem et gratiora sunt bona, quod
perseverant; et leviora incommoda, quod adsuevi.
Vale.

C. IV. (vi. 29.)

[Pliny's friend Quadratus had, it appears, consulted him as to the character of the causes which a high-minded and honourable advocate should undertake. This letter is Pliny's reply. The causes in question are those of friends, those which are likely to establish an important precedent, and those the pleading of which is certain to bring with it fame and distinction. Pliny, however, admits that he had himself occasionally yielded to necessity, and undertaken cases at the bidding of the senate. He mentions some of the principal public trials in which his services had been engaged.

One other letter (A. VI.), in which Pliny gives us an account of his impeachment of the *delator* Publicius Certus before the senate, is addressed to Quadratus. He was, as it appears from *Ep.* vi. 11, a young man of promise; he was a rising advocate, and a man of letters. He is again mentioned *Ep.* vii. 24, from which we learn that he was the grandson of a rich lady, Ummidia Quadratilla, who left him two-thirds of her property, and who was very possibly the sister of the Ummidius Quadratus, Governor of Syria in the reign of Claudius, as appears from Tacitus, *Ann.* xii. 45. Her name also appears in an inscription discovered at Casinum in Campania (*Orelli Insc.* No. 781), for the inhabitants of which she built at her own expense an amphitheatre and temple.]

C. PLINIUS QUADRATO SUO S.

Avidius Quietus, qui me unice dilexit, et, quo non minimum gaudeo, probavit, ut multa alia Thraseae (fuit enim familiaris) ita hoc saepe referebat, praecipere solitum, *suscipiendas esse causas, aut amicorum, aut*
2 *destitutas, aut ad exemplum pertinentes.* Cur *amicorum?* Non eget interpretatione. Cur *destitutas?* Quod in illis maxime et constantia agentis et humanitas cerneretur. Cur *pertinentes ad exemplum?* Quia plu-
3 rimum referret, bonum an malum induceretur. Ad haec ego genera causarum, ambitiose fortasse, addam tamen *claras et illustres.* Aequum enim est, agere nonnunquam gloriae et famae, id est, suam causam. Hos terminos, quia me consuluisti, dignitati ac vere-

\.undiae tuae statuo.   Nec me practerit, usum et esse **4**
et haberi optimum dicendi magistrum.   Video etiam,
multos parvo ingenio, literis nullis, ut bene agerent,
agendo consecutos.   Sed et illud, quod vel Pollionis **5**
vel tanquam Pollionis accepi, verissimum experior :
Commode agendo factum est, ut saepe agerem ; saepe
agendo, ut minus commode : quia scilicet assiduitate
nimia facilitas magis quam facultas, nec fiducia, sed
temeritas paratur.   Nec vero Isocrati, quo minus **6**
haberetur summus orator, offecit, quod infirmitate
vocis, mollitie frontis, ne in publico diceret, impedie-
batur.   Proinde multum lege, scribe, meditare, ut
possis, cum voles, dicere ; dices, cum velle debebis.
Hoc fere temperamentum ipse servavi.   Nonnunquam **7**
necessitati, quae pars rationis est, parui.   Egi enim
quasdam a senatu iussus, quo tamen in numero fuerunt
ex illa Thraseae divisione, hoc est, ad exemplum pertinentes.   Adfui Baeticis contra Baebium Massam. **8**
Quaesitum est, an danda esset inquisitio : data est.
Adfui rursus iisdem querentibus de Caecilio Classico.
Quaesitum est, an provinciales ut socios ministrosque
proconsulis, plecti oporteret : poenas luerunt.   Ac- **9**
cusavi Marium Priscum, qui, lege repetundarum damnatus, utebatur clementia legis, cuius severitatem
immanitate criminum excesserat : relegatus est.   Tuitus **10**
sum Iulium Bassum, ut incustoditum nimis et incautum,
ita minime malum : iudicibus acceptis in senatu re-
mansit.   Dixi proxime pro Vareno, postulante, ut sibi **11**
invicem evocare testes liceret : impetratum est.   In
posterum opto, ut ea potissimum iubear, quae me deceat
vel sponte fecisse.   Vale.

C. V. (vi. 31.)

[This letter gives an account of the trials which had lately been heard by the Emperor Trajan. Pliny was acting as assessor to the Emperor at his special request. These cases were heard, not at Rome, but at Centum Cellae (Civita Vecchia), about forty-seven miles distant, where, as it appears, Trajan had a country house close to the sea. Pliny found his visit particularly agreeable, and speaks of the Emperor's kindness and courtesy in the warmest terms. He describes the place, where Trajan was at this time having a harbour constructed on a very considerable scale. Centum Cellae, of which we hear nothing before Trajan's reign, appears from that time to have become a town of some importance.]

C. PLINIUS CORNELIANO SUO S.

Evocatus in consilium a Caesare nostro ad Centum Cellas (hoc loco nomen) magnam cepi voluptatem.
2 Quid enim iucundius, quam principis iustitiam, gravitatem, comitatem in secessu quoque, ubi haec maxime recluduntur, inspicere? Fuerunt variae cognitiones, et quae virtutes iudicis per plures species experirentur.
3 Dixit causam Claudius Ariston, princeps Ephesiorum, homo munificus, et innoxie popularis: inde invidia, et ab dissimillimis delator immissus: itaque absolutus
4 vindicatusque est. Sequenti die audita est Galitta, adulterii rea. Nupta haec tribuno militum, honores petituro, et suam et mariti dignitatem centurionis amore maculaverat: maritus legato consulari, ille
5 Caesari scripserat. Caesar, excussis probationibus, centurionem exauctoravit, atque etiam relegavit. Supererat crimini, quod nisi duorum esse non poterat, reliqua pars ultionis: sed maritum, non sine aliqua reprehensione patientiae, amor uxoris retardabat; quam quidem, etiam post delatum adulterium, domi habuerat,
6 quasi contentus aemulum removisse. Admonitus, ut perageret accusationem, peregit invitus. Sed illam damnari, etiam invito accusatore, necesse erat; damnata, et Iuliae legis poenis relicta est. Caesar et nomen

centurionis, et commemorationem disciplinae militaris
sententiae adiecit, ne omnes eiusmodi causas revocare
ad se videretur. Tertio die inducta cognitio est, mul- 7
tis sermonibus et vario rumore iactata, de Iulii Tironis
codicillis, quos ex parte veros esse constabat, ex parte
falsi dicebantur. Substituebantur crimini Sempro- 8
nius Senecio, eques Romanus, et Eurythmus, Caesaris
libertus et procurator. Heredes, cum Caesar esset in
Dacia, communiter epistola scripta, petierant, ut sus-
ciperet cognitionem. Susceperat. Reversus diem dixe- 9
rat: et, cum ex heredibus quidam, quasi reverentia
Eurythmi, remitterent accusationem, pulcherrime dixerat, *Nec ille Polycletus est, nec ego Nero.* Indulserat
tamen petentibus dilationem; cuius tempore exacto,
consederat auditurus. A parte heredum intraverunt 10
duo; omnino postularunt, ut omnes heredes agere
cogerentur, cum detulissent omnes, aut sibi quoque
desistere permitteretur. Locutus est Caesar summa 11
gravitate, summa moderatione: cumque advocatus
Senecionis et Eurythmi dixisset, suspicionibus relinqui
reos, nisi audirentur. *Non curo,* inquit, *an isti suspicionibus relinquantur: ego relinquor.* Dein, conversus 12
ad nos: Ἐπιστήσατε, *quid facere debeamus? Isti
enim queri volunt, quod sibi licuerit non accusare.*
Tum ex consilii sententia iussit denuntiari heredibus
omnibus, aut agerent, aut singuli approbarent caussas
non agendi, alioqui se vel de calumnia pronuntiaturum.
Vides, quam honesti, quam severi dies, quos iu- 13
cundissimae remissiones sequebantur. Adhibebamur
quotidie coenae: erat modica, si principem cogites.
Interdum acroamata audiebamus: interdum iucundis-
simis sermonibus nox ducebatur. Summo die abe- 14
untibus nobis (tam diligens in Caesare humanitas fuit),
xenia sunt missa. Sed mihi, ut gravitas cognitionum,
consilii honor, suavitas simplicitasque convictus, ita
locus ipse periucundus fuit. Villa pulcherrima cin- 15
gitur viridissimis agris: imminet litori, cuius in sinu
fit cum maxime portus; cuius sinistrum brachium
firmissimo opere munitum est; dextrum elaboratur.
In ore insula adsurgit, quae illatum vento mare 16

obiacens frangat, tutumque ab utroque latere decur-
sum navibus praestet. Adsurgit autem arte visenda.
Ingentia saxa latissima navis provehit: contra haec
alia super alia deiecta ipso pondere manent, ac sensim
17 quodam velut aggere construuntur. Eminet iam et
apparet saxeum dorsum: impactosque fluctus in immensum elidit et tollit. Vastus illic fragor, canumque
circa mare. Saxis deinde pilae adiicientur, quae proce-
denti tempore enatam insulam imitentur. Habebit hic
portus et nomen auctoris, eritque vel maxime salutaris.
Nam per longissimum spatium litus importuosum hoc
receptaculo utetur. Vale.

Section D.

LETTERS CONNECTED WITH THE AUTHOR'S PRIVATE LIFE AND CHARACTER.

II

D. I. (iv. 8)

[Pliny had been congratulated by a friend on having been appointed by the Emperor to an augurship. He gives his reasons in this letter for feeling peculiar pleasure at his promotion. The office was ancient and dignified, and was bestowed for life It was also a gratifying circumstance to him that he was chosen in the place of an eminent man, who appears to have named Pliny as a worthy successor to himself. It should be understood that for a considerable period vacancies in the College of Augurs were filled up by the process of co-optatio, or self-election ; and though under the Empire the right of choice belonged to the Emperor, it is natural to suppose that, as is here suggested, the tradition of the old mode of appointment would still linger.]

C. PLINIUS ARRIANO SUO S.

Gratularis mihi, quod acceperim auguratum. Iure gratularis: primum, quod gravissimi principis iudicium in minoribus etiam rebus consequi pulchrum est: deinde quod sacerdotium ipsum cum priscum et religiosum, tum hoc quoque sacrum plane et insigne est, quod non adimitur viventi. Nam alia, quamquam dignitate 2 propemodum paria, ut tribuuntur, sic auferuntur: in hoc fortunae hactenus licet, ut dari possit. Mihi vero 3 etiam illud gratulatione dignum videtur, quod successi Iulio Frontino, principi viro, qui me nominationis die per hos continuos annos inter sacerdotes nominabat, tanquam in locum suum cooptaret; quod nunc eventus ita comprobavit, ut non fortuitum videretur. Te qui- 4 dem, ut scribis, hoc maxime delectat auguratus meus, quod Marcus Tullius augur fuit. Laetaris enim, quod honoribus eius insistam, quem aemulari studiis cupio. Sed utinam, ut sacerdotium idem et consulatum, multo 5 etiam invenior quam ille, sum consecutus, ita senex saltem ingenium eius aliqua ex parte adsequi possim! Sed nimirum quae sunt in manu hominum, et mihi et 6 multis contigerunt: illud vero, ut adipisci arduum, sic etiam sperare nimium est, quod dari non nisi a diis potest. Vale.

D. II. (iv. 13.)

[This interesting letter shows Pliny's kind feeling for his native town, and his sound judgment as to what would be most for its benefit. A youth who had come to pay his respects had said, in answer to a question, that he was about to study at Mediolanum (*Milan*). Thereupon Pliny asks his visitors : Why not have the means of study at home? He is ready himself to contribute a third part of any sum subscribed by the town. The parents should have the right of choosing the teachers ; if they secured men of eminence, they might make their town a centre of education to the district. He now asks Tacitus, whose reputation attracted men of education, to send down such as might be willing to become candidates.]

C. PLINIUS CORNELIO TACITO SUO S.

Salvum te in urbem venisse gaudeo. Venisti autem, si quando alias, nunc maxime mihi desideratus. Ipse pauculis adhuc diebus in Tusculano commorabor, ut
2 opusculum, quod est in manibus, absolvam. Vereor enim, ne, si hanc intentionem iam in fine laxavero, aegre resumam. Interim ne quid festinationi meae pereat, quod sum praesens petiturus, hac quasi praecursoria epistola rogo. Sed prius accipe causas ro-
3 gandi. Proxime cum in patria mea fui, venit ad me salutandum municipis mei filius praetextatus. Huic ego, *Studes?* inquam. Respondit, *Etiam.—Ubi?—Mediolani.—Cur non hic?* Et pater eius (erat enim una, atque etiam ipse adduxerat puerum), *Quia nullos*
4 *hic praeceptores habemus.— Quare nullos? Nam vehementer intererat vestra, qui patres estis* (et opportune complures patres audiebant), *liberos vestros hic potissimum discere. Ubi enim aut iucundius morarentur, quam in patria, aut pudicius continerentur, quam sub*
5 *oculis parentum, aut minore sumptu, quam domi? Quantulum est ergo, collata pecunia conducere praeceptores? quodque nunc in habitationes, in viatica, in ea quae peregre emuntur impenditis, adiicere mercedibus? Atque adeo ego, qui nondum liberos habeo, paratus sum pro republica nostra, quasi pro filia vel parente, tertiam*

partem eius, quod conferre vobis placebit, dare. Totum [6]
*etiam pollicerer, nisi timerem, ne hoc munus meum
quandoque ambitu corrumperetur, ut accidere multis in
locis video, in quibus praeceptores publice conducuntur.
Huic vitio uno remedio occurri potest, si parentibus* [7]
*solis ius conducendi relinquatur, isdemque religio recte
iudicandi necessitate collationis addatur.* Nam qui [8]
*fortasse de alieno negligentes, certe de suo diligentes
erunt, dabuntque operam, ne a me pecuniam non nisi
dignus accipiat, si accepturus et ab ipsis erit.* Proinde [9]
*consentite, conspirate, maioremque animum ex meo sumite,
qui cupio esse quam plurimum, quod debeam conferre.
Nihil honestius praestare liberis vestris, nihil gratius
patriae potestis. Educentur hic, qui hic nascuntur,
statimque ab infantia natale solum amare, frequentare
consuescant. Atque utinam tam claros praeceptores in-
ducatis, ut in finitimis oppidis studia hinc petantur,
utque nunc liberi vestri aliena in loca, ita mox alieni in
hunc locum confluant!* Haec putavi altius et quasi a [10]
fonte repetenda, quo magis scires, quam gratum mihi
foret, si susciperes, quod iniungo. Iniungo autem, et
pro rei magnitudine rogo, ut ex copia studiosorum,
quae ad te ex admiratione ingenii tui convenit, circum-
spicias praeceptores, quos solicitare possimus; sub ea
tamen conditione, ne cui fidem meam obstringam.
Omnia enim libera parentibus servo. Illi iudicent,
illi eligant: ego mihi curam tantum et impendium
vindico. Proinde si quis fuerit repertus, qui ingenio [11]
suo fidat, eat illuc ea lege, ut hinc nihil aliud certum,
quam fiduciam suam ferat. Vale.

D. III. (vii. 18.)

[In reply to a friend and fellow-townsman who wishes to
know how he may best secure the proper application after
his death of a fund which he was intending to devote to an
annual feast at Comum, Pliny explains the plan which in a
similar case he had himself adopted ; namely, to make a charge
for the purpose on an estate.]

C. PLINIUS CANINIO SUO S.

Deliberas mecum, quemadmodum pecunia, quam
municipibus nostris in epulum obtulisti, post te quoque salva sit.   Honesta consultatio, non expedita sententia.   Numeres reipublicae summam? Verendum est,
ne dilabatur.   Des agros?   Ut publici, negligentur.
2 Equidem nihil commodius invenio, quam quod ipse
feci.   Nam pro quingentis millibus nummum, quae in
alimenta ingenuorum ingenuarumque promiseram,
agrum ex meis, longe pluris, actori publico mancipavi :
eundem vectigali imposito recepi, tricena millia annua
3 daturus.   Per hoc enim et reipublicae sors in tuto, nec
reditus incertus, et ager ipse propter id, quod vectigali
large supercurrit, semper dominum, a quo exerceatur,
4 inveniet.   Nec ignoro, me plus aliquanto, quam don-
asse videor, erogavisse, cum pulcherrimi agri pretium
5 necessitas vectigalis infregerit.   Sed oportet privatis
utilitatibus publicas, mortalibus aeternas anteferre,
multoque diligentius muneri suo consulere, quam facul-
tatibus. Vale.

D. IV. (iv. 19.)

[Pliny here describes in terms of affectionate praise the good qualities of his wife Calpurnia, her intelligence, her affectionate disposition, and the keen interest which she felt in her husband's pursuits. Calpurnia was the writer's second wife, and had been educated by her aunt Hispulla, to whom this letter and viii. 11 are addressed.]

C. PLINIUS HISPULLAE CALPURNIAE SUAE S.

Cum sis pietatis exemplum, fratremque optimum et amantissimum tui pari caritate dilexeris, filiamque eius, ut tuam, diligas, nec tantum amitae eius, verum etiam patris amissi adfectum repraesentes, non dubito, maximo tibi gaudio fore, cum cognoveris, dignam patre, dignam te, dignam avo evadere. Summum est acumen, 2 summa frugalitas: amat me, quod castitatis indicium est. Accedit his studium literarum, quod ex mei caritate concepit. Meos libellos habet, lectitat, ediscit 3 etiam. Qua illa solicitudine, cum videor acturus, quanto, cum egi, gaudio adficitur! Disponit, qui nuntient sibi, quem adsensum, quos clamores excitarim, quem eventum iudicii tulerim. Eadem, si quando recito, in proximo discreta velo sedet laudesque nostras avidissimis auribus excipit. Versus quidem meos can- 4 tat formatque cithara, non artifice aliquo docente, sed amore, qui magister est optimus. His ex causis in 5 spem certissimam adducor, perpetuam nobis maioremque in dies futuram esse concordiam. Non enim aetatem meam, aut corpus, quae paullatim occidunt ac senescunt, sed gloriam diligit. Nec aliud decet tuis manibus 6 educatam, tuis praeceptis institutam, quae nihil in contubernio tuo viderit, nisi sanctum honestumque, quae denique amare me ex tua praedicatione consueverit. Nam cum matrem meam parentis loco vener- 7 arere, me a pueritia statim formare, laudare, talemque, qualis nunc uxori meae videor, ominari solebas. Cer- 8 tatim ergo tibi gratias agimus: ego, quod illam mihi, illa, quod me sibi dederis, quasi invicem elegeris. Vale.

D. V. (vi. 4.)

[This and the two following epistles are charming love-letters, addressed by Pliny to his wife, the same Calpurnia whose praises he celebrates in the preceding letter.]

C. PLINIUS CALPURNIAE SUAE S.

Nunquam sum magis de occupationibus meis questus, quae me non sunt passae aut proficiscentem te valetudinis causa in Campaniam prosequi, aut profec-
2 tam e vestigio subsequi. Nunc enim praecipue simul esse cupiebam, ut oculis meis crederem, quid viribus, quid corpusculo adparares, ecquid denique secessus voluptates, regionisque abundantiam, inoffensa trans-
3 mitteres. Equidem etiam fortem te non sine cura desiderarem. Est enim suspensum et anxium, de eo, quem ardentissime diligas, interdum nihil scire.
4 Nunc vero me cum absentiae, tum infirmitatis tuae ratio, incerta et varia solicitudine exterret. Vereor om nia, imaginor omnia, quaeque natura metuentium est,
5 ea maxime mihi, quae maxime abominor, fingo. Quo impensius rogo, ut timori meo quotidie singulis, vel etiam binis epistolis consulas. Ero enim securior, dum legam; statimque timebo, cum legero. Vale.

D. VI. (vi. 7.)

C. PLINIUS CALPURNIAE SUAE S.

Scribis, te absentia mea non mediocriter adfici, unumque habere solacium, quod pro me libellos meos
2 teneas, saepe etiam in vestigio meo colloces. Gratum est, quod nos requiris, gratum, quod his fomentis adquiescis: invicem ego epistolas tuas lectito, atque identidem in manus quasi novas sumo; sed eo magis ad desideri-
3 um tui accendor. Nam cuius literae tantum habent suavitatis, huius sermonibus quantum dulcedinis inest! Tu tamen frequentissime scribe, licet hoc ita me delectet, ut torqueat. Vale.

D. VII. (vii. 5.)

C. PLINIUS CALPURNIAE SUAE S.

Incredibile est, quanto desiderio tui tenear. In causa amor primum; deinde, quod non consuevimus abesse. Inde est, quod magnam partem noctium in imagine tua vigil exigo: inde, quod interdiu, quibus horis te visere solebam, ad diaetam tuam ipsi me, ut verissime dicitur, pedes ducunt: quod denique aeger et maestus, et similis excluso, a vacuo limine cedo. Unum tempus his tormentis caret, quo in foro et amicorum litibus conteror. Aestima tu, quae vita mea sit, cui requies in labore, in miseria curisque solacium. Vale. ₂

D. VIII. (iv. 1.)

[Pliny writes to his wife's grandfather, accepting an invitation, but explaining that the arrival of himself and his wife would be delayed by a duty which they had to perform in the dedication of a temple at Tifernum-on-Tiber, a town near his Tuscan estate.]

C. PLINIUS FABATO PROSOCERO SUO S.

Cupis post longum tempus neptem tuam meque una videre. Gratum est utrique nostrum, quod cupis; mutuo me Hercule. Nam invicem nos incredibili quodam desiderio vestri tenemur, quod non ultra differemus. Atque adeo iam sarcinulas alligamus, festinaturi, quantum itineris ratio permiserit. Erit una, sed brevis, mora: deflectemus in Tuscos, non ut agros remque familiarem oculis subiiciamus (id enim postponi potest), sed ut fungamur necessario officio. Oppidum est praediis nostris vicinum; nomen Tiferni Tiberini; quod me paene adhuc puerum patronum cooptavit, tanto maiore studio, quanto minore iudicio. Adventus meos celebrat, profectionibus angitur, honoribus gaudet. In hoc ego, ut referrem gratiam (nam vinci in

amore turpissimum est), templum pecunia mea exstru-
xi: cuius dedic tionem, cum sit paratum, differre lon-
6 gius, irreligiosum est.   Erimus ergo ibi dedicationis
die, quem epulo celebrare constitui.   Subsistemus fortasse et sequenti: sed tanto magis viam ipsam cor-
7 ripiemus.   Contingat modo te filiamque tuam fortes
invenire!   Nam continget hilares, si nos incolumes
receperitis.   Vale.

D. IX. (i. 6.)

[Pliny tells his friend Tacitus that he had been boar-
nunting with great success, not, however, forgetting his literary pursuits, but honouring Diana and Minerva at once by
carrying his tablets, &c. into the woods.]

C. PLINIUS CORNELIO TACITO SUO S.

Ridebis, et licet rideas.   Ego ille, quem nosti, apros
tres, et quidem pulcherrimos, cepi.   Ipse? inquis.   Ipse:
non tamen ut omnino ab inertia mea et quiete discede-
rem.   Ad retia sedebam.   Erant in proximo, non vena-
bulum aut lancea, sed stilus et pugillares.   Meditabar
aliquid enotabamque, ut, si manus vacuas, plenas tamen
2 ceras reportarem.   Non est, quod contemnas hoc
studendi genus.   Mirum est, ut animus agitatione mo-
tuque corporis excitetur.   Iam undique silvae et solitu-
do, ipsumque illud silentium, quod venationi datur,
3 magna cogitationis incitamenta sunt.   Proinde cum
venabere, licebit, auctore me, ut panarium et lagunculam, sic etiam pugillares feras.   Experieris, non Dianam
magis montibus, quam Minervam, inerrare.   Vale.

D. X. (ix. 10.)

[This letter has been attributed to Tacitus, and it certainly looks like a reply to the preceding, in which Pliny recommends his friend to unite the worship of Diana and Minerva. The writer would do so, he says, but there are no wild boars to be found. There is, however, an allusion to an opinion about the composition of poetry, of which we find no hint in D. IX. But it is possible that this opinion was expressed on some other occasion.]

C. PLINIUS TACITO SUO S.

Cupio praeceptis tuis parere; sed aprorum tanta penuria est, ut Minervae et Dianae, quas ais pariter colendas, convenire non possit. Itaque Minervae tan- **2** tum serviendum est; delicate tamen, ut in secessu, et aestate. In via plane nonnulla leviora, statimque delenda, ea garrulitate, qua sermones in vehiculo seruntur, extendi. His quaedam addidi in villa, cum aliud non liberet. Itaque poëmata quiescunt; quae tu inter nemora et lucos commodissime perfici putas. Oratiuncu- **3** lam unam, alteram retractavi; quamquam id genus operis inamabile, inamoenum, magisque laboribus ruris, quam voluptatibus simile. Vale.

D. XI. (ix. 36.)

[We are told in this letter how Pliny was accustomed to pass a summer day from its beginning to its close in the retirement of his Tuscan villa. He contrived, he says, to blend in an agreeable manner study and recreation.]

C. PLINIUS FUSCO SUO S.

Quaeris, quemadmodum in Tuscis diem aestate disponam. Evigilo cum libuit, plerumque circa horam primam, saepe ante, tardius raro: clausae fenestrae

2 manent. Mire enim silentio et tenebris ab iis, quae avocant, abductus, et liber, et mihi relictus, non oculos animo, sed animum oculis sequor, qui eadem, quae mens, vident, quoties non vident alia. Cogito, si quid in manibus, cogito ad verbum scribenti emendantique similis, nunc pauciora, nunc plura, ut vel difficile vel facile componi tenerive potuerunt. Notarium voco, et, die admisso, quae formaveram, dicto: abit, rursusque 3 revocatur, rursusque remittitur. Ubi hora quarta vel quinta (neque enim certum dimensumque tempus) ut dies suasit, in xystum me vel cryptoporticum confero; reliqua meditor et dicto. Vehiculum adscendo. Ibi quoque idem, quod ambulans aut iacens. Durat intentio, mutatione ipsa refecta: paullum redormio, dein ambulo, mox orationem Graecam Latinamve clare et intente, non tam vocis causa, quam stomachi, lego: pariter tamen et illa firmatur. Iterum ambulo, ungor, 4 exerceor, lavor. Coenanti mihi, si cum uxore vel paucis, liber legitur: post coenam, comoedus aut lyristes: mox cum meis ambulo, quorum numero sunt eruditi. Ita variis sermonibus vespera extenditur, et 5 quamquam longissimus dies cito conditur. Nonnunquam ex hoc ordine aliqua mutantur. Nam si diu tacui vel ambulavi, post somnum demum lectionemque non vehiculo, sed (quod brevius, quia velocius) equo gestor. Interveniunt amici ex proximis oppidis, partemque diei ad se trahunt, interdumque lassato mihi 6 opportuna interpellatione subveniunt. Venor aliquando, sed non sine pugillaribus, ut, quamvis nihil ceperim, nonnihil referam. Datur et colonis, ut videtur ipsis, non satis temporis, quorum mihi agrestes querelae literas nostras et haec urbana opera commendant. Vale.

D. XII. (v. 1.)

[This letter is about a legacy which Pliny had acquired under somewhat peculiar circumstances. Pomponia Gratilla, wife of Arulenus Rusticus, had for some reason or other disinherited her son, and bequeathed her property to Pliny and other distinguished men of the time. The son begged Pliny to give up his share, with a tacit understanding that it should ultimately pass into his possession. To this Pliny objected, as not being a straightforward proceeding, and declared that he was ready to waive all claim on the property in case it should appear that the mother had unjustly disinherited her son. The matter was referred to arbitration ; the son argued his cause, Pliny briefly defended the conduct of the mother. The decision of the arbitrators was that Pomponia had had reasonable grounds of displeasure with her son. The case was on the point of being carried into the court of the centumviri, when Pliny's coheirs, who were, as he said, afraid, not of the weakness of their cause, but of the peculiar dangers of the time (it was during Domitian's reign), requested him to talk the matter over with the son. This he did ; the matter was privately discussed in the Temple of Concord, and Pliny, having pointed out to him what he conceived to be a reasonable view of the matter, finally agreed to make him a present proportionate to the amount which he inherited under Pomponia's will. The son appears to have been perfectly satisfied, and to have acknowledged Pliny's kindness by leaving him a moderate legacy.]

C. PLINIUS SEVERO SUO S.

Legatum mihi obvenit modicum, sed amplissimo gratius. Cur amplissimo gratius ? Pomponia Gratilla, exheredato filio Asudio Curiano, heredem reliquerat me : dederat coheredes Sertorium Severum, praetorium virum, aliosque splendidos equites Romanos. 2 Curianus orabat, ut sibi donarem portionem meam, seque praeiudicio iuvarem : eandem tacita conventione salvam mihi pollicebatur. Respondebam, non conve- 3 nire moribus meis, aliud palam, aliud agere secreto : praeterea non esse satis honestum, donare et locupleti et orbo : in summa, non profuturum ei, si donassem,

profuturum, si cessissem, esse autem me paratum ce-
4 dere, si inique exheredatum mihi liqueret. Ad hoc ille,
Rogo cognoscas. Cunctatus paullum, *Faciam,* inquam :
*neque enim video, cur ipse me minorem putem, quam
tibi videor. Sed iam nunc memento, non defuturam mihi
constantiam, si ita fides duxerit, secundum matrem*
5 *tuam pronuntiandi. Ut voles,* ait : *voles enim, quod
aequissimum.* Adhibui in consilium duos, quos tunc
civitas nostra spectatissimos habuit, Corellium et Fron-
6 tinum. His circumdatus in cubiculo meo sedi. Dixit
Curianus, quae pro se putabat. Respondi paucis ego
(neque enim aderat alius, qui defunctae pudorem
tueretur), deinde secessi, et ex consilii sententia, *Videtur,* inquam, *Curiane, mater tua iustas habuisse causas
irascendi tibi.* Post hoc ille cum ceteris subscripsit centumvirale iudicium, mecum non subscripsit.
7 Appetebat iudicii dies : coheredes mei componere et
transigere cupiebant, non diffidentia caussae, sed
metu temporum. Verebantur, quod videbant multis
accidisse, ne ex centumvirali iudicio capitis rei exirent.
8 Et erant quidam in illis, quibus obici et Gratillae
amicitia et Rustici posset. Rogant me, ut cum
9 Curiano loquar. Convenimus in aedem Concordiae.
Ibi ego, *Si mater,* inquam, *te ex parte quarta scripsisset
heredem, num queri posses? Quid si heredem quidem
instituisset ex asse, sed legatis ita exhausisset, ut non
amplius apud te, quam quarta, remaneret? Igitur
sufficere tibi debet, si, exheredatus a matre, quartam partem ab heredibus eius accipias, quam tamen ego augebo.*
10 *Scis te non subscripsisse mecum, et biennium transisse,
omniaque me usu cepisse. Sed ut te coheredes mei trac-
tabiliorem experiantur, utque tibi nihil abstulerit reverentia mei, offero pro mea parte tantundem.* Tuli
fructum non conscientiae modo, verum etiam famae.
11 Ille ergo Curianus legatum mihi reliquit, et factum
meum, nisi forte blandior mihi, antiquum notabili
12 honore signavit. Haec tibi scripsi, quia de omnibus, quae me vel delectant vel angunt, non aliter
tecum, quam mecum, loqui soleo : deinde, quod durum
existimabam, te amantissimum mei fraudare voluptate,

quam ipse capiebam. Neque enim sum tam sapiens, 13
ut nihil mea intersit, an iis, quae honeste fecisse me
credo, testificatio quaedam, et quasi praemium accedat.
Vale.

D. XIII. (v. 19.)

[Pliny shows here his kind consideration for his dependants. Zosimus, a freedman, an accomplished and amiable man,
was suffering from cough and spitting of blood. He had
already been sent to Ægypt, and had come back apparently
restored. Over-exertion had, however, brought on a relapse,
and Pliny now wishes to send him to Forum Iulii, where his
friend Paullinus had a villa of which he begs the use.
Forum Iulii (Fréjus) was an important colony, the birthplace
of Agricola. Its climate would resemble that of Nice, from
which it was not far distant, and would therefore be suitable
to pulmonary complaints.

Paullinus (to whom other letters are addressed) was, as we
learn from Tacitus (*Hist.* iii. 42, 43), a native of Forum
Iulii, had been a tribune of the Praetorian guard, and was
Procurator of Gallia Narbonensis, A.D. 69.]

C. PLINIUS PAULLINO SUO S.

Video, quam molliter tuos habeas: quo simplicius
tibi confitebor, qua indulgentia meos tractem. Est 2
mihi semper in animo et Homericum illud, πατὴρ δ᾽ ὣς
ἤπιος ἦεν, et hoc nostrum, *pater familiae.* Quod si es-
sem natura asperior et durior, frangeret me tamen in-
firmitas liberti mei Zosimi, cui tanto maior humanitas
exhibenda est, quanto nunc illa magis eget. Homo 3
probus, officiosus, literatus, et ars quidem eius et quasi
inscriptio *comoedus,* in qua plurimum facit. Nam pronuntiat acriter, sapienter, apte, decenter etiam; utitur
et cithara perite, ultra quam comoedo necesse est.
Idem tam commode orationes et historias et carmina
legit, ut hoc solum didicisse videatur. Haec tibi 4
sedulo exposui, quo magis scires, quam multa unus
mihi et quam iucunda ministeria praestaret. Accedit
huc longa iam caritas hominis, quam ipsa pericula

5 auxerunt. Est enim ita natura comparatum, ut nihil
aeque amorem incitet et accendat, quam carendi metus,
6 quem ego pro hoc non semel patior. Nam ante
aliquot annos, dum intente instanterque pronuntiat,
sanguinem reiecit, atque ob hoc in Aegyptum missus
a me, post longam peregrinationem confirmatus rediit nuper : deinde dum per continuos dies nimis
imperat voci, veteris infirmitatis tussicula admonitus,
7 rursus sanguinem reddidit. Qua ex caussa desti-
navi eum mittere in praedia tua, quae Foro Iuli
possides. Audivi enim te saepe referentem, esse ibi et
aëra salubrem, et lac eiusmodi curationibus accommo-
8 datissimum. Rogo ergo, scribas tuis, ut illi villa,
ut domus pateat ; offerant etiam sumtibus eius, si quid
9 opus erit: erit autem opus medico. Est enim tam parcus et continens, ut non solum delicias, verum etiam
necessitates valetudinis, frugalitate restringat. Ego
proficiscenti tantum viatici dabo, quantum sufficiat
eunti in tua. Vale.

D. XIV. (viii. 16.)

[Pliny here speaks of the heavy trial which he had experienced in the illness and death of some of his slaves. He
finds some consolation in the thought that he has been an
exceptionally indulgent master to them.]

C. PLINIUS PATERNO SUO S.

Confecerunt me infirmitates meorum, mortes etiam,
et quidem iuvenum. Solatia duo, nequaquam paria
tanto dolori, solatia tamen : unum facilitas manumittendi (videor enim non omnino immaturos perdidisse,
quos iam liberos perdidi), alterum, cum permitto servis quoque quasi testamenta facere, eaque, ut legitima,
2 custodio. Mandant rogantque, quod visum : pareo
ut iussus. Dividunt, donant, relinquunt, dumtaxat
intra domum. Nam servis respublica quaedam et

quasi civitas domus est. Sed quamquam his solatiis 3
acquiescam, debilitor et frangor eadem illa humanitate,
quae me, ut hoc ipsum permitterem, induxit. Non
ideo tamen velim durior fieri. Nec ignoro, alios
huiusmodi casus nihil amplius vocare, quam damnum,
eoque sibi magnos homines et sapientes videri. Qui
an magni sapientesque sint, nescio: homines non sunt.
Hominis est enim adfici dolore, sentire, resistere 4
tamen et solatia admittere, non solatiis non egere.
Verum de his plura fortasse, quam debui, sed pau- 5
ciora, quam volui. Est enim quaedam etiam dolendi voluptas, praesertim si in amici sinu defleas,
apud quem lacrimis tuis vel laus sit parata, vel venia.
Vale.

SECTION E.

MISCELLANEOUS LETTERS.

E. I. (ii. 17.)

[This and the following letter have a special interest and value. They are elaborate descriptions of two of Pliny's principal villas with their various adjuncts. As indications of the general tone and character of Roman taste in such matters they may be studied with profit; but it is, we think, a mistake to attempt anything like the construction of an actual plan of the houses described and their grounds. We doubt whether a Roman architect would have undertaken to do this from the materials here supplied. In a folio volume, *On the Villas of the Ancients*, printed by private subscription in 1728 (the work of a Mr. Robert Castell), these two letters are translated with notes, to which are added plans and drawings in illustration of them. Much labour and ingenuity were evidently bestowed on the work, but it is easy to see that far too much has been attempted. It is not likely that Pliny intended to do more than to give the friends to whom he was writing a tolerably distinct idea of the situation, size, and arrangement of his Laurentine and Tuscan villas. This he has certainly succeeded in doing. We can at least get from these letters a good notion of the chief features of a Roman country house.

The first letter describes his Laurentine villa. Laurentum was about sixteen miles from Rome, and though apparently not so beautiful or fashionable a place as Baiae, it still had powerful attractions for the wealthy Roman nobles. It chiefly consisted at this time of the villas of such men, and thus resembled some of the more distant suburbs of London. In the strict sense of the Roman term, Pliny's seat at Laurentum was not a villa; that is to say, it had no estate or farm buildings attached to it. In iv. 6, he says of it, 'I have nothing in the place except the house and garden, and the beach.' All provisions had to be procured from the neighbouring town of Ostia; and a house so supplied Varro (*De Re Rustica*, iii. 1) will not allow to be a 'villa,' in which view Martial (iii. 36) concurs. Hence Pliny here speaks of it as merely a 'villula.' It had, in fact, simply gardens and pleasure-grounds. We gather from ix. 40, that he made it his residence during part of the autumn and winter. In i. 9, he calls it his μουσεῖον, as being a place specially favourable to study.

His Tuscan villa, described in the following letter, was in

the proper sense of the word a country house, and seems to
have been his principal seat. From D. X. he appears to have
always lived in it during the summer. It was surrounded by
a large estate, and was situated near the town of Tifernum
Tiberinum, under the shelter of the Appennine range, at a
distance of about 150 miles from Rome. It was in Etruria,
but close to the frontier of Umbria, in which country Tifernum stood (Comp. D. VIII.).]

C. PLINIUS GALLO SUO S.

Miraris, cur me Laurentinum, vel, si ita mavis,
Laurens meum tantopere delectet. Desines mirari, cum
cognoveris gratiam villae, opportunitatem loci, litoris
2 spatium. Decem et septem millibus passuum ab urbe
secessit, ut, peractis quae agenda fuerint, salvo iam et
composito die, possis ibi manere. Aditur non una via;
nam et Laurentina et Ostiensis eodem ferunt, sed Laurentina a quartodecimo lapide, Ostiensis ab undecimo re-
linquenda est. Utrimque excipit iter aliqua ex parte
arenosum, iunctis paullo gravius et longius, equo breve
3 et molle. Varia hinc atque inde facies. Nam modo
occurrentibus silvis via coarctatur, modo latissimis pra-
tis diffunditur et patescit. Multi greges ovium, multa
ibi equorum boumque armenta, quae, montibus hieme
4 depulsa, herbis et tepore verno nitescunt. Villa usibus capax, non sumptuosa tutela. Cuius in prima parte
atrium frugi, nec tamen sordidum: deinde porticus in
D litterae similitudinem circumactae, quibus parvula,
sed festiva, area includitur. Egregium hac adversus
tempestates receptaculum: nam specularibus, ac multo
5 magis imminentibus tectis muniuntur. Est contra
medias cavaedium hilare: mox triclinium satis pulchrum, quod in littus excurrit, ac si quando Africo
mare impulsum est, fractis iam et novissimis fluctibus
leviter adluitur. Undique valvas aut fenestras non
minores valvis habet: atque ita a lateribus a fronte quasi
tria maria prospectat: a tergo cavaedium, porticum, aream, porticum rursus, mox atrium, silvas et longinquos
6 respicit montes. Huius a laeva retractius paullo cubiculum est amplum, deinde aliud minus, quod altera fene-

stra admittit orientem, occidentem altera retinet, hac et
subiacens mare longius quidem, sed securius intuetur.
Huius cubiculi et triclini illius obiectu includitur 7
angulus, qui purissimum solem continet et accendit.
Hoc hibernaculum, hoc etiam gymnasium meorum est
Ibi omnes silent venti, exceptis qui nubilum inducunt,
et serenum ante, quam usum loci, eripiunt. Adnecti- 8
tur angulo cubiculum in ἀψῖδα curvatum, quod ambitum solis fenestris omnibus sequitur. Parieti eius in
bibliothecae speciem armarium insertum est, quod non
legendos libros, sed lectitandos capit. Adhaeret dor- 9
mitorium membrum, transitu interiacente, qui, suspensus et tubulatus, conceptum vaporem salubri tempera-
mento huc illuc digerit et ministrat. Reliqua pars lateris huius servorum libertorumque usibus detinetur,
plerisque tam mundis, ut accipere hospites possint.
Ex alio latere cubiculum est politissimum ; deinde vel 10
cubiculum grande, vel modica coenatio, quae plurimo
sole, plurimo mari lucet. Post hanc cubiculum cum
procoetone, altitudine aestivum, munimentis hibernum:
est enim subductum omnibus ventis. Huic cubiculo
aliud et procoeton communi pariete innguntur. Inde 11
balinei cella frigidaria spatiosa et effusa, cuius in contra-
riis parietibus duo baptisteria, velut eiecta, sinuantur,
abunde capacia, si mare in proximo cogites. Adiacet
unctorium, hypocauston, adiacet propnigeon balinei :
mox duae cellae, magis elegantes, quam sumptuosae.
Cohaeret calida piscina mirifice, ex qua natantes mare
adspiciunt. Nec procul sphaeristerium, quod cali- 12
dissimo soli, inclinato iam die, occurrit. Hic turris eri-
gitur, sub qua diaetae duae ; totidem in ipsa ; praeterea
coenatio, quae latissimum mare, longissimum littus,
amoenissimas villas prospicit. Est et alia turris : in 13
hac cubiculum, in quo sol nascitur conditurque : lata
post apotheca et horreum. Sub hoc triclinium, quod
turbati maris non nisi fragorem et sonum patitur, cumque iam languidum ac desinentem; hortum et gestatio-
nem videt, qua hortus includitur. Gestatio buxo, aut 14
rore marino, ubi deficit buxus, ambitur : nam buxus,
qua parte defenditur tectis, abunde viret; aperto caelo

apertoque vento, et quamquam longinqua adspergine
15 maris inarescit. Adiacet gestationi interiore circuitu vinea tenera et umbrosa, nudisque etiam pedibus
mollis etcedens. Hortum morus et ficus frequens vestit:
quarum arborum illa vel maxime ferax est terra, malig-
nior ceteris. Hac non deteriore, quam maris facie, coenatio remota a mari fruitur. Cingitur diaetis duabus
a tergo, quarum fenestris subiacet vestibulum villae,
16 et hortus alius, pinguis et rusticus. Hinc cryptoporticus, prope publici operis, extenditur. Utrinque
fenestrae, a mari plures, ab horto singulae, et alternis
pauciores. Hac, cum serenus dies et immotus, omnes,
cum hinc vel inde ventus inquietus, qua venti quies-
17 cunt, sine iniuria patent. Ante cryptoporticum xystus
violis odoratus. Teporem solis infusi repercussu cryptoporticus auget, quae ut tenet solem, sic aquiloneir.
inhibet submovetque: quantumque caloris ante, tantum
retro frigoris. Similiter Africum sistit, atque ita diver-
sissimos ventos, alium alio a latere, frangit et finit.
18 Haec iucunditas eius hieme, maior aestate. Nam
ante meridiem xystum, post meridiem gestationes hortique proximam partem umbra sua temperat: quae, ut
dies crevit decrevitque, modo brevior, modo longior hac
19 vel illac cadit. Ipsa vero cryptoporticus tum maxime
caret sole, cum ardentissimus culmini eius insistit.
Ad hoc patentibus fenestris Favonios accipit transmittit-
que, nec umquam aëre pigro et manente ingravescit.
20 In capite xysti deinceps cryptoporticus, horti diaeta
est, amores mei; re vera amores: ipse posui. In hac
heliocaminus quidem, alia xystum, alia mare, utraque
solem, cubiculum autem valvis, cryptoporticum fenestra
21 prospicit. Qua mare contra parietem medium, zotheca perquam eleganter recedit, quae specularibus et
velis obductis reductisve modo adiicitur cubiculo, modo
aufertur. Lectum et duas cathedras capit: a pedibus
mare, a tergo villae, a capite silvae: tot facies locorum
22 totidem fenestris et distinguit et miscet. Iunctum est
cubiculum noctis et somni. Non illud voces servulorum,
non maris murmur, non tempestatum motus, non ful-
gurum lumen, ac ne diem quidem sentit, nisi fenestris

apertis. Tam alti abditique secreti illa ratio, quod in-
teriacens andron parietem cubiculi hortique distinguit,
atque ita omnem sonum media inanitate consumit.
Applicitum est cubiculo hypocaustum perexiguum, 23
quod angusta fenestra suppositum calorem, ut ratio exi-
git, aut effundit aut retinet. Procoeton inde et cubiculum porrigitur in solem, quem orientem statim exceptum ultra meridiem, oblicum quidem, sed tamen
servat. In hanc ego diaetam cum me recipio, abesse 24
mihi etiam a villa mea videor, magnamque eius voluptatem, praecipue Saturnalibus, capio, cum reliqua
pars tecti licentia dierum festisque clamoribus personat.
Nam nec ipse meorum lusibus, nec illi studiis meis
obstrepunt. Haec utilitas, haec amoenitas deficitur 25
aqua salienti, sed puteos, ac potius fontes habet: sunt
enim in summo. Et omnino litoris illius mira natura:
quocunque loco moveris humum, obvius et paratus humor occurrit, isque sincerus ac ne leviter quidem tanta
maris vicinitate corruptus. Suggerunt affatim ligna 26
proximae silvae: ceteras copias Ostiensis colonia ministrat. Frugi quidem homini sufficit etiam vicus, quem
una villa discernit: in hoc balinea meritoria tria, magna
commoditas, si forte balineum domi vel subitus adventus, vel brevior mora calfacere dissuadeat. Littus 27
ornant varietate gratissima, nunc continua, nunc intermissa tecta villarum, quae praestant multarum urbium
faciem, sive mari, sive ipso litore utare: quod nonnunquam longa tranquillitas mollit, saepius frequens et
contrarius fluctus indurat. Mare non sane pretiosis 28
piscibus abundat: soleas tamen et squillas optimas sug-
gerit. Villa vero nostra etiam mediterraneas copias
praestat, lac in primis: nam illuc e pascuis pecora
conveniunt, si quando aquam umbramve sectantur.
Iustisne de causis cum tibi videor incolere, inhabitare, 29
diligere secessum? quem tu nimis urbanus es nisi concupiscis. Atque utinam concupiscas! ut tot tantisque
dotibus villulae nostrae maxima commendatio ex tuo
contubernio accedat. Vale.

E. II. (v. 6.)

C. PLINIUS APOLLINARI SUO S.

Amavi curam et solicitudinem tuam, quod, cum
audisses me aestate Tuscos meos petiturum, ne facerem
2 suasisti, dum putas insalubres.　Est sane gravis et
pestilens ora Tuscorum, quae per litus extenditur.　Sed
hi procul a mari recesserunt : quin etiam Appennino,
3 saluberrimo montium, subiacent.　Atque adeo, ut omnem pro me metum ponas, accipe temperiem caeli, regionis situm, villae amoenitatem ; quae et tibi auditu, et
4 mihi relatu iucunda erunt.　Caelum est hieme frigi-
dum et gelidum : myrtos, oleas, quaeque alia assiduo
tepore laetantur, aspernatur ac respuit : laurum tamen
patitur, atque etiam nitidissimam profert, interdum, sed
5 non saepius quam sub urbe nostra, necat.　Aestatis
mira clementia.　Semper aer spiritu aliquo movetur ;
6 frequentius tamen auras, quam ventos habet.　Hinc
senes multi : videas avos proavosque iam iuvenum, audias fabulas veteres sermonesque maiorum : cumque
7 veneris illo, putes alio te seculo natum.　Regionis forma
pulcherrima.　Imaginare amphitheatrum aliquod immensum, et quale sola rerum natura possit effingere :
lata et diffusa planities montibus cingitur : montes
summa sui parte procera nemora et antiqua habent.
8 Frequens ibi et varia venatio : inde caeduae silvae
cum ipso monte descendunt ; has inter pingues terreni-
que colles (neque enim facile usquam saxum, etiam si
quaeratur, occurrit) planissimis campis fertilitate non
cedunt, opimamque messem serius tantum, sed non mi-
9 nus percoquunt.　Sub his per latus omne vineae porri-
guntur, unamque faciem longe lateque contexunt ; quarum a fine imoque quasi margine arbusta nascuntur.
10 Prata inde campique : campi, quos non nisi ingentes
boves et fortissima aratra perfringunt.　Tantis glebis
tenacissimum solum, cum primum prosecatur, ad-
11 surgit, ut nono demum sulco perdometur.　Prata
florida et gemmea trifolium aliasque herbas, teneras

semper et molles, et quasi novas, alunt. Cuncta enim perennibus rivis nutriuntur : sed ubi aquae plurimum, palus nulla, quia devexa terra, quidquid liquoris accepit, nec absorbuit, effundit in Tiberim. Medios ille 12 agros secat, navium· patiens, omnesque fruges devehit in urbem, hieme dumtaxat et vere; aestate submittitur, immensique fluminis nomen arenti alveo deserit, auctumno resumit. Magnam capies voluptatem, si 13 hunc regionis situm ex monte prospexeris. Neque enim terras tibi, sed formam aliquam, ad eximiam pulchritudinem pictam, videberis cernere : ea varietate, ea descriptione, quocunque inciderint oculi, reficientur. Villa in colle imo sita prospicit quasi ex summo : ita 14 leniter et sensim clivo fallente consurgit, ut, cum adscendere te non putes, sentias adscendisse. A tergo Appenninum, sed longius, habet. Accipit ab hoc auras quamlibet sereno et placido die, non tamen acres et immodicas, sed spatio ipso lassas et infractas. Mag- 15 na sui parte meridiem spectat, aestivumque solem ab hora sexta, hibernum aliquanto maturius quasi invitat in porticum latam, et pro modo longam. Multa in hac membra; atrium etiam ex more veterum. Ante por- 16 ticum xystus concisus in plurimas species, distinctusque buxo ; demissus inde pronusque pulvinus, cui bestiarum effigies invicem adversas buxus inscripsit. Acanthus in plano mollis, et, paene dixerim, liquidus. Ambit hunc ambulatio pressis varieque tonsis viri- 17 dibus inclusa : ab his gestatio in modum circi, quae buxum multiformem, humilesque et retentas manu arbusculas circumit. Omnia maceria muniuntur : hanc gradata buxus operit et subtrahit. Pratum inde non 18 minus natura, quam superiora illa arte, visendum : campi deinde porro, multaque alia prata et arbusta. A capite porticus triclinium excurrit : valvis xystum 19 desinentem, et protinus pratum, multumque ruris, videt. Fenestris, hac latus xysti, et quod prosilit villae, hac adiacentis hippodromi nemus comasque prospectat. Contra mediam fere porticum diaeta paullum recedit, cingit areolam, quae quatuor platanis inumbratur. Inter has marmoreo labro aqua

exundat, circumiectasque platanos, et subiecta platanis
21 leni adspergine fovet. Est in hac diaeta dormitorium
cubiculum, quod diem, clamorem sonumque exclu-
dit; iunctaque ei quotidiana amicorum coenatio quae
areolam illam, porticum aliam, eademque omnia, quae
22 porticus, adspicit. Est et aliud cubiculum a proxima
platano viride et umbrosum, marmore excultum podio
tenus: nec cedit gratiae marmoris ramos insidentesque
23 ramis aves imitata pictura. Fonticulus in hoc; in
fonte crater; circa siphunculi plures miscent iucun-
dissimum murmur. In cornu porticus amplissimum
cubiculum a triclinio occurrit; aliis fenestris xystum,
aliis despicit pratum, sed ante piscinam, quae fenestris
24 servit ac subiacet, strepitu visuque iucunda. Nam ex
edito desiliens aqua, suscepta marmore, albescit. Idem
cubiculum hieme tepidissimum, quia plurimo sole per-
25 funditur. Cohaeret hypocauston, et, si dies nubilus,
immisso vapore, solis vicem supplet. Inde apodyterium balinei laxum et hilare excipit cella frigidaria;
in qua baptisterium amplum atque opacum. Si natare
latius aut tepidius velis, in area piscina est, in proximo
puteus, ex quo possis rursus adstringi, si poeniteat
26 teporis. Frigidariae cellae connectitur media, cui sol
benignissime praesto est; caldariae magis: prominet
enim. In hac tres descensiones: duae in sole, tertia
27 a sole longius, a luce non longius. Apodyterio super-
positum est sphaeristerium, quod plura genera exercitationis, pluresque circulos capit. Non procul a
balineo scalae, quae in cryptoporticum ferunt, prius ad
diaetas tres. Harum alia areolae illi, in qua platani
quatuor, alia prato, alia vineis imminet, diversasque
28 caeli partes, ut prospectus, habet. In summa cryptoporticu cubiculum, ex ipsa cryptoporticu excisum, quod
hippodromum, vineas, montes intuetur. Iungitur cubiculum obvium soli, maxime hiberno. Hinc oritur diaeta,
quae villae hippodromum adnectit. Haec facies, hic
29 usus a fronte. A latere aestiva cryptoporticus in
edito posita; quae non adspicere vineas, sed tangere
videtur. In media triclinium saluberrimum adflatum
ex Appenninis vallibus recipit: post latissimis fenestris

vineas, valvis aeque vineas, sed per cryptoporticum,
quasi admittit. A latere triclinii, quod fenestris caret, 30
scalae convivio utilia secretiore ambitu suggerunt. In
fine cubiculum, cui non minus iucundum prospectum
cryptoporticus ipsa, quam vineae praebent. Subest
cryptoporticus, subterraneae similis'; aestate incluso
frigore riget, contentaque aëre suo, nec desiderat auras
nec admittit. Post utramque cryptoporticum, unde 31
triclinium desinit, incipit porticus, ante medium diem,
hiberna, inclinato die, aestiva. Hac adeuntur diaetae
duae, quarum in altera cubicula quatuor, altera tria,
ut circumit sol, aut sole utuntur, aut umbra. Hanc 32
dispositionem amoenitatemque tectorum late longeque
praecedit hippodromus. Medius patescit, statimque
intrantium oculis totus offertur, platanis circumitur.
Illae hedera vestiuntur, utque summae suis, ita imae
alienis frondibus virent: hedera truncum et ramos
pererrat, vicinasque platanos transitu suo copulat;
has buxus interiacet; exteriores buxos circumvenit
laurus, umbraeque platanorum suam confert. Rectus 33
hippodromi limes in extrema parte hemicyclio frangi-
tur, mutatque faciem : cupressis ambitur et tegitur,
densiore umbra opacior nigriorque ; interioribus circulis (sunt enim plures) purissimum diem recipit.
Inde etiam rosas effert, umbrarumque frigus non in- 34
grato sole distinguit. Finito vario illo multiplicique
curvamine recto limiti redditur, nec huic uni. Nam
viae plures, intercedentibus buxis, dividuntur. Alibi 35
pratulum, alibi ipsa buxus intervenit in formas mille
descripta, literas interdum, quae modo nomen domini
dicunt, modo artificis: alternis metulae surgunt, alternis inserta sunt poma : et in opere urbanissimo subita
velut illati ruris imitatio. Medium spatium brevioribus
utrimque platanis adornatur. Post has acanthus hinc 36
inde lubricus et flexuosus, deinde plures figurae plu-
raque nomina. In capite stibadium candido marmore,
vite protegitur. Vitem quatuor columellae Carystiae
subeunt. E stibadio aqua, velut expressa cubantium
pondere, siphunculis effluit ; cavato lapide suscipitur,
gracili marmore continetur, atque ita occulte tempe-

126 C. PLINI SECUNDI

37 ratur, ut impleat, nec redundet. Gustatorium gra-
viorque coena margini imponitur; levior naucularum
et avium figuris innatans circuit. Contra fons egerit
aquam et recipit: nam expulsa in altum in se cadit,
iunctisque hiatibus et absorbetur et tollitur. E regione stibadi adversum cubiculum tantum stibadio
38 reddit ornatus, quantum accipit ab illo. Marmore
splendet, valvis in viridia prominet et exit: alia
viridia superioribus inferioribusque fenestris sus-
picit despicitque. Mox zothecula refugit quasi in
cubiculum idem atque aliud. Lectus hic, et undique
fenestrae, et tamen lumen obscurum umbra premente.
39 Nam laetissima vitis per omne tectum in culmen
nititur et adscendit. Non secus ibi, quam in nemore,
iaceas: imbrem tantum, tanquam in nemore, non sentias. Hic quoque fons nascitur, simulque subducitur.
40 Sunt locis pluribus disposita sedilia e marmore, quae
ambulatione fessos, ut cubiculum ipsum, iuvant. Fon-
ticuli sedilibus adiacent; per totum hippodromum
inducti fistulis strepunt rivi, et, qua manus duxit,
sequuntur. His nunc illa viridia, nunc haec, interdum
simul omnia, iuvantur. Vitassem iamdudum, ne vi-
derer argutior, nisi proposuissem omnes angulos tecum
41 epistola circumire. Neque enim verebar, ne laboriosum esset legenti tibi, quod visenti non fuisset; praesertim cum interquiescere, si liberet, depositaque
epistola, quasi residere saepius posses. Praeterea in-
dulsi amori meo. Amo enim, quae maxima ex parte
42 ipse inchoavi, aut inchoata percolui. In summa (cur
enim non aperiam tibi vel iudicium meum vel errorem?)
primum ego officium scriptoris existimo, ut titulum
suum legat, atque identidem interroget se, quid coeperit scribere, sciatque, si materiae immoratur, non
esse longum; longissimum, si aliquid accersit atque
43 adtrahit. Vides, quot versibus Homerus, quot Ver-
gilius arma, hic Aeneae, Achillis ille, describat: brevis
tamen uterque est, quia facit, quod instituit. Vides,
ut Aratus minutissima etiam sidera consectetur et colli-
gat: modum tamen servat. Non enim excursus hic
44 eius, sed opus ipsum est. Similiter nos, ut parva

magnis, cum totam villam oculis tuis subiicere conamur, si nihil inductum et quasi devium loquimur, non epistola, quae describit, sed villa, quae describitur, magna est. Verum illuc, unde coepi, ne secundum legem meam iure reprehendar, si longior fuero in hoc, in quod excessi. Habes caussas, cur ego Tuscos meos 45 Tusculanis, Tiburtinis, Praenestinisque meis praeponam. Nam super illa, quae rettuli, altius ibi otium et pinguius, eoque securius; nulla necessitas togae; nemo accersitor ex proximo. Placida omnia et quiescentia, quod ipsum salubritati regionis, ut purius caelum, ut aër liquidior, accedit. Ibi animo, ibi corpore maxime valeo. Nam studiis animum, venatu corpus exerceo. Mei quoque nusquam salubrius degunt; usque adhuc 46 certe neminem ex iis, quos eduxeram mecum (venia sit dicto) ibi amisi. Dii modo in posterum hoc mihi gaudium, hanc gloriam loco servent. Vale.

E. III. (ix. 7.)

[Pliny playfully describes in this letter his two villas on the lake of Como, which he distinguished, according to their lighter or more severe attractions, by the names of Comedy and Tragedy.]

C. PLINIUS ROMANO SUO S.

Aedificare te scribis. Bene est: inveni patrocinium. Aedifico enim iam ratione, quia tecum. Nam hoc quoque non dissimile, quod ad mare tu, ego ad Larium lacum. Huius in litore plures villae meae. 2 sed duae ut maxime delectant, ita exercent. Altera imposita saxis, more Baiano, lacum prospicit: altera, aeque more Baiano, lacum tangit. Itaque 3 illam, tragoediam; hanc, appellare comoediam soleo: illam, quod quasi cothurnis, hanc, quod quasi socculis sustinetur. Sua utrique amoenitas, et utraque possidenti ipsa diversitate iucundior. Haec lacu 4 propius, illa latius utitur: haec unum sinum molli curvamine amplectitur, illa editissimo dorso duos diri-

mit: illic recta gestatio longo limite super litus extenditur, hic spatiosissimo xysto leviter inflectitur:
illa fluctus non sentit, haec frangit: ex illa possis de-
spicere piscantes, ex hac ipse piscari, hamumque e
cubiculo, ac paene etiam de lectulo, ut e naucula,
iacere. Hae mihi causae utrique, quae desunt, ad-
5 struendi, ob ea quae supersunt. Etsi quid ego rationem tibi? apud quem pro ratione erit, idem facere.
Vale.

E. IV. (viii. 20.)

[Pliny describes in this letter a remarkable lake which he
had lately seen (the Lacus Vadimonis, now *Laghetto di Bas-
sano*). It was in Etruria, amongst the Ciminian hills, and
not far from the Tiber. A number of floating islands were
its principal feature. It was considered sacred. It had its
historical associations, though there is no allusion to them in
this letter. The Etruscans were twice defeated on the spot by
the Romans, in B.C. 309 and 283. Livy (ix. 39) describes
the former of the two engagements.]

C. PLINIUS GALLO SUO S.

Ad quae noscenda iter ingredi, transmittere mare
solemus, ea sub oculis posita negligimus, seu quia ita
natura comparatum, ut, proximorum incuriosi, longinqua sectemur, seu quod omnium rerum cupido languescit, cum facilis occasio est, seu quod differimus
tanquam saepe visuri, quod datur videre, quoties velis
2 cernere. Quacunque de causa, permulta in urbe
nostra, iuxtaque urbem, non oculis modo, sed ne
auribus quidem novimus: quae si tulisset Achaia,
Aegyptus, Asia, aliave quaelibet miraculorum ferax
commendatrixque terra, audita, perlecta, lustrataque
3 haberemus. Ipse certe nuper, quod nec audieram
ante, nec videram, audivi pariter et vidi. Exegerat
prosocer meus, ut Amerina praedia sua inspicerem.
Haec perambulanti mihi ostenditur subiacens lacus,
nomine Vadimonis: simul quaedam incredibilia nar-
4 rantur. Perveni ad ipsum. Lacus est in similitu-

dinem iacentis rotae circumscriptus, et undique aequalis:
nullus sinus, obliquitas nulla, omnia dimensa, paria, et
quasi artificis manu cavata et excisa. Color caerulo
albidior, viridior, et pressior; sulphuris odor saporque
medicatus : vis, qua fracta solidantur. Spatium modicum, quod tamen sentiat ventos, et fluctibus intu-
mescat. Nulla in hoc navis (sacer enim) sed in- 5
natant insulae, herbidae omnes arundine et iunco,
quaeque alia foecundior palus, ipsaque illa, extre-
mitas lacus effert. Sua cuique figura, ut modus :
cunctis margo derasus, quia frequenter vel litori vel
sibi illisae terunt terunturque. Par omnibus altitudo,
par levitas : quippe in speciem carinae humili radice
descendunt. Haec ab omni latere perspicitur, eadem- 6
que suspensa pariter et mersa. Interdum iunctae
copulataeque et continenti similes sunt; interdum dis-
cordantibus ventis digeruntur: nonnunquam destitutae
tranquillitate singulae fluitant. Saepe minores ma- 7
ioribus, velut cymbulae onerariis, adhaerescunt, saepe
inter se maiores minoresque quasi cursum certamenque
desumunt; rursus omnes in eundem locum appulsae,
qua steterunt, promovent terram, et modo hac, modo
illac, lacum reddunt auferuntque : ac tum demum,
cum medium tenuere, non contrahunt. Constat, pe- 8
cora herbas secuta, sic in insulas illas, ut in extremam
ripam, procedere solere, nec prius intelligere mobile
solum, quam litore abrepta, quasi illata et imposita,
circumfusum undique lacum pavent ; mox quo tulerit
ventus egressa, non magis se descendisse sentire, quam
senserint adscendisse. Idem lacus in flumen egeritur ; 9
quod ubi se paulisper oculis dedit, specu mergitur, alte-
que conditum meat : ac, si quid, antequam subduceretur, accepit, servat et profert. Haec tibi scripsi, quia 10
nec minus ignota, quam mihi, nec minus grata credebam. Nam te quoque, ut me, nihil aeque ac naturae
opera delectant. Vale.

E. V. (viii. 8.)

[This letter is a very exact and picturesque description of the source of the Clitumnus, a small river in the south of Umbria, which unites its waters with the Tinia, a tributary of the Tiber. The surrounding scenery seems to have been singularly beautiful. The source itself was in a hill covered with cypresses; hence Propertius (ii. 19, 25) speaks of it as hidden in a grove :—

‘ Qua formosa suo Clitumnus flumina luco
Integit, et niveos abluit unda boves.’

In the second of the above lines is an allusion to the effect which the clearness and purity of the water was supposed to have on the flocks and herds in its neighbourhood. To this there is also reference in Virgil, *Georg.* ii. 146, Hinc albi, Clitumne, greges; and it is noticed by the elder Pliny, *N. H.* ii. 103, 106. The river, it appears, was worshipped with peculiar honour; there was an ancient temple on the spot, and a number of little chapels around it. The margin of the stream was dotted with country houses.]

C. PLINIUS ROMANO SUO S.

Vidistine aliquando Clitumnum fontem? Si nondum (et puto nondum : alioqui narrasses mihi), vide, 2 quem ego (poenitet tarditatis) proxime vidi. Modicus collis adsurgit, antiqua cupresso nemorosus et opacus. Hunc subter fons exit, et exprimitur pluribus venis, sed imparibus, eluctatusque quem facit gurgitem lato gremio patescit purus et vitreus, ut numerare iactas 3 stipes et relucentes calculos possis. Inde non loci devexitate, sed ipsa sui copia et quasi pondere impellitur. Fons adhuc, et iam amplissimum flumen atque etiam navium patiens, quas, obvias quoque et contrario nisu in diversa tendentes, transmittit et perfert : adeo validus, ut illa, qua properat ipse, quamquam per solum planum, remis non adiuvetur; idem aegerrime 4 remis contisque superetur adversus. Iucundum utrumque per iocum ludumque fluitantibus, ut flexerint cursum, laborem otio, otium labore variare. Ripae

fraxino multa, multa populo vestiuntur, quas perspicuus amnis, velut mersas, viridi imagine adnumerat.
Rigor aquae certaverit nivibus; nec color cedit.   Ad- 5
iacet templum, priscum et religiosum.   Stat Clitumnus
ipse, amictus ornatusque praetexta.   Praesens numen,
atque etiam fatidicum, indicant sortes.   Sparsa sunt
circa sacella complura, totidemque dii.   Sua cuique
veneratio, suum nomen, quibusdam vero etiam fontes.
Nam praeter illum, quasi parentem ceterorum, sunt
minores capite discreti; sed flumini miscentur, quod
ponte transmittitur.   Is terminus sacri profanique.   In 6
superiore parte navigare tantum, infra etiam natare
concessum.   Balineum Hispellates, quibus illum locum
divus Augustus dono dedit, publice praebent, praebent
et hospitium.   Nec desunt villae, quae secutae fluminis
amoenitatem, margini insistunt.   In summa, nihil erit, 7
ex quo non capias voluptatem.   Nam studebis quoque,
et leges multa multorum omnibus columnis, omnibus
parietibus inscripta, quibus fons ille deusque celebra-
tur.   Plura laudabis, nonnulla ridebis ; quamquam tu
vero, quae tua humanitas, nulla ridebis.   Vale.

E. VI. (iii. 6.)

[A graphic description of a Corinthian bronze statue—the
figure of an old man—which Pliny, not generally accustomed
to indulge himself in such purchases, had lately bought out of
a legacy which had come to him.]

C. PLINIUS SEVERO SUO 8.

Ex hereditate, quae mihi obvenit, emi proxime Corinthium signum, modicum quidem, sed festivum et
expressum, quantum ego sapio, qui fortasse in omni re,
in hac certe perquam exiguum sapio : hoc tamen signum
ego quoque intelligo.   Est enim nudum, nec aut vitia, 2
si qua sunt, celat, aut laudes parum ostentat.   Effingit
senem stantem : ossa, musculi, nervi, venae, rugae

etiam ut spirantis apparent: rari et cedentes capilli, lata
frons, contracta facies, exile collum, pendent lacerti.
3 papillae iacent, recessit venter. A tergo quoque eadem
aetas, ut a tergo. Aes ipsum, quantum verus color indicat, vetus et antiquum. Talia denique omnia, ut
possint artificum oculos tenere, delectare imperito-
4 rum. Quod me, quamquam tirunculum, solicitavit ad
emendum. Emi autem, non ut haberem domi (neque
enim ullum adhuc Corinthium domi habeo), verum ut
5 in patria nostra celebri loco ponerem, ac potissimum in
Iovis templo. Videtur enim dignum templo, dignum
deo domum. Tu ergo, ut soles omnia, quae a me tibi
iniunguntur, suscipe hanc curam, et iam nunc iube ba-
sim fieri, ex quo voles marmore, quae nomen meum
honoresque capiat, si hos quoque putabis addendos.
6 Ego signum ipsum, ut primum invenero aliquem, qui
non gravetur, mittam tibi: vel ipse, quod mavis, adfe-
ram mecum. Destino enim (si tamen officii ratio
7 permiserit) excurrere isto. Gaudes, quod me venturum
esse polliceor, sed contrahes frontem, cum adiecero,
ad paucos dies. Neque enim diutius abesse me eadem
haec, quae nondum exire, patiuntur. Vale.

E. VII. (iv. 28.)

[This letter is a request from Pliny to one of his friends,
that he would undertake to procure portraits of Cornelius
Nepos and Titus Cassius for a distinguished man of letters
who wished to place them in his library. Pliny's friend came
from the same town as Nepos and Cassius, and would be able
to procure copies of any such likenesses, if they existed, on
the spot. Verona, if, as seems probable, Nepos was a native
of that place, would be the town in question.]

C. PLINIUS SEVERO SUO S.

Herennius Severus, vir doctissimus, magni aesti-
mat in bibliotheca sua ponere imagines municipum tuorum, Corneli Nepotis et Titi Cassi, petitque, si sunt
istic, ut esse credibile est, exscribendas pingendasque

delegem. Quam curam tibi potissimum iniungo, pri- 2
mum quia desideriis meis amicissime obsequeris, deinde, quia tibi studiorum summa reverentia, summus
amor studiosorum, postremo, quod patriam tuam omnesque qui nomen eius auxerunt, ut patriam ipsam, 3
veneraris et diligis. Peto autem, ut pictorem quam
diligentissimum adsumas. Nam cum est arduum, similitudinem effingere ex vero, tum longe difficillima
est imitationis imitatio; a qua, rogo, ut artificem,
quem elegeris, ne in melius quidem sinas aberrare.
Vale.

E. VIII. (i. 12.)

[Corellius Rufus, whose death under peculiarly painful circumstances is described at length in this letter, is spoken of
with affectionate praise in *Epp.* iv. 17 ; vii. 11, etc. He was
many years older than Pliny, and, as we are here told, was
regarded by him almost as a father. We find, too, from *Ep.*
iv. 17, that Pliny attributed his success in life in a great
measure to his friend's advice and influence. In the present
letter we have a touching description of the tedious sufferings
of Corellius, and of his determination to end them by voluntary starvation. From the age of 32 he had been afflicted
with hereditary gout, which as he advanced in years became
intolerably acute. His earnest wish to survive the tyrant
Domitian was gratified, and it may be inferred from a passage
in *Ep.* iv. 17, that he lived to see the better times of Nerva
and Trajan. His death must have occurred at the beginning
of the latter Emperor's reign. Pliny's letters are our only
source of information respecting him.

Calestrius Tiro (to whom several letters are addressed) was
one of Pliny's most intimate friends, having been associated
with him in military service and in the Quaestorship.]

C. PLINIUS CALESTRIO TIRONI SUO S.

Iacturam gravissimam feci, si iactura dicenda est
tanti viri amissio. Decessit Corellius Rufus, et quidem
sponte, quod dolorem meum exulcerat. Est enim luc-
tuosissimum genus mortis, quae non ex natura, **nec**

2 fatalis videtur. Nam utcunque in illis, qui morbo finiuntur, magnum ex ipsa necessitate solatium est, in iis vero, quos arcessita mors aufert, hic insanabilis do-
3 lor est, quod creduntur potuisse diu vivere. Corellium quidem summa ratio, quae sapientibus pro necessitate est, ad hoc consilium compulit, quamquam plurimas vivendi caussas habentem, optimam conscientiam, optimam famam, maximam auctoritatem, praeterea filiam, uxorem, nepotem, sorores, interque tot pignora, veros
4 amicos. Sed tam longa, tam iniqua valetudine conflictabatur, ut haec tanta pretia vivendi mortis rationibus vincerentur. Tertio et tricesimo anno (ut ipsum praedicantem audiebam) pedum dolore correptus est. Patrius hic illi : nam plerumque morbi quoque per
5 successiones quasdam, ut alia, traduntur. Hunc abstinentia, sanctitate, quoad viridis aetas, vicit et fregit : novissime cum senectute ingravescentem viribus animi
6 sustinebat, cum quidem incredibiles cruciatus et indignissima tormenta pateretur. Iam enim dolor non pedibus solis, ut prius, insidebat, sed omnia membra pervagabatur. Veni ad eum Domitiani temporibus, in
7 suburbano iacentem. Servi e cubiculo recesserunt (habebat is hoc moris, quoties intrasset fidelior amicus): quin etiam uxor, quamquam omnis secreti capacissima,
8 digrediebatur. Circumtulit oculos, et, *Cur*, inquit, *me putas hos tantos dolores tamdiu sustinere? ut scilicet isti latroni vel uno die supersim.* Dedisses huic animo par corpus, fecisset quod optabat. Adfuit tamen deus voto, cuius ille compos, ut iam securus liberque moriturus, multa illa vitae, sed minora, retinacula ab-
9 rupit. Increverat valetudo, quam temperantia mitigare tentavit: perseverantem constantia fugit. Iam dies alter, tertius, quartus: abstinebat cibo. Misit ad me uxor eius Hispulla communem amicum C. Geminium cum tristissimo nuntio, *destinasse Corellium mori, nec aut suis aut filiae precibus flecti; solum superesse me,*
10 *o quo revocari posset ad vitam.* Cucurri: perveneram in proximum, cum mihi ab eadem Hispulla Iulius Atticus nuntiat, nihil iam ne me quidem impetraturum : tam obstinate magis ac magis induruisse. Dixerat sane

medico admoventi cibum, Κέκρικα, quae vox, quantum admirationis in animo meo, tantum desiderii reliquit. Cogito, quo amico, quo viro caream. Implevit quidem 11 annum septimum et sexagesimum, quae aetas etiam robustissimis satis longa est : scio. Evasit perpetuam valetudinem : scio. Decessit superstitibus suis, florente republica, quae illi omnibus suis carior erat : et hoc scio. Tamen tanquam et juvenis et firmissimi mortem 12 doleo ; doleo autem, licet me imbecillum putes, meo nomine. Amisi enim, amisi vitae meae testem, rectorem, magistrum. In summa, dicam, quod, recenti dolore, contubernali meo Calvisio dixi : *vereor ne negligentius vivam.* Proinde adhibe solatia mihi ; non haec, 13 *senex erat, infirmus erat* (haec enim novi), sed nova aliqua sed magna, quae audierim nunquam, legerim nunquam. Nam quae audivi, quae legi, sponte succurrunt, sed tanto dolore superantur. Vale.

E. IX. (v. 16.)

[This is a particularly pleasing letter, exhibiting as it does the tender and affectionate side of Pliny's character. His friend Fundanus had just lost his younger daughter, a charming and sprightly girl, who had not yet completed her fourteenth year. She seems to have been a universal favourite, and to have been as good and amiable as she was, for her years, intelligent and accomplished. She was patient and resigned throughout her last illness. Her death was all the sadder, as she was betrothed to a young man of great promise, and the very day of the marriage was fixed. The father, though according to Pliny he had from his earliest youth fortified himself with the study of philosophy, was utterly inconsolable under this heavy affliction. Pliny begs his friend, in case of his writing a letter of condolence, to use the language of the tenderest sympathy, and carefully to avoid any expression which might seem to savour of censure or reproof.]

C. PLINIUS MARCELLINO SUO S.

Tristissimus haec tibi scribo, Fundani nostri filia minore defuncta, qua puella nihil unquam festivius,

amabilius, nec modo longiore vita, sed prope immorta-
2 litate, dignius vidi.   Nondum annos quattuordecim
impleverat, et iam illi anilis prudentia, matronalis gravitas erat, et tamen suavitas puellaris cum virginali
3 verecundia.   Ut illa patris cervicibus inhaerebat! ut
nos amicos paternos et amanter et modeste complecte-
batur! ut nutrices, ut paedagogos, ut praeceptores, pro
suo quemque officio, diligebat!   Quam studiose, quam
intelligenter lectitabat! ut parce custoditeque ludebat!
Qua illa temperantia, qua patientia, qua etiam constan-
4 tia novissimam valetudinem tulit!   Medicis obseque-
batur, sororem, patrem adhortabatur, ipsamque se des-
titutam corporis sui viribus vigore animi sustinebat.
5 Duravit hic illi usque ad extremum, nec aut spatio
valetudinis aut metu mortis infractus est, quo plures
gravioresque nobis causas relinqueret et desiderii et
6 doloris.   O triste plane acerbumque funus! o morte
ipsa mortis tempus indignius! Iam destinata erat egre-
gio iuveni, iam electus nuptiarum dies, iam nos vocati.
7 Quod gaudium quo moerore mutatum est!   Non possum exprimere verbis, quantum animo vulnus acceperim, cum audivi Fundanum ipsum (ut multa luctuosa
dolor invenit) praecipientem, quod in vestes, marga-
rita, gemmas, fuerat erogaturus, hoc in thura et un-
8 guenta et odores impenderetur.   Est quidem ille eruditus et sapiens, ut qui se ab ineunte aetate altioribus
studiis artibusque dediderit: sed nunc omnia, quae
audiit saepeque dixit, aspernatur, expulsisque virtuti-
9 bus aliis, pietatis est totus.   Ignosces, laudabis etiam,
si cogitaveris, quid amiserit. Amisit enim filiam, quae
non minus mores eius, quam os vultumque referebat,
10 totumque patrem mira similitudine exscripserat.   Proinde si quas ad eum de dolore tam iusto litteras
mittes, memento adhibere solatium, non quasi castiga-
torium et nimis forte, sed molle et humanum. Quod ut
facilius admittat, multum faciet medii temporis spatium.
11 Ut enim crudum adhuc vulnus medentium manus re-
formidat, deinde patitur, atque ultro requirit; sic
recens animi dolor consolationes reiicit ac refugit, mox
desiderat, et clementer admotis acquiescit. Vale.

E. X. (viii. 23.)

[This letter tells us all that we know about Pliny's friend Junius Avitus. His career, which was one of singular promise, was, to the great grief of Pliny, who loved him almost as if he had been his son, cut short by death.]

C. PLINIUS MARCELLINO SUO S.

Omnia mihi studia, omnes curas, omnia avocamenta exemit, excussit, eripuit dolor, quem ex morte Iuni Aviti gravissimum cepi.   Latum clavum in domo 2 mea induerat: suffragio meo adiutus in petendis honoribus fuerat: ad hoc, ita me diligebat, ita verebatur, ut me formatore morum, me quasi magistro uteretur. Rarum hoc in adolescentibus nostris.   Nam quotus- 3 quisque vel aetati alterius, vel auctoritati, ut minor, cedit?   Statim sapiunt, statim sciunt omnia: neminem verentur, imitantur neminem, atque ipsi sibi exempla sunt.   Sed non Avitus, cuius haec praecipua prudentia, quod alios prudentiores arbitrabatur; haec praecipua eruditio, quod disce e volebat.   Semper ille aut de 4 studiis aliquid, aut de officiis vitae consulebat: semper ita recedebat, ut melior factus: et erat factus vel eo, quod audierat, vel quod omnino quaesierat.   Quod 5 ille obsequium Serviano, exactissimo viro, praestitit! quem legatum tribunus ita et intellexit et cepit, ut ex Germania in Pannoniam transeuntem, non ut commilito, sed ut comes adsectatorque sequeretur.   Qua industria, qua modestia quaestor consulibus suis (et plures habuit) non minus iucundus et gratus, quam usui fuit! Quo discursu, qua vigilantia, hanc ipsam aedilitatem, cui praereptus est, petiit! Quod vel maxime dolorem meum exulcerat.   Obversantur oculis cassi labores, et infruc- 6 tuosae preces, et honor quem meruit tantum.   Redit animo ille latus clavus in penatibus meis sumptus? redeunt illa prima, illa postrema suffragia mea, illi sermones, illae consultationes.   Afficior adolescentia ipsius, ad- 7 ficior necessitudinum casu.   Erat illi grandis natu parens: erat uxor, quam ante annum virginem acceperat;

erat filia, quam ante annum sustulerat. Tot spes, tot gaudia dies unus in diversa convertit. Modo designatus aedilis, recens maritus, recens pater, intactum honorem, orbam matrem, viduam uxorem, filiam pupillam, ignaram avi, patris, reliquit. Accedit lacrimis meis, quod absens, et impendentis mali nescius, pariter aegrum, pariter decessisse, cognovi, ne gravissimo dolori timore consuescerem. In tantis tormentis eram, cum scriberem haec, scriberem sola. Neque enim nunc aliud aut cogitare aut loqui possum. Vale.

E. XI. (i. 22.)

[In this letter we have a sketch of the character and attainments of Titus Aristo, an eminent lawyer for whose learning Pliny had the highest respect. Elsewhere (viii. 14) Pliny submits to him an intricate question in connection with the forms of procedure in the Senate on which he desires an opinion. We learn from the present letter that Aristo was suffering from prolonged sickness, and had resolved, should the physicians hold out no hope of his recovery, to put an end to his life. Such hope, however, there was; Pliny rejoices in it, and hopes soon to be sufficiently free from anxiety about his friend as to feel justified in leaving Rome for his Laurentine Villa.]

C. PLINIUS CATILIO SEVERO SUO S.

Diu iam in urbe haereo, et quidem attonitus. Perturbat me longa et pertinax valetudo Titi Aristonis, quem singulariter et miror et diligo. Nihil est enim illo gravius, sanctius, doctius: ut mihi non unus homo, sed literae ipsae omnesque bonae artes in uno homine summum periculum adire videantur. Quam peritus ille et privati iuris et publici! Quantum rerum, quantum exemplorum, quantum antiquitatis tenet! Nihil est, quod discere velis, quod ille docere non possit: mihi certe, quoties aliquid abditum quaero, ille the-

saurus est. Iam quanta sermonibus eius fides! quanta 3
auctoritas! quam pressa et decora cunctatio! quid est,
quod non statim sciat? Et tamen plerumque haesitat,
dubitat, diversitate rationum, quas acri magnoque iudicio ab origine causisque primis repetit, discernit, ex-
pendit. Ad hoc quam parcus in victu! quam modicus 4
in cultu! Soleo ipsum cubiculum eius, ipsumque lectum, ut imaginem quandam priscae frugalitatis adspicere. Ornat haec magnitudo animi, quae nihil ad 5
ostentationem, omnia ad conscientiam refert, recteque
facti non ex populi sermone mercedem sed ex facto
petit. In summa, non facile quis quemquam ex istis, 6
qui sapientiae studium habitu corporis praeferunt, huic
viro comparabit. Non quidem gymnasia sectatur aut
porticus, nec disputationibus longis aliorum otium su-
umque delectat, sed in toga negotiisque versatur, multos advocatione, plures consilio iuvat. Nemini tamen 7
istorum castitate, pietate, iustitia, fortitudine etiam,
primo loco cesserit. Mirareris, si interesses, qua patientia hanc ipsam valetudinem toleret, ut dolori resistat, ut
sitim differat, ut incredibilem febrium ardorem immotus opertusque transmittat. Nuper me paucosque 8
mecum, quos maxime diligit, advocavit, rogavitque,
ut medicos consuleremus de summa valetudinis, ut, si
esset insuperabilis, sponte exiret e vita: sin tantum dif-
ficilis et longa, resisteret maneretque; dandum enim 9
precibus uxoris, dandum filiae lacrymis, dandum etiam
nobis amicis, ne spes nostras, si modo non essent inanes, voluntaria morte desereret. Id ego arduum in primis, et praecipua laude dignum puto. Nam impetu 10
quodam et instinctu procurrere ad mortem, commune
cum multis: deliberare vero et causas eius expendere,
utque suaserit ratio, vitae mortisque consilium suscipere vel ponere, ingentis est animi. Et medici quidem 11
secunda nobis pollicentur: superest, ut promissis deus
adnuat, tandemque me hac solicitudine exsolvat; qua
liberatus, Laurentinum meum, hoc est libellos et pugillares, studiosumque otium repetam. Nunc enim nihil
legere, nihil scribere aut adsidenti vacat, aut anxio
libet. Habes quid timeam, quid optem, quid etiam 12

in posterum destinem : tu quid egeris, quid agas, quid
velis agere, invicem nobis, sed laetioribus epistolis,
scribe. Erit confusioni meae non mediocre solatium,
si tu nihil quereris. Vale.

E. XII. (vii. 19.)

[Fannia, the second wife of Helvidius Priscus, a lady whom
Pliny held in high esteem, was suffering from a severe illness
which she had contracted while attending on the sick bed of
one of the Vestal virgins. Pliny expresses in this letter his
deep grief at the prospect of the heavy loss which the State
will sustain by the death of so noble a woman. She had
twice accompanied her husband into exile, first in the reign
of Nero, a second time in that of Vespasian. She was herself
sentenced to banishment by Domitian. Pliny here gives us
her courageous answer to the delator Metius Carus, on the
occasion of the trial of Senecio, whose crime consisted in
having written a laudatory memoir of her husband's life. (See
Tacit. *Agr.* 2.) She appears from this letter to have been as
gentle and amiable as she could be firm and fearless. We
may conclude that she with many others returned from banishment after Domitian's death.]

C. PLINIUS PRISCO SUO S.

Angit me Fanniae valetudo. Contraxit hanc, dum
adsidet Iuniae virgini, sponte primum (est enim adfi-
2 nis), deinde etiam ex auctoritate pontificum. Nam
Virgines, cum vi morbi atrio Vestae coguntur excedere, matronarum curae custodiaeque mandantur. Quo
munere Fannia dum sedulo fungitur, hoc discrimine
3 implicita est. Insident febres, tussis increscit, summa
macies, summa defectio: animus tantum et spiritus viget, Helvidio marito, Thrasea patre dignissimus: reliqua labuntur, meque non metu tantum, verum etiam
4 dolore conficiunt. Doleo enim, maximam feminam
eripi oculis civitatis, nescio an aliquid simile visuris.
Quae castitas illi! quae sanctitas! quanta gravitas!

quanta constantia! Bis maritum secuta in exsilium
est, tertio ipsa propter maritum relegata. Nam, cum 5
Senecio reus esset, quod de vita Helvidii libros composuisset, rogatumque se a Fannia in defensione dixisset,
quaerente minaciter Metio Caro, an rogasset, respondit,
Rogavi; an commentarios scripturo dedisset, *Dedi*; an
sciente matre, *Nesciente*. Postremo nullam vocem ce-
dentem periculo emisit. Quin etiam illos ipsos libros, 6
quamquam ex necessitate et metu temporum abolitos
SC., publicatis bonis, servavit, habuit, tulitque in exilium exilii caussam. Eadem quam iucunda, quam 7
comis, quam denique (quod paucis datum est) non minus amabilis, quam veneranda! Eritne, quam postea
uxoribus nostris ostentare possimus? erit, a qua viri
quoque fortitudinis exempla sumamus? quam sic cer-
nentes audientesque miremur, ut illas, quae leguntur?
Ac mihi domus ipsa nutare, convulsaque sedibus suis 8
ruitura supra videtur, licet adhuc posteros habeat.
Quantis enim virtutibus quantisque factis adsequentur,
ut haec non novissima occiderit? Me quidem illud 9
etiam adfligit et torquet, quod matrem eius, illam (nihil
possum illustrius dicere) tantae feminae matrem, rursus videor amittere, quam haec, ut reddit ac refert
nobis, sic auferet secum, meque et novo pariter et rescisso vulnere adficiet. Utramque colui, utramque 10
dilexi: utram magis, nescio: nec discerni volebant.
Habuerunt officia mea in secundis, habuerunt in adversis. Ego solatium relegatarum, ego ultor rever-
sarum: non feci tamen paria, atque eo magis hanc
cupio servari, ut mihi solvendi tempora supersint. In 11
his eram curis, cum scriberem ad te; quas si deus aliquis in gaudium verterit, de metu non querar. Vale.

E. XIII. (vi. 25.)

[A somewhat singular incident, which seems to show that travelling in Italy was occasionally dangerous, forms the subject of this letter. It is in reply to a communication received from one of Pliny's friends, to the effect that a Roman knight had mysteriously disappeared shortly after leaving Ocriculum, a town in Umbria, about forty-four miles from Rome. Pliny fears that he has been murdered, and mentions a similar circumstance in connection with a fellow-townsman of his own, for whom he had procured a military command, giving him at the same time about 350*l*. for his outfit. Nothing was ever heard of the man afterwards; and Pliny can only account for his disappearance by the supposition of foul play.]

C. PLINIUS HISPANO SUO S.

Scribis, Robustum, splendidum equitem Romanum, cum Attilio Scauro, amico meo, Ocriculum usque commune iter fecisse, deinde nusquam comparuisse: petis, ut Scaurus veniat, nosque, si potest, in aliqua inquisi-
2 tionis vestigia inducat. Veniet; vereor ne frustra. Suspicor enim tale nescio quid Robusto accidisse, quale
3 aliquando Metilio Crispo, municipi meo. Huic ego ordinem impetraveram, atque etiam proficiscenti quadraginta millia nummum ad instruendum se ornandumque donaveram; nec postea aut epistolas eius, aut ali-
4 quem de exitu nuntium accepi. Interceptusne sit a suis, an cum suis, dubium: certe non ipse, non quisquam ex servis eius apparuit. Utinam ne in Robusto
5 idem experiamur! Tamen arcessamus Scaurum. Demus hoc tuis, demus optimi adolescentis honestissimis precibus, qui pietate mira, mira etiam sagacitate, patrem quaerit. Di faveant, ut sic inveniat ipsum, quemadmodum iam, cum quo fuisset, invenit! Vale.

E. XIV. (vii. 27.)

[Pliny seems, from this amusing letter, which closely re-
sembles some modern ghost stories, to have been by no means
free from superstitious tendencies. He avers his belief in the
reality of apparitions, and supports it with four instances
which had come to his ears. One of them is the case of a
haunted house at Athens, in which, he says, some human
bones with chains about them were discovered on a spot to
which the apparition had been traced and where it suddenly
disappeared. He mentions a singular fact in connection with
himself at the end of the letter. It appears that an information had been actually lodged against him by Carus Metius,
and the paper containing it was found in Domitian's portfolio
after the Emperor's death.

Pliny's friend and correspondent, Licinius Sura, was a man
of considerable importance in the reigns of Nerva, Trajan,
and Hadrian; and he appears, from the allusions we have
to him in Dio Cassius, Aurelius Victor, and Spartianus' *Life of
Hadrian*, to have been to a great extent instrumental in ad-
vancing Trajan and Hadrian to the throne. He was employed
by Trajan to write his speeches, and in the Dacian war was
sent as an ambassador to the Dacian King Decebalus.]

C. PLINIUS SURAE SUO S.

Et mihi discendi, et tibi docendi facultatem otium
praebet. Igitur perquam velim scire, esse phantasmata
et habere propriam figuram numenque aliquod putes,
an inania et vana ex metu nostro imaginem accipere.
Ego ut esse credam, in primis eo ducor, quod audio 2
accidisse Curtio Rufo. Tenuis adhuc et obscurus
obtinenti Africam comes haeserat: inclinato die spatia-
batur in porticu: offertur ei mulieris figura humana
grandior pulchriorque: perterrito, *Africam se, futurorum praenuntiam*, dixit: *iturum enim Romam, honoresque gesturum, atque etiam cum summo imperio in
eandem provinciam reversurum, ibique moriturum.* Facta 3
sunt omnia. Praeterea accedenti Carthaginem, egre-
dientique navem, eadem figura in litore occurrisse
narratur. Ipse certe implicitus morbo, futura praeteritis, adversa secundis auguratus, spem salutis, nullo
suorum desperante, proiecit. Iam illud nonne et 4

magis terribile et non minus mirum est? quod ex
5 ponam, ut accepi. Erat Athenis spatiosa et capax
domus, sed infamis et pestilens. Per silentium noctis
sonus ferri, et, si attenderes acrius, strepitus vincu-
lorum longius primo, deinde e proximo reddebatur:
mox apparebat idolon, senex macie et squalore con-
fectus, promissa barba, horrenti capillo: cruribus
compedes, manibus catenas gerebat quatiebatque. In-
6 de inhabitantibus tristes diraeque noctes per metum
vigilabantur: vigiliam morbus et crescente formidine
mors sequebatur. Nam interdiu quoque, quamquam
abscesserat imago, memoria imaginis oculis inerrabat, longiorque caussa timoris timor erat. Deserta
inde et damnata solitudine domus, totaque illi monstro
relicta; proscribebatur tamen, seu quis emere, seu
7 quis conducere, ignarus tanti mali, vellet. Venit
Athenas philosophus Athenodorus, legit titulum: au-
ditoque pretio, quia suspecta vilitas, percunctatus,
omnia docetur, ac nihilo minus, immo tanto magis con-
ducit. Vbi coepit advesperascere, iubet sterni sibi in
prima domus parte, poscit pugillares, stilum, lumen:
suos omnes in interiora dimittit, ipse ad scribendum
animum, oculos, manum intendit, ne vacua mens audita
8 simulacra et inanes sibi metus fingeret. Initio, quale
ubique, silentium noctis, deinde concuti ferrum, vin-
cula moveri: ille non tollere oculos, non remittere
stilum, sed obfirmare animum, auribusque praetendere:
tum crebescere fragor, adventare etiam, et iam ut in
limine, iam ut intra limen audiri: respicit, videt, agno-
9 scitque narratam sibi effigiem. Stabat innuebatque
digito, similis vocanti: hic contra, ut paullum exspec-
taret, manu significat, rursusque ceris et stilo incumbit:
illa scribentis capiti catenis insonabat: respicit rursus
idem, quod prius, innuentem: nec moratus, tollit lumen,
10 et sequitur. Ibat illa lento gradu, quasi gravis vinculis; postquam deflexit in aream domus, repente dilapsa
deserit comitem: desertus herbas et folia concerpta
11 signum loco ponit. Postero die adit magistratus, monet, ut illum locum effodi iubeant. Inveniuntur ossa
inserta catenis et implicita, quae corpus aevo terraque

putrefactum nuda et exesa reliquerat vinculis: collecta publice sepeliuntur: domus postea rite conditis manibus caruit. Et haec quidem adfirmantibus credo. Illud 12 adfirmare aliis possum. Est libertus mihi, non illiteratus. Cum hoc minor frater eodem lecto quiescebat. Is visus est sibi cernere quendam in toro residentem, admoventemque capiti suo cultros, atque etiam ex ipso vertice amputantem capillos. Ubi illuxit, ipse circa verticem tonsus, capilli iacentes reperiuntur. Exiguum temporis medium, et rursus simile aliud 13 priori fidem fecit. Puer in paedagogio mistus pluribus dormiebat: venerunt per fenestras (ita narrat) in tunicis albis duo, cubantemque detonderunt; et qua venerant, recesserunt. Hunc quoque tonsum, sparsosque circa capillos dies ostendit. Nihil notabile secutum, 14 nisi forte, quod non fui reus: futurus, si Domitianus, sub quo haec acciderunt, diutius vixisset. Nam in scrinio eius datus a Caro de me libellus inventus est; ex quo coniectari potest, quia reis moris est submittere capillum, recisos meorum capillos depulsi, quod imminebat, periculi signum fuisse. Proinde rogo, eruditionem tuam intendas. Digna res est, quam diu mul- 15 tumque considere: ne ego quidem indignus, cui copiam scientiae tuae facias. Licet etiam utramque in 16 partem, ut soles, disputes: ex altera tamen fortius, ne me suspensum incertumque dimittas, cum mihi consulendi caussa fuerit, ut dubitare desinerem. Vale.

E. XV. (iii. 1.)

[This pleasant and interesting letter describes the manner of life which Vestricius Spurinna followed in the retirement of his old age. Pliny had lately been on a visit to his house, and had been impressed with the regularity of his habits, the refinement of his taste, and his general mental and bodily vigour.]

C. PLINIUS CALVISIO SUO S.

Nescio, an ullum iucundius tempus exegerim, quam

L

quo nuper apud Spurinnam fui; adeo quidem, ut neminem magis in senectute (si modo senescere datum
est) aemulari velim: nihil est enim illo vitae genere
2 distinctius. Me autem ut certus siderum cursus, ita vita
hominum disposita delectat, senum praesertim. Nam
iuvenes confusa adhuc quaedam et quasi turbata non in-
decent: senibus placida omnia et ordinata conveniunt.
3 quibus industria sera, turpis ambitio est. Hanc regu-
lam Spurinna constantissime servat; quin etiam parva
haec, (parva, si non cotidie fiant) ordine quodam et
4 velut orbe circumagit. Mane lectulo continetur: hora
secunda calceos poscit, ambulat millia passuum tria.
Nec minus animum quam corpus exercet. Si adsunt
amici, honestissimi sermones explicantur: si non, liber
legitur: interdum etiam praesentibus amicis, si tamen
5 illi non gravantur. Deinde considit, et liber rursus,
aut sermo libro potior: mox vehiculum ascendit, adsu-
mit uxorem singularis exempli, vel aliquem amicorum,
6 ut me proxime. Quam pulchrum illud, quam dulce
secretum! quantum ibi antiquitatis! quae facta, quos
viros audias! quibus praeceptis imbuare! quamvis ille
hoc temperamentum modestiae suae indixerit, ne prae-
7 cipere videatur. Peractis septem millibus passuum,
iterum ambulat mille, iterum residit, vel se cubiculo ac
stilo reddit. Scribit enim, et quidem utraque lingua,
lyrica doctissima. Mira illis dulcedo, mira suavitas,
mira hilaritas, cuius gratiam cumulat sanctitas scriben-
8 tis. Ubi hora balinei nuntiata est, (est autem hieme
nona, aestate octava) in sole, si caret vento, ambulat
nudus. Deinde movetur pila vehementer et diu: nam
hoc quoque exercitationis genere pugnat cum senectute.
Lotus accubat, et paullisper cibum differt: interim audit
legentem remissius aliquid et dulcius. Per hoc omne
tempus liberum est amicis vel eadem agere, vel alia, si
9 malint. Apponitur coena non minus nitida quam
frugi, in argento puro et antiquo. Sunt in usu et
Corinthia, quibus delectatur nec adficitur. Frequenter
comoedis coena distinguitur, ut voluptates quoque
studiis condiantur. Sumit aliquid de nocte et aestate.
Nemini hoc longum est: tanta comitate convivium

trahitur. Inde illi post septimum et septuagesimum 10
annum aurium oculorumque vigor integer; inde agile
et vividum corpus, solaque ex senectute prudentia.
Hanc ego vitam voto et cogitatione praesumo, ingres- 11
surus avidissime, ut primum ratio aetatis receptui
canere permiserit. Interim mille laboribus conteror,
quorum mihi et solatium et exemplum est idem Spurinna. Nam ille quoque, quoad honestum fuit, obiit
officia, gessit magistratus, provincias rexit; multoque
labore hoc otium meruit. Igitur eundem mihi cursum, 12
eundem terminum statuo: idque iam nunc apud te
subsigno, ut, si me longius evehi videris, in ius voces
ad hanc epistolam meam, et quiescere iubeas, cum
inertiae crimen effugero. Vale.

E. XVI. (i. 5.)

[This and the three following letters tell us some singular
anecdotes about a well-known man of the time, who had been
a conspicuously successful 'delator.' Regulus had made so
profitable a use of the opportunities afforded him by the reigns
of Nero and Domitian, that he had risen from obscure poverty
into almost fabulous wealth and an important social position.
He seems to have been a strange mixture of vindictiveness,
cowardice, preposterous affectation, and a certain sort of ability
which, coupled with indefatigable industry, brought him considerable success at the bar. It is generally supposed that he
was the same man as the Regulus of whom Martial more than
once speaks in very complimentary language (see *Epig.* i. 13,
83, 112; iv. 16). The poet always flattered the favourites of
Domitian, and looked to them for patronage.

In the present letter Pliny tells us with much self-compla-
cency how skilfully he contrived to avoid a trap laid for him
by Regulus on the occasion of a trial in which he and Regulus were counsel on opposite sides.]

C. PLINIUS VOCONIO ROMANO SUO S.

Vidistine quemquam Marco Regulo timidiorem humi-
lioremque post Domitiani mortem? sub quo non minora

L 2

flagitia commiserat, quam sub Nerone, sed tectiora.
Coepit vereri, ne sibi irasceret : nec fallebatur; irasce-
2 bar. Rustici Aruleni periculum foverat, exsultaverat
morte, adeo ut librum recitaret publicaretque, in quo
Rusticum insectatur, atque etiam *Stoicorum simiam*
3 appellat. Adicit *Vitelliana cicatrice stigmosum.* Ag-
noscis eloquentiam Reguli. Lacerat Herennium Sene-
cionem, tam intemperanter quidem, ut dixerit ei Metius
Carus : *Quid tibi cum meis mortuis? Numquid ego aut
Crasso aut Camerino molestus sum?* quos ille sub
4 Nerone accusaverat. Haec me Regulus dolenter tu-
lisse credebat, ideoque etiam, cum recitaret librum, non
adhibuerat. Praeterea reminiscebatur, quam capitali-
5 ter ipsum me apud centumviros lacessisset. Aderam
Arionillae, Timonis uxori, rogatu Aruleni Rustici.
Regulus contra. Nitebamur nos in parte causae sententia Metii Modesti, optimi viri : is tunc in exilio
erat, a Domitiano relegatus. Ecce tibi Regulus,
Quaero, inquit, *Secunde, quid de Modesto sentias.* Vides,
quod periculum, si respondissem, *bene* : quod flagitium,
si, *male.* Non possum dicere aliud tunc mihi, quam
deos adfuisse. *Respondebo,* inquam, *quid sentiam, si de
hoc centumviri iudicaturi sunt.* Rursus ille, *Quaero,
6 quid de Modesto sentias.* Iterum ego, *Solebant testes
in reos, non in damnatos interrogari.* Tertio ille, *Non
iam quid de Modesto, sed quid de pietate Modesti sentias.
7 Quaeris,* inquam, *quid sentiam? At ego ne interrogare
quidem fas puto, de quo pronuntiatum est.* Conticuit :
me laus et gratulatio secuta est ; quod nec famam
meam aliquo responso, utili fortasse, inhonesto tamen,
laeseram, nec me laqueis tam insidiosae interrogationis
8 involveram. Nunc ergo conscientia exterritus appre-
hendit Caecilium Celerem ; mox Fabium Iustum rogat,
ut me sibi reconcilient. Nec contentus, pervenit ad
Spurinnam ; huic suppliciter (ut est, quum timet, ab-
iectissimus) : *Rogo,* inquit, *mane videas Plinium domi :
sed plane mane ; neque enim diutius ferre sollicitudinem
possum ; et quoquo modo efficias, ne mihi irascatur.*
9 Evigilaveram. Nuntius a Spurinna : *Venio ad te.—
Immo ego ad te.* Coimus in porticu Liviae, cum alter

ad alterum tenderemus. Exponit Reguli mandata,
addit preces suas, ut decebat optimum virum pro dissi-
millimo, parce. Cui ego: *Dispicies ipse, quid renun-* 10
tiandum Regulo putes: te decipi a me non oportet. Exspecto *Mauricum* (nondum enim ab exilio venerat), *ideo
nihil alterutram in partem respondere tibi possum, fac-
turus quidquid ille decreverit.* Illum enim esse huius
consilii ducem, me comitem, decet. Paucos post dies 11
ipse me Regulus convenit in praetoris officio: illuc
me persecutus secretum petit. Ait, *timere se, ne animo
meo penitus haereret, quod in centumvirali iudicio aliquando dixisset,* cum responderet mihi et Satrio Rufo:
*Satrius Rufus, cui non est cum Cicerone aemulatio, et
qui contentus est eloquentia seculi nostri.* Respondi, 12
*nunc me intelligere maligne dictum, quia ipse confitere-
tur: ceterum potuisse honorificum existimari. Est enim,*
inquam, *mihi cum Cicerone aemulatio, nec sum contentus eloquentia seculi nostri. Nam stultissimum credo,* 13
ad imitandum non optima quaeque proponere. Sed
tu, *qui huius iudicii meministi, cur illius oblitus es,
in quo me interrogasti, quid de Meti Modesti pietate
sentirem?* Expalluit notabiliter, quamvis palleat semper: et haesitabundus inquit, *Interrogavi, non ut tibi
nocerem, sed ut Modesto.* Vide hominis crudelitatem,
qui se non dissimulet exuli nocere voluisse. Sub- 14
iunxit egregiam causam : *Scripsit,* inquit, *in epistola
quadam, quae apud Domitianum recitata est: Regulus,
omnium bipedum nequissimus;* quod quidem
Modestus verissime scripserat. Hic fere nobis ser- 15
monis terminus. Neque enim volui progredi longius,
ut mihi omnia libera servarem, dum Mauricus venit.
Nec me praeterit, esse Regulum δυσκαθαίρετον: est
enim locuples, factiosus; curatur a multis, timetur a
pluribus, quod plerumque fortius amore est. Potest
tamen fieri, ut haec concussa labantur. Nam gratia
malorum tam infida est, quam ipsi. Verum, ut idem 16
saepius dicam, exspecto Mauricum. Vir est gravis,
prudens, multis experimentis eruditus, et qui futura
possit ex praeteritis providere. Mihi et tentandi aliquid et quiescendi illo auctore ratio constabit. Haec 17

tibi scripsi, quia acquum erat, te pro amore mutuo non
solum omnia mea facta dictaque, verum etiam consilia
cognoscere. Vale.

E. XVII. (ii. 20.)

[Here we have anecdotes of Regulus in the capacity of a
captator, or legacy-hunter.]

C. PLINIUS CALVISIO SUO S.

Assem para, et accipe auream fabulam, fabulas
immo. Nam me priorum nova admonuit : nec refert,
2 a qua potissimum incipiam. Verania Pisonis graviter
iacebat ; huius dico Pisonis, quem Galba adoptavit.
Ad hanc Regulus venit. Primum impudentiam hominis, qui venerit ad aegram, cuius marito inimicis-
3 simus, ipsi invisissimus fuerat. Esto, si venit tantum :
at ille etiam proximus toro sedit : quo die, qua hora
nata esset, interrogavit. Ubi audivit, componit vultum,
intendit oculos, movet labra, agitat digitos, computat—
4 nihil : diu miseram exspectatione suspendit. *Habes*,
inquit, *climactericum tempus, sed evades. Quod ut tibi
magis liqueat, aruspicem consulam, quem sum fre-*
5 *quenter expertus.* Nec mora : sacrificium facit, adfirmat, exta cum siderum significatione congruere. Illa,
ut in periculo, credula, poscit codicillos : legatum Regulo scribit : mox ingravescit : clamat moriens, *o hominem nequam, perfidum, ac plus etiam quam periurum!*
6 qui sibi per salutem filii peierasset. Facit hoc Regulus
non minus scelerate quam frequenter. quod iram deorum,
quos ipse cotidie fallit, in caput infelicis pueri detes-
7 tatur. Velleius Blaesus ille locuples, consularis, novissima valetudine conflictabatur : cupiebat mutare
testamentum. Regulus, qui speraret aliquid ex novis
tabulis, quia nuper captare eum coeperat, medicos hortari, rogare, quoquo modo spiritum homini prorogarent.
8 Postquam signatum est testamentum, mutat personam,

vertit allocutionem, isdemque medicis, *Quousque mi-
serum cruciatis? quid invidetis bona morte, cui dare
vitam non potestis?* Moritur Blaesus, et tamquam
omnia audisset, Regulo ne tantulum quidem. Suffi- 9
ciunt duae fabulae, an scholastica lege tertiam poscis?
Est unde fiat. Aurelia, ornata femina, signatura tes- 10
tamentum, sumpserat pulcherrimas tunicas. Regulus
cum venisset ad signandum, *Rogo*, inquit, *has mihi
leges.* Aurelia ludere hominem putabat ; ille serio in-
stabat. Nec multa: coegit mulierem aperire tabulas, 11
ac sibi tunicas, quas erat induta, legare : observavit
scribentem, inspexit, an scripsisset. Et Aurelia quidem vivit : ille tamen istud tanquam morituram coegit.
Et hic hereditates, hic legata, quasi mercatur, accipit.
Ἀλλὰ τί διατείνομαι in ea civitate, in qua iampridem 12
non minora praemia, immo maiora, nequitia et impro-
bitas, quam pudor et virtus, habent? Adspice Regu- 13
lum, qui ex paupere et tenui ad tantas opes per flagitia
processit, ut ipse mihi dixerit, cum consuleret, quam
cito sestertium sexcenties impleturus esset, invenisse se
exta duplicia quibus portendi, millies et ducenties ha-
biturum. Et habebit, si modo, ut coepit, aliena testa- 14
menta, quod est improbissimum genus falsi, ipsis,
quorum sunt illa, dictaverit. Vale.

E. XVIII. (iv. 2.)

[Regulus had lately lost his son, a lad of some ability and
promise. By the legal process termed *emancipatio* he had
released the youth from his paternal power, and thus enabled
him to acquire the right of becoming heir to the property of
his mother, who, we suppose, was unwilling, from fear of the
consequences, to make him her heir as long as he was under
his father's control and could inherit nothing for himself.
According to Roman law, whatever was bequeathed to a son
still under the *patria potestas* belonged, as a matter of course,
to the father. Regulus, if popular gossip might be trusted, in his
anxiety to secure for himself his son's fortune, used to fawn upon

him with the most unseemly adulation. He made a singularly
grotesque show of sorrow on the occasion of his death. The
boy kept a number of pet animals : these the father had killed
on the funeral pile.]

C. PLINIUS CLEMENTI SUO S.

Regulus filium amisit : hoc uno malo indignus, quod
nescio an malum putet. Erat puer acris ingenii, sed
ambigui : qui tamen posset recta sectari, si patrem non
2 referret. Hunc Regulus emancipavit, ut heres matris
exsisteret. Mancipatum (ita vulgo ex moribus hominis
loquebantur) foeda et insolita parentibus indulgentiae simulatione captabat. Incredibile, sed Regulum
3 cogita. Amissum tamen luget insane. Habebat puer
mannulos multos, et iunctos et solutos : habebat canes
maiores minoresque : habebat luscinias, psittacos, me-
4 rulas : omnes Regulus circa rogum trucidavit. Nec
dolor erat ille, sed ostentatio doloris. Convenitur ad
eum mira celebritate. Cuncti detestantur, oderunt, et
quasi probent, quasi diligant, cursant, frequentant :
utque breviter, quod sentio, enuntiem, in Regulo de-
5 merendo Regulum imitantur. Tenet se trans Tiberim
in hortis, in quibus latissimum solum porticibus im-
mensis, ripam statuis suis occupavit, ut est in summa
avaritia sumptuosus, in summa infamia gloriosus.
6 Vexat ergo civitatem insaluberrimo tempore ; et quod
vexat, solatium putat. Dicit se velle ducere uxorem :
7 hoc quoque, sicut alia, perverse. Audies brevi nuptias lugentis, nuptias senis : quorum alterum immatu-
8 rum, alterum serum est. Unde hoc augurer, quaeris?
Non quia adfirmat ipse (quo mendacius nihil est), sed
quia certum est, Regulum esse facturum, quidquid
fieri non oportet. Vale.

E. XIX. (iv. 7.)

[This gives us additional anecdotes about the peculiar manner in which Regulus had manifested his sorrow for his son, as well as a remark on the oratorical success which, in spite of various defects, his self-confidence had gained for him.]

C. PLINIUS LEPIDO SUO S.

Saepe tibi dico, inesse vim Regulo. Mirum est, quam efficiat, in quod incubuit. Placuit ei lugere filium : luget, ut nemo. Placuit statuas eius et imagines quam plurimas facere : hoc omnibus officinis agit. Illum coloribus, illum cera, illum aere, illum argento, illum auro, ebore, marmore effingit. Ipse vero et nu- 2 per, adhibito ingenti auditorio, librum de vita eius recitavit, de vita pueri : recitavit tamen ; eundem in exemplaria transcriptum mille, per totam Italiam provinciasque dimisit. Scripsit publice, ut a decurionibus eligeretur vocalissimus aliquis ex ipsis, qui legeret eum populo : factum est. Hanc ille vim (seu quo alio 3 nomine vocanda est intentio, quidquid velis, obtinendi) si ad potiora vertisset, quantum boni efficere potuisset ! Quamquam minor vis bonis, quam malis, inest, ac sicut ἀμαθία μὲν θράσος, λογισμὸς δὲ ὄκνον φέρει, ita recta ingenia debilitat verecundia, perversa confirmat audacia. Exemplo est Regulus. Imbecillum latus, os 4 confusum, haesitans lingua, tardissima inventio, memoria nulla : nihil denique praeter ingenium insanum : et tamen eo impudentia ipsoque illo furore pervenit, ut orator habeatur. Itaque Herennius Senecio mirifice 5 Catonis illud de oratore in hunc e contrario vertit : *Orator est vir malus, dicendi imperitus.* Non, mehercule, Cato ipse tam bene verum oratorem, quam hic Regulum expressit. Habesne, quo tali epistolae parem 6 gratiam referas ? Habes, si scripseris, num aliquis in municipio vestro ex sodalibus meis, num etiam ipse tu hunc luctuosum Reguli librum, ut circulator, in foro

legeris, ἐπάρας scilicet, ut ait Demosthenes, τὴν φωνήν,
7 καὶ γεγηθώς, καὶ λαρυγγίζων. Est enim tam ineptus,
ut risum magis possit exprimere, quam gemitum.
Credas non de puero scriptum, sed a puero. Vale

E. XX. (i. 3.)

[Pliny in this letter urges his friend Caninius Rufus to take
advantage of his retirement amid the beautiful scenery of
Comum for the accomplishment of some great literary work.
Caninius was Pliny's neighbour at Comum, and an intimate
friend. We hear from B. XVIII. that he thought of comme-
morating Trajan's achievements in Dacia in an epic poem.
Letters B. XII., XVI., XVII., D. III., and E. XXVII. are addressed to him.]

C. PLINIUS CANINIO RUFO SUO S.

Quid agit Comum, tuae meaeque deliciae? quid
suburbanum amoenissimum? quid illa porticus verna
semper? quid platanon opacissimus? quid Euripus
viridis et gemmeus? quid subiectus et serviens lacus?
quid illa mollis et tamen solida gestatio? quid balineum illud, quod plurimus sol implet et circumit? quid
triclinia illa popularia, illa paucorum? quid cubicula
diurna nocturna? Possident te et per vices partiuntur?
2 an, ut solebas, intentione rei familiaris obeundae,
crebris excursionibus avocaris? Si te possident, felix
3 beatusque es: si minus, unus ex multis. Quin tu
(tempus est enim) humiles et sordidas curas aliis man-
das, et ipse te in alto isto pinguique secessu studiis
adseris? Hoc sit negotium tuum, hoc otium: hic
labor, haec quies: in his vigilia, in his etiam somnus
4 reponatur. Effinge aliquid et excude, quod sit per-
petuo tuum. Nam reliqua rerum tuarum post te alium
atque alium dominum sortientur: hoc numquam tuum
5 desinet esse, si semel coeperit. Scio, quem animum,
quod horter ingenium. Tu modo enitere, ut tibi ipse
eis tanti, quanti videberis aliis, si tibi fueris. Vale.

E. XXI. (i. 9.)

[Pliny draws a contrast between city life, so busy and so unsatisfactory, and the quiet and satisfying enjoyments and occupations of the country.]

C. PLINIUS MINUCIO FUNDANO SUO S.

Mirum est quam singulis diebus in urbe ratio aut constet aut constare videatur, pluribus cunctisque non constet. Nam si quem interroges, *Hodie quid egisti?* 2 respondeat, *Officio togae virilis interfui, sponsalia aut nuptias frequentavi; ille me ad signandum testamentum, ille in advocationem, ille in consilium rogavit.* Haec quo die feceris necessaria; eadem, si cotidie 3 fecisse te reputes, inania videntur, multo magis cum secesseris. Tunc enim subit recordatio, *Quot dies quam frigidis rebus absumpsi!* Quod evenit mihi postquam 4 in Laurentino meo aut lego aliquid aut scribo, aut etiam corpori vaco cuius fulturis animus sustinetur. Nihil audio quod audisse, nihil dico quod dixisse poe- 5 niteat. Nemo apud me quemquam sinistris sermonibus carpit, neminem ipse reprehendo, nisi tamen me, cum parum commode scribo; nulla spe, nullo timore sollicitor, nullis rumoribus inquietor: mecum tantum et cum libellis loquor. O rectam sinceramque vitam! 6 o dulce otium, honestumque ac paene omni negotio pulchrius! O mare, o litus, verum secretumque μουσεῖον! quam multa invenitis, quam multa dictatis! Proinde tu quoque strepitum istum inanemque dis- 7 cursum, et multum ineptos labores, ut primum fuerit occasio, relinque, teque studiis vel otio trade. Satius 8 est enim, ut Attilius noster eruditissime simul et facetissime dixit, otiosum esse, quam nihil agere. Vale.

E. XXII. (i. 15.)

[Pliny jokingly tells his friend Septicius, who had broken an engagement to dinner, that he should bring an action against him for damages. He hints that his friend had preferred more sumptuous fare elsewhere to the simplicity of his own entertainment, but avows that he could not have enjoyed himself more thoroughly.]

C. PLINIUS SEPTICIO CLARO SUO S.

Heus tu, promittis ad coenam, nec venis! Dicetur ius: ad assem impendium reddes, nec id modicum. 2 Paratae erant lactucae singulae, cochleae ternae, ova bina, alica cum mulso et nive (nam hanc quoque computabis, immo hanc in primis, quae perit in ferculo), olivae, betacei, cucurbitae, bulbi, alia mille non minus lauta. Audisses comoedum, vel lectorem, vel lyristen, 3 vel, quae mea liberalitas, omnes. At tu apud nescio quem, ostrea, vulvas, echinos, Gaditanas, maluisti. Dabis poenas, non dico quas. Dure fecisti: invidisti, nescio an tibi, certe mihi, sed tamen et tibi. Quantum nos lu- 4 sissemus, risissemus, studuissemus! Potes apparatius coenare apud multos: nusquam hilarius, simplicius, incautius. In summa, experire: et nisi postea te aliis potius excusaveris, mihi semper excusa. Vale.

E. XXIII. (ii. 6.)

[Pliny tells us in this letter that he had lately dined at the house of a man who had been guilty of the bad taste of treating some of his guests differently from others. There were three kinds of wine, the first and best for the host and a select few, the second best for his inferior friends, the last and worst kind for his freedmen. Pliny takes care to let his friend know that, whenever he entertained, he put only one kind of wine on table, and warns him, as a young man, against being

imposed on by any such pitiful attempt to combine vulgar
show with economy.

Two of Pliny's friends, it appears, bore the cognomen of
Avitus. They were probably brothers. Both were young men
of singular promise, and both died young. In *Ep.* v. 21, we have
mention of the death of a Julius Avitus, who died at sea as he
was on his return from a province where he had been quaestor.
He is spoken of as a youth of wonderful literary attainments,
and as certain to have risen to the highest honours of the state
had he lived. But a yet more intimate friend of Pliny would
seem to have been a Junius Avitus, of whom a short account is given in E. X. It was in Pliny's house that he
assumed the distinguishing dress of a senator; and he seems
to have regarded Pliny almost as a father. He had served as
a military tribune in Germany and Pannonia, had risen to the
quaestorship, and was a candidate for the aedileship at the
time of his death. We may reasonably suppose him to be
the friend to whom the present letter is addressed.]

C. PLINIUS AVITO SUO S.

Longum est altius repetere, nec refert, quemadmodum acciderit, ut homo minime familiaris coenarem
apud quendam, ut sibi videbatur, lautum et diligentem;
ut mihi, sordidum simul et sumptuosum. Nam sibi et **2**
paucis opima quaedam; ceteris vilia et minuta ponebat.
Vinum etiam parvulis lagunculis in tria genera descri-
pserat, non ut potestas eligendi, sed ne ius esset recusandi: et aliud sibi et nobis, aliud minoribus amicis (nam
gradatim amicos habet), aliud suis nostrisque libertis.
Animadvertit, qui mihi proximus recumbebat, et, an **3**
probarem, interrogavit. Negavi. *Tu ergo*, inquit, *quam
consuetudinem sequeris?—Eadem omnibus pono. Ad
coenam enim, non ad notam, invito: cunctisque rebus
exaequo, quos mensa et toro aequavi.—Etiamne li-* **4**
*bertos?—Etiam. Convictores enim tunc, non libertos,
puto.* Ille: *Magno tibi constat?—Minime.—Qui fieri potest?—Quia scilicet liberti mei non idem quod ego,
sed idem ego, quod liberti.*—Et Hercule, si gulae tem- **5**
peres, non est onerosum, quo utaris ipse, communicare
cum pluribus. Illa ergo reprimenda, illa quasi in ordinem redigenda est, si sumptibus parcas, quibus aliquan-

to rectius tua continentia, quam aliena contumelia, con-
6 sulas. Quorsum haec? Ne tibi, optimae indolis iuveni, quorundam in mensa luxuria specie frugalitatis im-
ponat. Convenit autem amori in te meo, quoties tale
aliquid inciderit, sub exemplo praemonere, quid debeas
7 fugere. Igitur memento, nihil magis esse vitandum,
quam istam luxuriae et sordium novam societatem,
quae cum sint turpissima discreta ac separata, turpius
iunguntur. Vale.

E. XXIV. (iii. 12.)

[Pliny accepts an invitation to dinner on the condition that
the entertainment be of a moderate kind, and seasoned with
intellectual conversation, and illustrates what he says by an
anecdote of Cato.]

C. PLINIUS CATILIO SUO S.

Veniam ad coenam, sed iam nunc paciscor, sit expedita, sit parca: Socraticis tantum sermonibus abundet:
2 in his quoque teneat modum. Erunt officia antelucana, in quae incidere impune ne Catoni quidem licuit,
quem tamen C. Caesar ita reprehendit, ut laudet.
3 Scribit enim, eos, quibus obvius fuerit, cum caput
ebrii retexissent, erubuisse: deinde adiicit, *Putares,
non ab illis Catonem, sed illos a Catone deprehensos.*
Potuitne plus auctoritatis tribui Catoni, quam si ebrius
4 quoque tam venerabilis erat? Nostrae tamen coenae
ut apparatus et impendii, sic temporis modus constet.
Neque enim ii sumus, quos vituperare ne inimici quidem possint, nisi ut simul laudent. Vale.

E. XXV. (viii. 22.)

[This letter is directed against that numerous class of persons who, while they are slaves of their own caprices, cannot bear with patience the faults of others. It may be compared with Hor. *Sat.* i. 3, presenting an almost exact parallel to the lines :—

'Aequum est
Peccatis veniam poscentem reddere rursus.']

C. PLINIUS GEMINIO SUO S.

Nostine hos, qui omnium libidinum servi sic aliorum vitiis irascuntur, quasi invideant, et gravissime puniunt, quos maxime imitantur? cum eos etiam, qui non indigent clementia ullius, nihil magis quam lenitas deceat. Atque ego optimum et emendatissimum existimo, qui 2 ceteris ita ignoscit, tanquam ipse cotidie peccet: ita peccatis abstinet, tanquam nemini ignoscat. Proinde 3 hoc domi, hoc foris, hoc in omni vitae genere teneamus, ut nobis implacabiles simus, exorabiles istis etiam, qui dare veniam, nisi sibi, nesciunt; mandemusque memoriae, quod vir mitissimus, et ob hoc quoque maximus, Thrasea, crebro dicere solebat : *qui vitia odit, homines odit.* Fortasse quaeris, quo commotus haec scribam. Nuperquidam ... Sed melius coram; quamquam ne tunc 4 quidem. Vereor enim, ne id, quod improbo, insectari, carpere, referre, huic, quod cum maxime praecipimus, repugnet. Quisquis ille, qualiscumque, sileatur ; quem insignire, exempli nihil, non insignire, humanitatis plurimum refert. Vale.

E. XXVI. (ix. 6.)

[We have in this letter Pliny's views about the famous Circensian games, which were annually celebrated at Rome during the early part of September. He found, he says, so little attraction in them that he did not care to leave his literary work for the sake of witnessing them. Even the spectators themselves were not drawn so much by the sight itself as by the gambling spirit which made them back the green or the red, &c. In the time of Domitian, six chariots ran in the course, and to these there corresponded six companies (*factiones*), distinguished as *prasina, russata, veneta, alba, aurata,* and *purpura.* Of these the four first colours were meant to represent the seasons of the year. We gather from allusions to the games in Martial and Juvenal that they formed at that time a conspicuous element in Roman life. Cicero in one of his letters (*Epist. ad Fam.* vii. 1) speaks somewhat contemptuously of the games; and Pliny may perhaps be here reproducing his sentiments.]

C. PLINIUS CALVISIO SUO S.

Omne hoc tempus inter pugillares ac libellos iucundissima quiete transmisi. *Quemadmodum,* inquis, *in urbe potuisti?* Circenses erant; quo genere spectaculi ne levissime quidem teneor. Nihil novum, nihil

2 varium, nihil quod non semel spectasse sufficiat. Quo magis miror, tot millia virorum tam pueriliter identidem currentes equos, insistentes curribus homines videre. Si tamen aut velocitate equorum, aut hominum arte traherentur, esset ratio nonnulla: nunc favent panno, pannum amant, et si in ipso cursu medioque certamine hic color illuc, ille huc transferatur, studium favorque transibit, et repente agitatores illos, equos illos, quos procul noscitant, quorum clamitant nomina, relinquent. Tanta gratia, tanta auctoritas in una vilis-

3 sima tunica; mitto apud vulgus, quod vilius tunica est, sed apud quosdam graves homines, quos ego cum recordor in re inani, frigida, assidua, tam insatiabiliter desidere, capio aliquam voluptatem, quod hac volup-

4 tate non capior. Ac per hos dies libentissime otium meum in literis colloco, quos alii otiosissimis occupationibus perdunt. **Vale.**

E. XXVII. (ix. 33.)

[Pliny tells in this letter a curious story about a dolphin ac Hippo, which became wonderfully tame and familiar. A similar story is to be found in Aulus Gellius.]

C. PLINIUS CANINIO SUO S.

Incidi in materiam veram, sed simillimam fictae, dignamque isto laetissimo, altissimo, planeque poëtico ingenio. Incidi autem, dum super coenam varia miracula hinc inde referuntur. Magna auctoris fides: tametsi quid poëtae cum fide? Is tamen auctor, cui bene vel historiam scripturus credidisses. Est in Africa 2 Hipponensis colonia, mari proxima: adiacet navigabile stagnum, ex quo, in modum fluminis, aestuarium emergit, quod vice alterna, prout aestus aut repressit, aut impulit, nunc infertur mari, nunc redditur stagno. Omnis hic aetas piscandi, navigandi, atque etiam na- 3 tandi studio tenetur: maxime pueri, quos otium ludusque solicitant. Iis gloria et virtus altissime provehi: victor ille, qui longissime, ut litus, ita simul natantes, reliquit. Hoc certamine puer quidam, audentior ce- 4 teris, in ulteriora tendebat. Delphinus occurrit, et nunc praecedere puerum, nunc sequi, nunc circumire, postremo subire, deponere, iterum subire, trepidantemque perferre primum in altum: mox flectit ad litus, redditque terrae et aequalibus. Serpit per coloniam 5 fama: concurrere omnes, ipsum puerum tanquam miraculum adspicere, interrogare, audire, narrare. Postero die obsident littus, prospectant mare, et si quid est mari simile. Natant pueri: inter hos ille, sed cautius. Delphinus rursus ad tempus, rursus ad puerum venit. Fugit ille cum ceteris. Delphinus, quasi invitet et revocet, exsilit, mergitur, variosque orbes implicitat expeditque. Hoc altero die, hoc tertio, hoc pluribus, donec 6 homines innutritos mari subiret timendi pudor. Accedunt, et adludunt, et appellant: tangunt etiam, pertrectantque praebentem. Crescit audacia experimento.

M

Maxime puer, qui primus expertus est, adnatantis insilit
tergo: fertur referturque, agnosci se, amari putat, amat
ipse: neuter timet, neuter timetur: huius fiducia,
7 mansuetudo illius augetur. Nec non alii pueri dextra
laevaque simul eunt hortantes monentesque. Ibat
una (id quoque mirum) delphinus alius, tantum spec-
tator et comes. Nihil enim simile aut faciebat aut
patiebatur: sed alterum illum ducebat, reducebat,
8 ut puerum ceteri pueri. Incredibile (tam verum
tamen, quam priora) delphinum gestatorem colluso-
remque puerorum in terram quoque extrahi solitum,
arenisque siccatum, ubi incaluisset, in mare revolvi.
9 Constat Octavium Avitum, legatum proconsule, in
litus educto religione prava superfudisse unguentum,
cuius illum novitatem odoremque in altum refugisse:
nec nisi post multos dies visum languidum et moestum;
mox, redditis viribus, priorem lasciviam et solita minis-
10 teria repetisse. Confluebant ad spectaculum omnes
magistratus, quorum adventu et mora modica res
publica novis sumtibus atterebatur. Postremo locus
ipse quietem suam secretumque perdebat. Placuit
occulte interfici, ad quod coibatur. Haec tu qua mise-
11 ratione, qua copia deflebis, ornabis, attolles! Quamquam non est opus adfingas aliquid aut adstruas:
sufficit, ne ea, quae sunt vera, minuantur. Vale.

E. XXVIII. (viii. 17.)

[This letter describes an inundation of the Tiber, which
appears to have been greatly increased by the simultaneous
overflowing of the Anio, one of the Tiber's chief tributaries.
Serious injury was inflicted on the rural population generally,
and on the country houses with which the banks of the Anio
were studded. The elder Pliny (iii. 5, 9) alludes to the
well-known superstitious fears which the Roman mind invariably associated with such a calamity: ' Tiberis vates quodam-
modo intelligitur ac monitor, aucto semper religiosus.' Tacitus

(*Hist.* i. 76) in speaking of an inundation of the river during
Otho's reign gives us a similar hint. It seems that the
damage done on the occasion here described was confined to the
country districts, and was most extensive in the region now
known as the Campagna.]

C. PLINIUS MACRINO SUO S.

Num istic quoque immite et turbidum caelum? Hic
assiduae tempestates et crebra diluvia. Tiberis alveum
excessit, et demissioribus ripis alte superfunditur.
Quamquam fossa, quam providentissimus imperator 2
fecit, exhaustus, premit valles, innatat campis; quaque
planum solum, pro solo cernitur. Inde, quae solet flumina accipere, et permista devehere, velut obvius sistere
cogit; atque ita alienis aquis operit agros, quos ipse
non tangit. Anio, delicatissimus amnium, ideoque 3
adiacentibus villis velut invitatus retentusque, magna
ex parte nemora, quibus inumbratur, et fregit et rapuit.
Subruit montes, et decidentium mole pluribus locis
clausus, dum amissum iter quaerit, impulit tecta, ac se
super ruinas ejecit atque extulit. Viderunt, quos ex- 4
celsioribus terris illa tempestas deprehendit, alibi divi-
tum apparatus, et gravem supellectilem, alibi instru-
menta ruris; ibi boves, aratra, rectores, hic soluta et
libera armenta; atque inter haec arborum truncos, aut
villarum trabes varie lateque fluitantia. Ac ne illa 5
quidem loca malo vacaverunt, quae non adscendit
amnis. Nam pro amne imber assiduus, et deiecti
nubibus turbines: proruta opera, quibus pretiosa rura
cinguntur: quassata atque etiam decussa monimenta.
Multi eiusmodi casibus debilitati, obruti, obtriti, et
aucta luctibus damna. Ne quid simile istic, pro men- 6
sura periculi, vereor: teque rogo, si nihil tale est,
quam maturissime solicitudini meae consulas: sed et si
tale, id quoque nunties. Nam parvulum differt, patia-
ris adversa, an exspectes: nisi quod tamen est dolendi
modus, non est timendi. Doleas enim, quantum scias
accidisse; timeas, quantum possit accidere. Vale.

E. XXIX. (x. 4.)

[Pliny begs from the Emperor the promotion of his friend Voconius Romanus to senatorial rank. The same request had been preferred to Nerva, but some difficulty had been interposed by delay in transferring to him the property necessary to give him a senator's qualification. This had now been done, and all that was wanted was the Emperor's assent.]

C. PLINIUS TRAIANO IMP.

Indulgentia tua, Imperator optime, quam plenissimam experior, hortatur me, ut audeam tibi etiam pro amicis obligari; inter quos sibi vel praecipuum locum vindicat Voconius Romanus, ab ineunte aetate condis-
2 cipulus et contubernalis meus.   Quibus ex caussis et a divo patre tuo petieram, ut illum in amplissimum ordinem promoveret.   Sed hoc votum meum bonitati tuae reservatum est, quia mater Romani liberalitatem sestertii quadringenties, quod conferre se filio codicillis ad patrem tuum scriptis professa fuerat, nondum satis legitime peregerat : quod postea fecit, admonita a no-
3 bis.   Nam et fundos emancipavit, et cetera, quae in emancipatione implenda solent exigi, consummavit.
4 Cum sit ergo finitum, quod spes nostras morabatur, non sine magna fiducia subsigno apud te fidem pro moribus Romani mei, quos et liberalia studia exornant, et eximia pietas, quae hanc ipsam matris liberalitatem, et statim patris hereditatem, et adoptionem a vitrico
5 meruit.   Auget haec et natalium et paternarum facultatum splendor; quibus singulis multum commendationis accessurum etiam ex meis precibus, indulgentiae
6 tuae credo.   Rogo ergo, Domine, ut me exoptatissimae mihi gratulationis compotem facias, et honestis, ut spero, affectibus meis praestes, ut non in me tantum, verum et in amico gloriari iudiciis tuis possim.

E. XXX. (x. 39.)

[In the former of these letters Pliny puts before Trajan his difficulties with regard to a new theatre which was in process of construction at Nicaea, and which seemed so insecurely built that it was doubtful whether it would be well to continue the work, and to a bath which was being made at Claudiopolis, where a public grant of money seemed in danger of being injudiciously spent. Trajan's answer remits both matters to the judgment of Pliny. He is told that he can find a competent architect in the province to inspect the works, and need not seek one from Rome.]

C. PLINIUS TRAIANO IMP.

Theatrum, Domine, Nicaeae maxima iam parte constructum, imperfectum tamen, sestertium, ut audio (neque enim ratio [plus] excussa est), amplius centies hausit: vereor, ne frustra. Ingentibus enim rimis de-2 scendit et hiat, sive in caussa solum humidum et molle, sive lapis ipse gracilis et putris: dignum est certe deliberatione, sitne faciendum, an sit relinquendum, an etiam destruendum. Nam fulturae ac substructiones, quibus subinde suscipitur, non tam firmae mihi quam sumptuosae videntur. Huic theatro ex privatorum 3 pollicitationibus multa debentur, ut basilicae circa, ut porticus supra caveam. Quae nunc omnia differuntur, cessante eo, quod ante peragendum est. Iidem Ni- 4 caeenses gymnasium, incendio amissum, ante adventum meum restituere coeperunt, longe numerosius laxiusque, quam fuerat, et iam aliquantum erogaverunt: periculum est, ne parum utiliter; incompositum enim et sparsum est. Praeterea architectus, sane aemulus eius, a quo opus inchoatum est, affirmat parietes, quamquam viginti et duos pedes latos, imposita onera sustinere non posse, quia sint caemento medio farti, nec testaceo opere praecincti. Claudiopolitani quoque in depresso 5 loco, imminente etiam monte, ingens balineum defodiunt magis, quam aedificant, et quidem ex ea pecunia, quam buleutae additi beneficio tuo, aut iam obtulerunt ob introitum, aut nobis exigentibus conferunt. Ergo cum 6

timeam, ne illic publica pecunia, hic, quod est omni
pecunia pretiosius, munus tuum male collocetur; cogor petere a te, non solum ob theatrum, verum etiam
ob haec balinea, mittas architectum, dispecturum, utrum
sit utilius post sumptum, qui factus est, quoquo modo
consummare opera, ut inchoata sunt: an quae videntur
emendanda, corrigere, quae transferenda, transferre,
ne, dum servare volumus, quod impensum est, male
impendamus, quod addendum est.

E. XXXI. (x. 40.)

TRAIANUS PLINIO S.

Quid oporteat fieri circa theatrum, quod inchoatum
apud Nicaenses est, in re praesenti optime deliberabis
et constitues.   Mihi sufficiet indicari, cui sententiae
accesseris.   Tunc autem a privatis exigi opera tibi
curae sit, cum theatrum, propter quod illa promissa
2 sunt, factum erit.   Gymnasiis indulgent Graeculi:
ideo forsitan Nicaenses maiore animo constructionem
eius aggressi sunt: sed oportet illos eo contentos esse,
3 quod possit illis sufficere.   Quid Claudiopolitanis circa
balineum, quod parum, ut scribis, idoneo loco inchoa-
verunt, suadendum sit, tu constitues.   Architecti tibi
deesse non possunt.   Nulla provincia est, quae non
peritos et ingeniosos homines habeat: modo ne exis-
times, brevius esse ab urbe mitti, cum ex Graecia
etiam ad nos venire soliti sint.

E. XXXII. (x. 65.)

[These two letters are interesting as bearing on the subject
of infanticide, a very prevalent custom in the days of the
Empire.   Pliny asks what is to be done with a class of persons called θρεπτοί, who had been exposed as children, brought
up as slaves by persons who had found them, and about whom
the question often afterwards arose, whether or no they were
free.   To this question Trajan replies.]

C. PLINIUS TRAIANO IMP.

Magna, Domine, et ad totam provinciam pertinens quaestio est de conditione et alimentis eorum, quos vocant θρεπτούς. In qua ego, auditis constitutionibus [2] Principum, quia nihil inveniebam aut proprium, aut universale, quod ad Bithynos ferretur, consulendum te existimavi, quid observari velles. Neque enim putavi, posse me in eo, quod auctoritatem tuam posceret, ex- [3] emplis esse contentum. Recitabatur autem apud me edictum, quod dicebatur divi Augusti, ad Anniam pertinens : recitatae et epistolae divi Vespasiani ad Lacedaemonios, et divi Titi ad eosdem et ad Achaeos, et Domitiani ad Avidium Nigrinum et Armenium Brocchum proconsules, item ad Lacedaemonios : quae ideo tibi non misi, quia et parum emendata, et quaedam non certae fidei videbantur, et quia vera et emendata in scriniis tuis esse credebam.

E. XXXIII. (x. 66.)

TRAIANUS PLINIO S.

Quaestio ista, quae pertinet ad eos, qui liberi nati, expositi, deinde sublati a quibusdam, et in servitute educati sunt, saepe tractata est : nec quidquam invenitur in commentariis eorum Principum, qui ante me fuerunt, quod ad omnes provincias sit contitutum. Epistolae sane sunt Domitiani ad Avidium Nigrinum, [2] et Armenium Brocchum, quae fortasse debeant observari : sed inter eas provincias, de quibus rescripsit, non est Bithynia . et ideo nec assertionem denegandam iis, qui ex eiusmodi causa in libertatem vindicabuntur, puto : neque ipsam libertatem redimendam pretio alimentorum.

NOTES.

A. I. (iii. 16.)

4. *exsequias*—sc. 'the funeral procession.'

commodiorem—sc. 'going on more favourably.' An unusual meaning of 'commodus.' The phrase 'commodior valetudo' occurs in Celsus, viii. 1. Comp. the expression, 'commode vales,' A. XVI. 11.

quid ageret puer—sc. 'how the boy was going on.'

6. *tanquam ... reliquisset*—that is, 'she seemed to have laid aside her sorrow at the bereavement, and to have left it outside the door of the room.' The turn of expression is somewhat rhetorical, and for this reason Ernesti thought it unworthy of Pliny on such an occasion. It has however at least the merit of very forcibly depicting Arria's self-control.

Paete, non dolet—comp. Martial's Epigram (i. 14), in which these memorable words are introduced.

7. *Scribonianus ... moverat.* This incident is noticed by Suetonius (*Claudius*, 13), Tacitus, *Ann.* xii. 52; *Hist.* ii. 75. Scribonianus, it appears, was governor of Dalmatia, which in the time of the Empire politically coincided with Illyricum, the province being sometimes spoken of under the first name, sometimes, as here, under the latter. The revolt of Scribonianus occurred during the reign of Claudius. It was very brief, and was crushed in four days.

8. *nempe enim daturi estis*, &c.—'of course you are going to give,' &c. Arria meant simply that she would relieve the soldiers of the trouble and expense of providing slaves to wait on her husband. 'Nempe' often implies indignation; here it need not be so understood.

9. *profiteretur indicium*—for the phrase 'profiteri indicium' (to turn queen's evidence), comp. Sallust, *Jug.* 35, Tacit. *Ann.* vi. 3.

11. *male moriar*—this is explained by the context as meaning a hard and painful death (dura ad mortem via).

12. *Focillata*—'Having been revived.' A post-Augustan word.

13. *Videnturne*—'Do they not seem?' Comp. for this use of 'ne' E. I. 29, '*Justisne* de causis eum tibi videor incolere?' and B. XIII. 6, 'Meritone eum qui haec de me scripsit, defunctum esse doleo?'

A. II. (vi. 16.)

2. *quamvis ... occiderit.* The meaning, which is not quite clearly expressed, is this: ' Although it was in a memorable catastrophe which brought ruin on the fairest regions of the earth that he perished, destined ever to live in history, just as much as nations and as cities (which have perished in like manner), &c., &c. ' Memorabili casu' should be taken as in apposition with 'clade.' His uncle's death, Pliny means, was just as famous from its circumstances as the downfall of a nation or city.

4. *classem.* Two fleets, both called praetorian, were stationed respectively at Misenum on the Tyrrhene Sea, and at Ravenna on the Adriatic. This, we learn from Tacitus, *Ann.* iv. 5, and Suetonius, *Oct.* 49, was the policy of Augustus, and may very possibly have had for its design the prompt suppression of any disturbances at Rome, which with the mixed and disorderly city-population were continually to be apprehended.

5. *usus ille sole—*' having taken a turn in the sun.' Comp. B. XI. 11, 'post *solem* plerumque frigida lavabatur.'

gustaverat—' he had lunched.' Comp. B. XI. 11, 'gustabat,' &c., and see note.

*pinus—*sc. the Italian pine, with a top like an umbrella.

6. *recenti ... destituta—*' carried upwards by a breath of wind just sprung up, then afterwards, as the wind fell, being left unsupported,' &c. This metaphorical use of ' senescere ' is common enough.

*in latitudinem vanescebat—*sc. 'the cloud became thinner as it broadened.'

7. *Liburnicam—*sc. a species of cutter. It was called indifferently ' liburna' or 'liburnica,' from the Liburni, an Illyrian tribe noted for piracy. The term had become thoroughly naturalised in the Latin language from the time of the battle of Actium, in which these vessels formed the fleet of Augustus.

8. *egrediebatur ... orabat—*there is here such confusion in the MSS., that we have but a choice of difficulties. To the common reading which has a stop at ' codicillos,' Retinae for Rectinae. villa ea for villa ejus, there are serious objections. It assumes that ' codicilli,' which nearly always means a note, a short letter, &c., can be used for ' pugillares,' which is the regular word for small writing tablets such as literary Romans carried about with them. It implies that the crews of the fleet were stationed at Retina (now Resina), a village some way from the coast. It describes their station by the inappropriate word ' villa ;' and it strangely represents that they could have escaped from it only on shipboard. These difficulties have led us to adopt Gierig's reading as on the whole the most satisfactory. According to this, Pliny's uncle received a short hurried note from a lady named Rectina, whose villa was close to the scene of danger, begging for assistance from the ships. She was, it seems, the wife of Caesius Bassus, a lyric poet mentioned by Quintilian, who, if we may trust the Scholiast

on Persius (whose sixth satire is addressed to him), perished in this eruption of Vesuvius.

9. *quod studioso . . . maximo*—sc. what he had begun to do from the thirst of knowledge, he now carries out in a noble and generous spirit.

10. *omnes figuras*—sc. all the various phenomena attendant on the eruption.

11. *radum subitum*—the effect of the eruption was to make the sea retire, leaving the ships in shallow water and in danger of running aground. Comp. the passage in the next letter, where this effect is described at length (mare in se resorberi, &c.).

ruina montis litora obstantia—understand by 'ruina montis' the mass of stones, ashes, &c., descending from the mountain and falling on the shore, and blocking it up so that it was difficult to land. This is the meaning of 'obstantia.'

fortes fortuna juvat—an old proverb. Comp. Virg. *Aen.* x. 284.

Pomponianum. He was very possibly the son of the Pomponius Secundus, whose life the elder Pliny is said to have written. See B. XI. 3. It is a pure conjecture that he was second in command of the fleet.

12. *Stabiis*—Stabiae was a mere village at this time. The elder Pliny himself says (*N. H.* iii. 5, 10) that it was entirely destroyed by Sulla. The name, however, did not disappear ; Seneca speaks of the littus *Stabianum.* We may suppose that it consisted of nothing more than a few scattered country houses. It was about four miles south of Pompeii.

sinu medio—'by the intervening bay.

infunditur—sc. 'runs up into the land and forms a bay.'

certus fugae—a post-Augustan construction. It is common in Tacitus.

13. *excitabatur*—'was thrown into clear relief.'

meatus animae—'his breathing.'

14. *area . . . surrexerat*—by 'area' is meant 'the open space in front of the house.'

15. *tremoribus*—'tremor terrae' is a somewhat poetical expression for an earthquake, which is usually described as 'motus terrae.'

16. *levium exesorumque*—'light and hollow.'

quod tamen . . . elegit—'this alternative, however (that of going into the open air), a comparison of dangers selected (as the best).' They weighed the risk of remaining in the house and that of leaving it, and decided that the latter was the least. The use of the abstract subject (collatio periculorum) is hardly in accordance with Latin idiom.

apud illum . . . vicit—the meaning is: 'He as a philosopher acted as he did because the reason for so doing outweighed to his mind the reason for remaining where they were ; with others it was a mere conflict between their fears.'

17. *solabantur*—this is the emendation of Cortius, and is now generally accepted with good reason, as it actually appears in one of the best MSS. (that of Prague). The common reading 'solvebant'

would imply that the darkness was quite dispersed by the 'faces variaque lumina.' This is absurd. To say that they consoled themselves amid the darkness with the light of torches is a somewhat poetical expression which Pliny would have been likely to use. By 'varia lumina' (as distinguished from 'faces') it would seem we are to understand the flames issuing from the mountain, and the light from the burning houses in the surrounding district.

ecquid . . . admitteret—' whether now the sea would at all allow us to embark.'

rastum—referring not merely to the size of the waves, but to the generally appalling look of the sea. The word denotes somewhat vaguely the kindred notions of loneliness and terror.

19. *caligine*—here 'vapour,' which would cause suffocation by filling the lungs.

stomacho—' the windpipe.' This is the original meaning of the Greek στόμαχος; and the word is so used by Homer. It appears too to have been the proper meaning of 'stomachus' from Cicero, *De Nat. D.* ii. 54, ' linguam ad radices ejus haerens excipit *stomachus.*' It is however but very rarely that we find it in this sense.

frequenter aestuans—' often inflamed.' It would seem that he suffered habitually from a weak and often a sore throat, and his death was indirectly due to this circumstance.

22. *omnia me . . . persecutum*—' that I have described in detail every incident at which I was present and every thing which I heard on the spot, when the account was to be perfectly relied on.'

(A. III. vi. 20.)

1. *adductum . . . cupere*—' cupere' depends on 'ais,' not on 'adductum.'

id enim ingressus abruperam—' for I broke off this part of the subject after I had but just entered on it.' He refers to the conclusion of the preceding letter : 'interim Miseni ego et mater ; sed nihil ad historiam,' &c.

quanquam . . . incipiam—Virg. *Aen.* ii. 12. With these words Aeneas introduces the tale of Troy.

2. *tempus studiis impendi*—in Cicero the regular construction is ' impendere tempus, curam, &c., *in aliquid.*' Later writers commonly used the *dative.*

3. *quia Campaniae solitus*—Pompeii had been almost destroyed by an earthquake A.D. 62. See Tacit. *Ann.* xv. 22. Seneca (*Q. N.* vi. 1) alludes to this calamity, and speaks of Campaniae as ' numquam securam hujus mali.'

4. *ita invaluit . . . crederentur*—'the shock was so violent that it seemed that everything was being not merely shaken but actually overturned.' The preceding letter says nothing of these premonitory shocks ; it merely states that the eruption was accompanied with an earthquake.

5. *posco librum T. Livi,* &c. &c. It has been ingeniously conjec-

tured that we have here an allusion to the work entitled ' Viri
Illustres,' which has been attributed to our author.

ut coeperam, excerpo—comp. the account, in B. XI. 10, of the
elder Pliny's practice of making extracts; 'nihil legit quod non
excerperet.'

ex Hispania—the elder Pliny had been proconsul of Spain.
See B. XI. 17.

6. *dubius dies*—dies = daylight. Comp. D. XI. 2, admisso *die.*
So Statius, *Theb.* i. 2. For the expression *dubius* dies comp. Ovid,
Met. iv. 401, ' *dubiae* confinia noctis.'

8. *egressi tecta*—' having gone beyond the limits of,' &c. This is
the force of the accusative; comp. A. V. 10, historia non debet
egredi veritatem. The stepping out of a *particular* building would
be expressed by an *ablative.*

9. *ab altero latere . . . majores erant.* The black cloud, broken as
it was by what seemed flashes of *forked* lightning (tortis vibratisque
discursibus) parted continually and showed great masses of flame
of various shape as a fiery background. These latter phenomena
Pliny compares to *sheet* lightning (fulguribus) though they were,
he says, on a larger scale.

' Tortus ' expresses the zigzag movement; ' vibratus ' its rapidity. Ab altero latere = landwards, the sea being in front as
described above.

10. *si frater . . . vivit.* We have followed Döring in not repeating
the pronoun ' tuus.' The single use of the word seems more appropriate to the haste of the speaker as he turns from the mother
to the son.

11. *aufertur*—' carries himself out of.'

14. *quiritatus*—the *monotonous* cry of infants, though the word is
not confined to this use, comp. Cic. *Epp. ad Fam.* ix. 32, ' illi
misero *quiritanti* (saying over and over again), " Civis Romanus
natus sum." '

noscitabant—' sought to recognize,' a not uncommon meaning
of frequentatives.

miserabantur—miseror = to *express* compassion.

15. *metu mortis mortem precarentur*—comp. Ovid. *Met.* vii. 604,
' mortisque timorem morte fugant.'

nusquam jam deos . . . interpretabantur. This final annihilation
of the universe, in which the gods themselves were to be included,
was a not uncommon notion among the ancients. So Seneca,
Thyestes, 831 :

        ' Iterumque deos hominesque premat
           Deforme Chaos.'

See also Virgil, *Georg.* i. 468 :

    ' Impiaque aeternam timuerunt saecula noctem.
The belief also occurs in the Scandinavian mythology. Closely
connected with it was the notion that the destruction of a city
involved the departure of its tutelary gods.

illud . . . illud—different points indicated by the narrator as he
spoke.

16. *nuntiabant*—the indicative is used because certain definite persons, present to the writer's mind, are spoken of.

ignis quidem . . . substitit—'And there was fire, but it stopped at some distance from us.'

17. *nisi me cum omnibus . . . credidissem*—comp. for a similar sentiment Seneca, *Thyest.* iv.:

> 'Abeant questus,
> Discede timor. Vitae est avidus
> Quisquis non vult, mundo secum
> Pereunte, mori.'

19. *curatis utcunque corporibus*—' having refreshed ourselves as we could.'

suspensam noctem—'a night of anxiety.' This use of 'suspensus' is quite in the style of Tacitus, who is always fond of transferring the epithets expressive of human feeling to surrounding circumstances.

plerique . . . ludificabantur—that is, the predictions of many persons were so full of extravagant terror as to make their own calamities and those of others seem positively ludicrous. Terrificis vaticinationibus is an instrumental ablative to be construed with 'lymphati.'

20. *non scripturus leges*—'you will read them, though you will not incorporate them with your history.'

A. IV. (iv. 11.)

1. *profiteri*—'to be a professor of rhetoric.' This *absolute* use of the word is post-Augustan. Comp. ii. 18, cum omnes qui *profitentur*, audiero.

2. *praefatione*—a 'praefatio' answered to what later writers called a 'prolusio,' and to our 'essay.' It is not to be taken in its strict meaning. Comp. its use in B. XIV. 1.

ex professoribus senatores—alluding to Quintilian, who had been raised by Domitian to the rank of a 'consularis.' For a precisely similar sentiment comp. Juvenal, vii. 198,

> 'Si fortuna volet, fies de rhetore consul,
> Si volet haec eadem, fies de consule rhetor.'

The profession of a teacher, though pursued at this time by many clever and distinguished men, was considered quite beneath the dignity of a Roman and a senator. It was confined almost exclusively to Greeks.

amaritudinis—the bitterness of the speech consisted specially in its sarcastic allusion to Quintilian.

3. *Graeco pallio amictus.* As an exile, Licinianus did not dare to wear the 'toga,' which was a distinctively Roman dress. The 'pallium,' which was originally and strictly Greek, was commonly worn by the provincials, who in Suetonius (*Jul. Caes.* 48) are described by the term '*palliati.*' Plays representing Greek life and manners were called fabulae *palliatae.*

quibus . . . interdictum—the regular formula in which the judicial sentence of 'exsilium' was expressed. It referred only to the limits of Italy.

se . . . *habitum suum*—comp. Ovid. *Met.* iv. 317 (Ante) quam
se composuit, quam circumspexit amictus.

5. *aestuabat ingenti invidia*—' was boiling with intense indignation.'

destitutus—'being left in the lurch,' as we should say. Domitian wished Cornelia to be convicted, but witnesses would not come
forward, and the evidence of Licinianus was all that could be
obtained against her.

6. *Vestalium maximam*—the eldest of the Vestals was also distinguished as virgo maxima, vetustissima. She appears also to
have been occasionally designated 'primigenia' (Symmachus,
Epp. ix. 129). Maxima vestalis is the title given to her in
inscriptions.

defodere vivam. See Livy ii. 42; viii. 15; xxiii. 57; Juv. vi.
10. The guilty vestal was buried alive near the 'porta Collina,'
in a spot known as the 'Campus Sceleratus.'

ut qui . . . arbitraretur—comp. Suet. *Domit.* viii.: 'incesta vestalium
virginum, a patre suo quoque et fratre neglecta, varie ac severe
coëreuit (Domitianus) more veteri.' Domitian was not like some
emperors content with the mere title of pontifex maximus; he
actually exercised the duties of the office, among which was the
punishment of unchaste vestals.

Albanam villam—Domitian's palace at the foot of the Mons
Albanus on the Via Appia. It is the subject of frequent allusion.
See Suet. *Domit.* iv.; Martial, viii. 36; Juvenal, iv. 145; Tacit. *Agr.*
45. Domitian made a practice of summoning the senators thither
instead of to the senate-house, the proper place of assembly.

cum ipse—the reference is to Julia, the daughter of Domitian's brother, Titus. She was 'vidua' at the time of his intrigue
with her; this explains the motive which prompted Domitian's act,
as described by the word 'occidisset.'

8. *irridens*—Cornelia, it is suggested, might have meant to ridi-
cule Domitian's celebration of triumphs over enemies whom he
had not seen, much less conquered. See Tacit. *Agr.* 39: 'inerat
(Domitiano) conscientia derisui super falsum e Germania trium-
phum.'

tamquam innocens—that is, all the circumstances of her death
pointed to the conclusion that she was really innocent, and such
was the general belief.

9. *quasi plane*—Connect this with casto puroque corpore.

omnibusque numeris pudoris—This expression implies a 'pudor'
as perfect as it could be. Comp. Cicero (*De Fin.* iii. 7), omnes
numeros virtutis continet. Pliny elsewhere praises a book as being
omnibus numeris absolutus.

10. πολλήι, &c.—from Euripides, *Hec.* 569, in the account of the
death of Polyxena. Ovid (*Met.* xiii. 476) has thus imitated the
passage :

　　　' Tunc quoque cura fuit partes velare tegendas
　　　　Cum caderet castique decus servare pudoris.'

11. *arripit*—' arripere ' is used in Cicero and the best writers in

the sense of 'suddenly coming down upon a man with an accusation.'

12. *κεῖται Πάτροκλος*—Homer, *Il.* xviii. (*σ'*) 20. In these words Antilochus announces to Achilles the death of Patroclus. They were always admired for their nervous conciseness. See Quintil. x. 1, 49. With similar brevity Senecio announced the departure of Licinianus from Italy.

13. *non esse ... instandum*—Domitian meant that there was no necessity for pressing Licinianus to throw aside his 'verecundia' and return from exile with the view of defending himself. It was to the emperor's interest that he should remain in exile, as his doing so would seem to be a confession of his guilt and consequently of that of Cornelia.

exsilium molle—Suetonius (*Aug.* 5) calls this 'exilium leve.' It means exile under tolerably favourable conditions, as in a moderately pleasant country.

14. *seque ... vindicat*—'and avenges himself on fortune by his essays,' of which we have had a specimen at the beginning of the letter. 'Vindicare de aliquo' is a rare construction; comp. Florus, iii. 21, 19, quanta saevitia opus erat ut Marius *de* Sulla *vindicaretur.*

16. *versus*—'lines.' Comp. B. XI. 12.

A. V. (vii. 33.)

3. *publicis actis*—also called 'acta senatus,' 'acta populi,' 'acta diurna,' &c.; sometimes simply termed 'acta.' These public registers belonged to the imperial period of Rome, and they furnished important material for history. Hence we have frequent allusions to them in Tacitus, Suetonius, &c.

cuius ... crevit—'the popularity of which was heightened by its danger.'

4. *dederat me*, &c. See C. IV. 8, where Pliny alludes to this occasion.

postulationibus vacaturos—'would be at leisure to hear claims for restitution.' 'Postulatio' was a legal term which meant 'a citation,' 'an impeachment,' or as here 'a claim for damages.' In this case several of the provincials of Baetica would have claims to make on the property of Massa, which the Senate on the conclusion of the trial had directed should be taken charge of by the State.

quorum ... debent—this expression of Senecio might be interpreted as a sort of side allusion to the emperor; hence the charge of 'impietas' preferred against him by Massa.

5. *ex beneficio tuo*—by 'beneficium' Senecio meant Pliny's services as counsel to the province.

7. *dicit ... ferebat*—'Senecio makes some observations which the circumstances of the case suggested.'

implesse—we have a similar use of 'implere' in Tacit. *Ann.* iv. 38, satis habeo si locum principem *impleam*; *Hist.* i. 16, im-

pletum est omne consilium ; *Agr.* 44, vera bona . . . *impleverat.*
This use of the word is found chiefly in the silver-age writers.

8. *impietatis reum postulat.* 'Impietas' here means something
more than 'vindictiveness,' which might intelligibly be laid to the
charge of Senecio for thus pursuing Massa. No definite legal
complaint could be made on such a ground, nor would there have
been the 'horror omnium' which Pliny says resulted from
Massa's attack on Senecio. 'Impietas' must imply an offence
against the sacred person of the emperor, and although Senecio
escaped on the present occasion, we know from E. XII. 5, and
Tacit. *Agr.* 2, that it was a charge of this nature which ultimately
proved fatal to him. Pliny would as a matter of course be involved in the peril thus brought on Senecio, as he had supported
him throughout the entire case ; hence the 'periculum' to which
he has already alluded as rendering his act the more popular.

ne mihi . . . obiecerit—that is, 'Massa by not naming me has
virtually charged me with being in collusion with him.'

9. *privatus.* Nerva was probably at this time, by the order of
Domitian, who was afraid of him, living at Tarentum.

A. VI. (ix. 13.)

1. *de Helvidii ultione.* Pliny refers to these books in vii. 30, and
says that his friend Genitor had compared them to the famous
speech of Demosthenes against Meidias.

quae . . . libros—sc. 'matters not alluded to in the books at all
(extra), and matters which though connected with the subject of
the books (circa), were not fully related in them.'

2. *statui mecum ac deliberavi*—comp. Cic. *Verr.* ii. 1, 1, quod
iste *statuerat* ac *deliberaverat* non adesse. Deliberare signifies, the
final act of 'resolving on a thing' as well as the previous mental
process. So Horace, *C.* i. 37, 29 (of Cleopatra), *deliberata* morte
erocior.

se proferendi—'of bringing oneself into notice.'

manus intulisset—comp. Tacit. *Agr.* 45, mox nostrae duxere
Helvidium in carcerem manus, where it is implied that the accusation and ruin of Helvidius was the united act of the senate. It
seems to have taken place A.D. 94, the year after Agricola's
death.

4. *postulaverant . . . oppresserant*—'had no sooner impeached
than they had crushed.'

modestius et constantius—'more reasonable and more effectual.'
Comp. for this use of 'constans' Tacitus, *Hist.* iii. 1, an ire com-
minus et certare pro Italia *constantius* foret (whether to meet the
enemy and to fight for Italy would be the more effective policy).

communi temporum invidia—sc. 'the universal feeling of hatred
for the times of Domitian.'

proprio crimine—'a specific charge.'

defremuisset—so most modern editors, after Cortius. The reading is confirmed by the circumstance that 'defremere' occurs in

N

Sidonius Apollinaris (ix. 9), who was a well-known imitator of Pliny.

5. *adscribi facto*—sc. 'to associate themselves in the prosecution.' This was called 'subscribere,' and the person so acting 'subscriptor.' The name of the leading prosecutor would stand first, and the names of his supporters would come next in order.

societate—the ablative is regularly used with 'invidere' by Pliny and his contemporaries. Comp. Tacit. *Ger.* 33, 'ne *spectaculo* quidem praelii *invidere*.'

6. *providentissimum*—'most far-sighted.'

sed non sustinui . . . indicarem—'I could not, however, bring myself to the resolution of not informing Corellius on the same day that I was about so to do,' &c. &c. 'Sustinere' here as elsewhere answers exactly to the Greek τλῆναι. 'Non sustinui,' 'I had not the heart,' 'I could not prevail on myself.'

7. *reum destinare.* 'Destinare' here signifies 'to fix on as a mark,' 'to aim at,' &c. Pliny at first merely pointed in his remarks to Certus, but did not single him out by name; he was really aiming at him, but not clearly and unmistakably.

de quo extra ordinem referas—'about whom you are bringing a motion before the house in an informal manner.' The meaning is that due notice of the prosecution and the defendant's name ought to have been previously given in, failing which, Pliny's present proceeding was irregular.

quis est ante relationem reus? By 'relatio' was meant the formal notice to the senate of a motion to be brought forward. In the present case, such a notice would have specified the name of the man to be accused and the crime or crimes laid to his charge. The 'jus relationis,' as it was called, rested with the emperor. It was argued against Pliny that no person could be the subject of a prosecution before the matter had been duly referred by the emperor to the senate.

8. *susceptae rei honestas*—'creditable nature of the undertaking.'

9. *sententiae loco*—'in your proper turn.' That is, when the time comes for asking the opinion of the senators, you shall say what you please.

permiseris. By this expression Pliny did not merely make a request; he asserted a claim. Render, 'you must grant me,' &c. The reference is to the 'jus censendi,' as it was technically termed.

10. *curato sermone*—'in an earnest conversation.' Comp. Tacit. *Ann.* i. 13, *curatissimae* preces (very earnest entreaties).

11. *praesentibus*—sc. the good times of Nerva, which encouraged such an attempt as Pliny was making.

praefectum aerarii—this was a very high office, and was conferred on praetors or ex-praetors. See Tacit. *Hist.* iv. 9.

12. *omnia . . . peregi*—Virg. *Aen.* vi. 105 (the words of Aeneas to the Sibyl).

13. *quasi in medio relictum*—that is, the precise charge had not

been specified by Pliny ; it had been left by him a matter of conjecture, though there could not be really much doubt about it.

14. *sum enim . . . persecutus*—'I have given it all at length in their own words.'

15. *Avidius Quietus*—he was an intimate friend of Thrasea, and was much attached to Pliny. See C. IV. 1.

Cornutus Tertullus—Pliny's colleague in the consulate. See *Paneg.* 90.

16. *Helvidi filiae*—her death in child-birth is mentioned iv. 21.

officii sui—sc. ' his duty as guardian.'

optimarum feminarum—sc. Arria and Fannia.

modestissimum adfectum—understand by 'adfectus' affection for Helvidius. The next sentence explains ' modestissimum.' Arria and Fannia's affection might be spoken of as very reasonable and moderate, inasmuch as it was satisfied with a comparatively slight vengeance on Certus.

cruentae adulationis — sc. flattery of Domitian, which necessarily involved cruel and murderous deeds.

poena flagitii—sc. exile or transportation to an island.

17. *puto, inquit,* &c. Rufus argued that for the present at least Certus was entitled to an acquittal, inasmuch as he had not been named by Pliny but only by others, and that no injustice could thus be done which, in the event of anything being proved against him, might not be subsequently redressed. Therefore (he implies) the senate need not be troubled with any anxiety lest justice should be defeated.

18. *quibus clamoribus*—sc. ' applause.'

proventum orationis—'the successful progress of the speech.'

19. *Veiento.* Although one of the worst of the ' delatores ' in Domitian's time, he enjoyed Nerva's friendship.

auxilium tribunorum. This was to enable any citizen to assert his rights against oppression or intimidation. Veiento was exercising the 'jus censendi,' which belonged to all senators.

20. *peracta discessione*—sc. ' having ascertained the vote of the house by a division.' ' Discessio ' is a well-known technical term in this sense.

ὦ γέρον, &c.—Hom. *Il.* viii. 102 (the opening line of Diomed's address to Nestor, in which he intreats the aged warrior to retire from the battle).

21. *intermissum . . . reduxissem*—Pliny in what he had done in this case had broken through the regular precedent of the time, according to which a matter could be brought under the notice of the senate only by means of a ' relatio ' from the emperor. In publicum consulendi, ' consulting the senate with a view to the public good.' Susceptis propriis simultatibus, sc. ' at the cost of private enmities.'

22. *et relationem . . . remisit.* The effect of this, of course, was that Pliny's intended impeachment of Certus was dropped. Pliny, however, represents that he was satisfied with having been the means of disgracing him to a certain extent.

A. VII. (iv. 22.)

1. *cognitioni*—'cognoscere' and 'cognitio' were legal terms for extraordinary cases tried, not by the ordinary judges, but by a special commission of distinguished men. Comp. C. V. for a similar compliment paid to Pliny.

Agon—comp. Suet. *Nero*, 22, 23, where the expression 'musicus *agon*' occurs.

duumviratu. The 'duumviri' in a 'colonia' or 'municipium' occupied a similar position among the 'decuriones,' or town council, to that of the consuls in the Roman senate, and were thus important local functionaries. It is clear, however, from the context, that their actual powers were very moderate, and that they were regarded simply as representatives of the wishes and intentions of their fellow-townsmen.

2. *mature et graviter*—'judiciously and impressively.'

3. *verius*—'more truth-speaking.' This is a rare use of 'verus.'

4. *Veiento.* See Juvenal iii. 185, iv. 113 (where he is coupled with Catullus), vi. 113. The mention of his name, as Pliny here hints, recalled one of the worst and most crafty of Domitian's favourites.

5. *Catullo Messalino*—Juvenal (iv. 113) calls him a caecus adulator. He was one of the most infamous of the 'delatores' in Domitian's time, and as such is alluded to by Tacitus, *Agr.* 45. As governor of Cyrenaica, known also as the Libyan Pentapolis, he was guilty of atrocious cruelties towards the Jewish inhabitants, which, according to Josephus (*De Bello Judaico*, 7), he expiated by a miserable death. When it is said that 'to a cruel disposition he added the evils of blindness,' Pliny's meaning is, that his cruelty was intensified by the circumstance of his blindness; consequently 'he was a stranger to fear, to shame, to compassion,' emotions which blindness makes it physically impossible to exhibit.

7. *nobiscum coenaret.* This was said in sarcastic allusion to Nerva's very mild and tolerant disposition, which seems almost to have amounted to what Aristotle calls ἀοργησία.

A. VIII. (ii. 1.)

1. *perinde felicis*—sc. 'as fortunate as he was great and illustrious.'

2. *gloriae suae*—'gloria' must here be understood *concretely* of Verginius's one specially great achievement.

posteritati suae interfuit—that is, 'he saw and enjoyed the renown which is commonly posthumous.' For a similar expression comp. ix. 3, certus *posteritatis* cum futura gloria vixit.

privati hominis. Under the republic a citizen who held no state office was 'privatus.' But under the empire, even the consuls and officers of the highest rank were, relatively to the emperor, 'privati.' So Tacitus uses the word.

3. *optimum*—Nerva, in whose reign Tacitus succeeded Verginius in the consulate.

citra dolorem—'not amounting to pain.' A post-Augustan use of 'citra.' Comp. Tacit. *Agr.* i., *citra* fidem, and 35, *citra* Romanum sanguinem.

5. *vocem praepararet*—sc. practising his voice, and studying the elocution to be adopted in the delivery of his speech.

acturus . . . gratias. It was usual for the consul to acknowledge in a formal speech before the senate his gratitude to the emperor for his promotion, and it was in this character that Pliny's Panegyric was delivered, as he himself tells us, iii. 18, officium consulatus injunxit mihi ut reipublicae nomine principi gratias agerem.

dum sequitur colligitque—'while he is trying to recover it and picking it up.'

parum apte collocata—'being clumsily set.'

6. *laudatus est.* The 'laudatio funebris' would in the natural course of things be delivered by the nearest relative of the deceased. If he were not qualified to undertake it, the senate (as in this case) specially commissioned some distinguished speaker to do so. See Quintilian, iii. 7, 1, 'funebres laudationes pendent frequenter ex publico aliquo officio atque ex senatusconsulto magistratibus saepe mandantur.' This was done at Sulla's funeral, his son Faustus being too young to discharge the duty.

cumulus—'the culminating point,' 'that which crowns,' &c. The *primary* meaning of the word appears to be, not a 'pile' or 'heap,' but the highest point or apex.

8. *suffragio ornavit*—sc. he acted the part of what was termed a 'suffragator,' one who interested himself on behalf of a candidate for office.

eadem . . . finitima—the 'municipium' of Verginius was Alsium (see next letter). This was in the same 'regio,' the country of the Insubres, as Comum.

officiis—answering to our 'levées.' Comp. in praetoris *officio* (E. XVI. 11).

illo die quo sacerdotes—probably January 1, or at any rate an early day in the year. By 'sacerdotes' Pliny means the College of Augurs, who, although the actual choice (cooptatio) of new members really belonged to the emperor, still exercised the privilege of recommendation (nominatio), as we see by D. 1. 3.

9. *quinqueviros*—commissioners appointed by Nerva to investigate the state of the public finances, which had been utterly deranged by Domitian.

hujus aetatis—'of this generation.'

12. *recentibus*—'lively,' 'vivid.' So (A. XIV. 12), inveni ita erectos animos senatus, ita *recentes*, &c.

A. IX. (vi. 10.)

1. *Alsiensem*—Alsium was a town on the coast of Etruria, where many wealthy Romans had villas. Comp. Cicero *pro Milone*, 20, where Pompeius Magnus is mentioned as having a villa in the place, and *Epp. ad Fam.* ix. 6, where the same is said of Caesar. Pliny's mother-in-law was Pompeia Celerina (see i. 4), and the property of Pompeius Magnus may have come to her by inheritance.

senectutis suae nidulum—comp. Hor. *Epist.* I. 10, 6, tu *nidum* servas, &c.

2. *requirebant*—comp. Ovid, *Met.* iv. 129, iuvenemque oculis animoque *requirit.* The word is more picturesque than 'desiderare,' but sometimes expresses less. Comp. C. III. 1, where Pliny says that he misses Regulus without regretting him.

3. *post decimum annum*—this marks the date of the letter, as Verginius died A.D. 97.

sine titulo, sine nomine—there was not only no enumeration of honours, but not even the name.

5. *parata oblivio*—'Paratus' is often used absolutely as equivalent to 'facilis.' Comp. Livy, v. 6, '*parata* victoria.'

conditoria—Conditorium, a post-Augustan word, commonly means 'coffin,' here 'tomb and monument.'

praesumere—'To undertake by anticipation.'

A. X. (ix. 19.)

1. *Frontinum.*]—Comp. D. I. 3; D. XII. 5, where we have evidence of the mutual esteem and affection which had existed between Frontinus and Pliny.

2. *immortalitatem . . sectantur.* Pliny very possibly had in his mind Cicero's speech for the poet Archias, in which we meet with a very similar sentiment (11), 'optimus quisque maxime gloria ducitur.'

3. *supremis titulis*—sc. an epitaph.

4. *prorogare*—sc. 'to extend into the future.'

in praedicando verecundia—we have the same expression in Tacitus, *Agr.* 8. This absolute use of 'praedicare' belongs to late Latin.

5. *semel . . . referret*—'that once and once only he went so far in my hearing as to mention this single circumstance in connexion with his own affairs,' &c.

Cluvium—he is referred to as a historian by Tacitus, *Ann.* xiii. 20 (where he is coupled with Pliny), and xiv. 2. He wrote, it seems, an account of the reigns of Nero, Galba, Otho, and Vitellius. The name Cluvius Rufus frequently occurs in Tacitus. He is spoken of, *Hist.* vi. 43, as famous for his wealth and eloquence, and under Galba he was governor of Spain. This Cluvius Rufus is generally supposed to have been the historian.

quae historiae fides debeatur—'what truthfulness is demanded by history.'

me fecisse quod feci. In allusion to his having twice declined the empire when offered him by the army.

6. *parcior*—sc. 'more sparing of his own praise.'

pressior — comp. iv. 14, describimus aliquid modo *pressius* modo elatius; iii. 18, *pressius* et adstrictius scripsi. The notion of pruning (premere) a luxuriant tree or that of pursuing a person closely (premere vestigia), is the clue to this use of the word.

supervacuo—supervacaneus is the form used by the Augustan writers.

restrictius—nearly the same as 'pressius.' The word suggests the idea of 'reticence' and 'self-control.'

7. *habeo propositum.* A phrase belonging to the later Latinity.

apud te—'in your judgment.'

A. XI. (ii. 11.)

2. *quibus . . . praefuit.* The province of Africa included the ancient Carthaginian territory, which was known as Old Africa, or Africa propria or Zeugitana, and New Africa, as it was called, or Numidia. It was often spoken of simply as Provincia Proconsularis, and its governor as Proconsul. It was a very important province, as Rome drew large supplies of corn from it.

omissa . . . petiit. He gave up the defence (knowing the exposure it would involve), and asked for the appointment of judges who should undertake what was termed 'litis aestimatio,' that is, assess the amount of compensation to be paid by him to the provincials. Such judges were called 'recuperatores.'

iussi—'ordered by the senate.'

crimina . . . possent—'crimes for the trial of which "iudices" could be assigned.' The crimes of Marius were too serious to be dealt with in the way of 'litis aestimatio' by the praetor's court.

3. *vela . . . impleret.* This comparison of a vehement speaker to a ship in full sail, is to be found in Cicero, who uses metaphorically the phrases, vela dare, facere, pandere. Comp. also iv. 20, 'in quo tu ingenii simul dolorisque *velis* latissime veheris,' and A. XVIII. 5, 'immitte rudentes, pande *vela*, ac si quando alias, toto ingenio vehere.'

4. *lege conclusam.* Some argued that further judicial proceedings on the part of the senate were barred by law. By lege we are not to understand the lex repetundarum (to which Marius was amenable), or indeed any *special* law, but the general principle of law, which in this case would, it was argued, screen Priscus from worse consequences than those involved in the crime of extortion (res repetundae).

5. *quantumque . . . vindicandum*—'and that the full extent of the defendant's guilt ought to be punished.'

6. *evocandos . . . vendidisse*—'that those persons ought to be

summoned (as witnesses) to whom he was said to have sold
punishments of innocent people.' One of these persons is said,
a little further on, to have bought (emisse) the punishment of a
certain 'eques.'

8. *qui . . . iussi*—sc. the persons alluded to above, 'evocandos,'
&c.

9. *inductus est*—'was brought to trial.' This is a post-Augustan use of 'inducere.'

iure senatorio—' on the strength of his privilege as a senator,' by
which, when asked his opinion, he could decline to give it at the
moment.

ut Priscus certior fieret—'that Priscus should be informed' (of
the impeachment of Marcianus).

11. *imaginare*—' picture to yourself.' A post-Augustan word.

12. *obversabatur*—' was continually before my mind.'

stabat—'there was standing before me one who had lately been
a consul,' &c.

iam neutrum. This usage seems strange and hardly classical.

13. *accusare damnatum.* Priscus was already 'damnatus,' inasmuch as he had given up his defence, and had so pleaded guilty to
a charge of res repetundae.

quem . . . tuebantur—' weighed down as he was by the frightful
character of the accusation, he was still, as it were, screened by
the pity felt for him in respect of a conviction already obtained.'
'Quasi' seems better taken with the entire sentence than construed solely with 'peractae.' We understand by peractae damnationis miseratio, the sympathy felt for the criminal in *consequence*
of the condemnation he had undergone on the minor charge of
simple extortion.

15. *studium*—' kind feeling.'

voci . . . consulerem—'that I should spare my voice and lungs.'

me . . . intendi—'that I was exerting myself.' The middle
voice.

16. *neque enim . . . actio*—sc. 'no new speech could be begun,' &c.

dispositus. Said of a speaker who arranges his matter well.
Comp. E XV. 2, ' vita hominum *disposita* delectat.'

18. *huius . . . abrumperet*—sc. his speech was terminated by
evening, but not terminated abruptly.

probationes—sc. proofs drawn from evidence.

19. *advocatione*—sc. the defence of the provincials, which involved the prosecution of Priscus. The duty had been imposed
(*iniuncta*) on Pliny and Tacitus, adesse provincialibus *iussi*.

20. *relegandum*—' relegatio ' was a mitigated form of banishment, first introduced by Augustus, and frequently employed by the
emperors. The ' relegatus' forfeited neither his rights as a citizen
nor his property.

21. *solutiore vel molliore*—'solutus' conveys the notion of *culpable* laxity ; ' mollis,' merely that of leniency.

23. Λιτουργιον—' a matter of public business.' The diminutival
form, which does not occur in Greek literature, seems used to ex-

press that the affair, though not insignificant (non leve), was a trifle compared with the great case of which it was but an offshoot.

nam et . . . probabatur—' for both by the accounts of Martianus and by a speech which he (Martianus) made before the town council of Leptis, he (Firminus) was proved to have lent his assistance to Priscus for a most shameful service, and to have bargained to receive from Martianus 50,000 denarii (or about 1770*l.*). There was a Leptis Magna and a Leptis Parva on the north coast of Africa; both were Phœnician colonies. See Sall. *Jug.* 19 and 78. It is the first of these which is here referred to. It was on the coast of Africa Zeugitana, to the east of Carthage, and near Adrumetum.

nomine unguentarii—' under the head of perfume-money.' Unguentarium is formed on the analogy of such words as clavarium, calcearium, salarium, congiarium, &c., &c., and points to one of the many unscrupulous ways in which Roman governors and their underlings continued to wring money out of the provincials. It reminds us of the pin-money which in modern times was granted to royal ladies.

pumicati—pumicatus (rubbed smooth with pumice) is applied by Martial (i. 67) to a book, the binding of which had been polished by this process. Here it stands for a fop or dandy. Such persons at Rome shaved close and carefully cultivated excessive smoothness of skin.

25. *oves delicatissimae*—' delicatus,' in its good sense (in which it is here used) means ' choice,' ' beautiful.' Pliny (E. XXVIII. 3) calls the Anio *delicatissimus* amnium. There is here also perhaps the notion which Virgil expresses in *molle* pecus, and which comes near to our ' softness,' ' delicacy,' &c. It should be noted that the favourable sense of ' delicatus ' is found chiefly in post-Augustan writers. In Cicero the word commonly implies censure.

A. XII. (ii. 12.)

1. λιτούργιον—see note 23 in preceding letter.

circumcisum . . . adrasum—the first word is the stronger of the two, and implies a more complete finish and termination. The notion of circumcidere is paring a thing all round, and so giving a finish to it; that of adradere is merely paring off certain portions of it. Pliny means to say, ' The affair is decided; I don't say finished as it should be, but still it is finished in a way.' Lord Orrery, in his translation, renders the passage thus : ' The perfumer is shaved, whether close enough or not I cannot say.' This supposed allusion to the ' unguentarium ' of the preceding letter seems far-fetched. Possibly Pliny may be using a metaphor derived from the treatment of wounds, in which ' circumcidere ' would denote a more vigorous application of the knife than ' adradere.'

2. *noto*—sc. known from the previous trial.

ordine movendum—' to be expelled from the senate.'

Acutius Nerva—this reading for ' acutius,' which has little meaning, is confirmed by the fact that there appears to have been an Acutia gens at Rome. It is now generally adopted.

3. *exsectum*—as we say, 'cut out of.' Properly, the word denotes the 'cutting out of diseased portions of the body.'

4. *notatum*—properly, 'marked with the nota censoria;' here simply equivalent to 'censured.'

5. *sordium*—sordes commonly signifies the meanness of a stingy householder; here it is used for avarice or rapacity on a great scale, as in Tacitus, *Hist.* i. 52, sordem et avaritiam Fonteii Capitonis, &c.; and thus denotes an actual crime.

numerantur . . . ponderantur—'votes are merely counted, their value is not estimated.' Speaking of actions which injure a few and benefit many, Cicero (*De Off.* ii. 22) says, 'Non *numero* haec judicantur sed *pondere*,' precisely the reverse of what we have here.

6. *prioris . . . exsolvi*—'I have fulfilled the pledge given in my former letter.'

A. XIII. (iii. 9.)

1. *quantum . . . exhauserim*—this was the *second* occasion on which Pliny was counsel for the provincials of Baetica. Comp. A. V. 4.

2. *fuit multiplex*—sc. the cause involved several issues.

3. *dolor . . . facit*—comp. Cicero *in Verrem*, iv. 43, where he says that the people of Sicily are never so badly off that they cannot make a joke (numquam tam male est Siculis quin aliquid facete et commode dicant). Dolor is here the pain arising from a sense of wrong. Venustus (here equivalent to our 'witty') is used by the best writers of intellectual as well as of physical grace.

6. *provisum hoc legibus*—sc. the laws provided for this impeachment of one already deceased.

addiderunt Baetici—sc. 'they added to the impeachment of Classicus, who was now dead, that of his agents,' &c.

7. *diligerem . . . amare*—the distinction between 'diligere' and 'amare' is well marked in this sentence. The first denotes moral preference for one person over another; the second, affection.

8. *in studiis*—sc. '*forensic* studies and pursuits.'

ἀκοινώνητον—the meaning is that in glory as in empire *one* must be supreme; there is something about it which is incommunicable.

pari iugo—this is a common figure of speech with both Greek and Roman writers. Comp. Theocritus, xii. 15, ἀλλήλους δ' ἐφίλησαν ἴσῳ ζυγῷ. The expression is equivalent to pari studio, labore, &c.

cuius et magnitudo . . . subiremus—the meaning is that in the judgment of Pliny and his fellow-counsel, Lucceius, the case was too heavy to be dealt with by a single process. It was better, they thought, to separate the charges and proceed against the defendants one by one.

9. *ne gratia . . . acciperet*—if all the defendants were put on their

trial together, there was reason to fear that each would get the benefit of the collective influence of all. Pro singulis, ' on behalf of each (defendant).'

vilissimo . . . dato—'all the most insignificant (of the defendants) being given up as scapegoats,' &c.

11. *erat in consilio*—'there came into my mind.'

Sertorianum illud, &c. The incident in question is related by Plutarch in his life of Sertorius. It appears that Sertorius tried to teach his soldiers the good effects of patience in the following manner. He brought out in their presence two horses; one was old and feeble, the other in its full vigour and with a singularly fine tail. Near the first he placed a tall and powerful soldier; near the second, one of the weakest and most diminutive. Each was to pull out the tail of his respective horse; the strong soldier by a sudden effort, the weak, by gradually plucking the hairs. The failure of the one and the success of the other taught the wisdom of attempting a difficult work gradually and in detail. See Horace, *Epist.* ii. 1, 45, and Orelli's note. Pliny means that the defendants, who were very numerous, must be proceeded against singly, as the hairs of the horse's tail were plucked out one by one. ' Vellere ' is to be understood after ' caudam equi.'

12. *carperetur*—' carpere ' is here used with reference to the incident explained above. There may too perhaps be an allusion to its military sense, in which it signified the action of light troops in harassing an army on its march.

probari—understand 'nocentes,' from the following 'nocente.'

duos . . . iunximus—sc. 'two we put on their trial along with Classicus.'

14. *iam sestertium . . . Baeticorum*—'I have now got in 4,000,000 sesterces (about 34,000*l*.) by having sold up half the people of Baetica.' ' Redigere ' is ' to call in debts,' and is used of getting in money lent on interest.

15. *neque enim . . . negarent*—that is, the line which their de-fence took was not to deny that they had been agents of Classicus, &c.

16. *vigilans*—this is said of a speaker who seizes all the points of a case, and keeps a sharp look-out for flaws in his opponent's arguments.

18. *tribunus cohortis*—this was an officer peculiar to the later times of the empire. It was confined to the first and strongest cohort of a legion, which numbered over 1000 men. A 'tribunus legionis ' held a higher rank.

19. *plures congregare*—sc. ' to put several on their trial.'

cognoscentium—sc. 'the judices holding the cognitio.'

minores rei—' the less influential defendants.'

Classici uxore—comp. Tacitus, *Ann.* iii. 33, where the liability of a governor's wife to be involved in charges of repetundae brought against her husband, and other ill consequences arising from her presence in a province, are dwelt upon at length. A motion, however, to provide a remedy by legal enactment failed. This was in the reign of Tiberius. It was an attempt to revive the policy of Augustus, who, as we learn from Suetonius, *Oct.* 24, legislated on the matter. Subsequently no such attempts appear to have been made, and governors of provinces were at perfect liberty to have their wives with them if they pleased.

20. *ne suspicionibus quidem haerebat*—sc. 'was not even so much as involved in suspicion.'

21. *Iudicas ergo?*—sc. 'Do you then take upon yourself the function of a "iudex"?' Pliny's answer implies that being selected out of the 'iudices' as counsel of the province, he might fairly exercise his discretion as to the accusation of Classicus' wife and daughter.

22. *numerosissimae causae*—sc. 'a case with very numerous ramifications.' This is a post-Augustan sense of 'numerosus,' which in the Augustan writers always means 'rhythmical.' Comp. *numerosum agmen* in this letter.

23. *dignum . . . par*—both adjectives are to be construed with 'laboris.'

24. *altercandum*—we are to understand by this word the disputes arising from time to time between the counsel on one side and the other.

sublevandi—sc. 'to be helped through with their evidence,' referring to the witnesses who were confused by the cross-examination of the opposing counsel.

26. *fides . . . offendit*—sc. 'good faith (the honest discharge of one's duty) gives offence at the time to those whose wishes it thwarts.'

in rem praesentem—this expression, which had passed into a proverb, was taken from a legal custom, according to which the judges or the plaintiff and defendant went to the very place with which the suit was connected, so as to see with their own eyes the actual state of affairs.

28. *facit hoc Homerus*—so Cicero, *Epp. ad Att.* ὕστερον πρότερον Ὁμηρικῶς.

29. *inquisitorem*—sc. one who collects evidence with a view to a prosecution. Comp. Cic. *Verr.* i. 2, 6, and Tacit. *Ann.* xv. 66.

tanquam . . . praevaricaretur—'praevaricatio' is the crime of one who plays into the hands of the opposite party and so defeats justice. Norbanus was charged with this crime in regard to the wife of Classicus, who, as we have been told, was an object of suspicion, and as such was included in the prosecution, although sufficiently clear proof of her guilt was not forthcoming. Her acquittal, it was suggested, was due to 'praevaricatio' on the part of Norbanus.

30. *reus . . . peragatur*—'agere reum,' 'to prosecute a person;' 'peragere reum,' 'to carry the prosecution through and convict him.'

31. *ordo legis*—sc. the ordinary legal procedure by which, as has been above explained, the 'praevaricator' was not tried till the original prosecution had been successful.

Domitiani temporibus usus—Domitian's reign was notoriously favourable to the ' delatores.' Of these Norbanus, it appears, had been one, not without success.

ad inquirendum—sc. to do the work of an ' inquisitor.' See note 29.

32. *dari sibi diem et edi crimina*—comp. Tacit. *Hist.* ii. 10, dari tempus, edi crimina. Norbanus requested (1) that time should be given him for his defence; (2) that the charges against him should be definitely stated.

malum pravumque—the combination of these epithets marks the complete type of wickedness which is made up of both moral and intellectual perversity.

33. *confidenter an constanter*—'confidenter' may have a good or bad sense; ' constanter' is limited to ' courage in a *good* cause.' ' Confidenter' here = audaciter. Comp. context, ' vel audaciam vel *constantiam* pertulit.'

tanquam . . . adfuisset. The evidence of Rufus and Frugi seems to have shown that Norbanus had helped on the accusation of Salvius Liberalis by influencing one of the ' iudices.'

34. *res contraria et nova*—that is, it was contrary to legal procedure, as explained already. In consequence, the prosecution of Casta (wife of Classicus) fell through.

35. *indicavimus . . . probaretur*—' we (Pliny and his fellow-counsel) explained to the senate that it was from Norbanus we had received our instructions in the case, which was a public one, and that we ought to have fresh instructions in the event of Norbanus being convicted of ' praevaricatio,' &c.

dum . . . sedimus—sc. during the trial of Norbanus for praevaricatio, we simply sat as spectators.

36. *tanquam . . . peregissent*—' because they had not secured the conviction of all the persons whom they had been deputed by the province to prosecute.'

A. XIV. (iv. 9.)

1. *laboriosus*—sc. ' full of troubles.' The word thus used answers to the Greek πονηρός, μοχθηρός.

ad senatum remissus—this was a bad omen for Bassus, as only exceptionally serious crimes were referred to the senate. See the letter on the prosecution of Marius Priscus, A. XI. 2.

pependit—' he was in suspense.' Usually with ' animi' or ' animo.'

2. *Titum . . . amicus*—Suetonius' account (*Tit.* ix.) of the relations between Titus and Domitian hardly agrees with what these words suggest. Titus according to that account did not regard his brother with fear or jealousy though he was perfectly well aware of his treasonable designs.

varias sententias habuit—that is, as we are told further on in the letter, there was much difference of opinion in the senate about his conduct.

3. *Pomponius Rufus*—see v. 20, where he is spoken of as Pom-

ponius Rufus Varenus, and from which it appears that he succeeded Bassus in the proconsulate of Bithynia and was himself impeached by the province, and defended by Pliny. The case proved a tedious one; it seems to have been ultimately dropped by the accusing parties. See vi. 5, 13; vii. 6, 10.

paratus—this is rather a favourite expression with Pliny. In A. XIII. 16, he describes a pleader as quamlibet subitis *paratus*, and characterises the style of a reply by the word ' paratissime.' It seems to be decidedly preferable to ' peritus,' which some editors have substituted for it, and to be more naturally coupled with ' vehemens.'

fax accusationis—' fax' is generally applied to persons who originate or stir up something bad and mischievous. Comp. *Panegyr.* viii. 5, *fax* tumultus; Tacit. *Hist.* ii. 86, acerrimam *facem* bello praetulit; Cic. *Philipp.* ii. 19, Antonius omnium Clodi incendiorum fax.

ornamentis suis—' his distinctions.' Comp. B. XXV. 1, ' praecipua seculi *ornamenta*.'

5. *quam in quaestu habebant*—' which they were treating as a source of profit.' The accusers, if successful, secured for themselves a fourth part of the property of the accused. Hence they were called ' quadruplatores,' a word which naturally became identified with the notion of chicanery.

6. *furta.* His accusers tried to bring the acts of Bassus within the legal definition of furtum by suggesting that he had received and given presents with ' dolus malus.' Furtum was a very comprehensive term, and covered every species of action in which anything like fraud or dishonest intention seemed to be an element.

lex—no specific ' lex,' but a general principle of law which from obvious motives of public expediency would forbid governors of provinces to receive presents.

quod iter defensionis—as we say, ' what *line* of defence.'

7. *nihil . . . reliquisset*—that is, Bassus by his admissions (as explained in the next sentence) had not left his defence at the full direction of his counsel. ' Mihi integrum est ' (' it is in my power ') is a Ciceronian phrase.

11. *iungere*—sc. ' to go through continuously.' Equivalent to ' continuare.'

frigus—either ' a cold reception from the audience ' or ' a tame and spiritless manner on the part of the speaker,' as opposed to ' dicentis calor.' Comp. B. XXIII. 4, Paullo aliena deliratio aliquantum *frigoris* attulit, where the word is susceptible of both meanings.

dimissum—sc. ' neglected,' and consequently extinguished. It might seem that the word would be more aptly joined with ' concussio,' but by a not unusual construction it is referred to ' ignis.'

remissione—' remissio ' is precisely antithetical to ' intentio.'

13. *contextum*—a word occasionally found in Cicero, and regularly accepted by the post-Augustan writers. Cicero explains its

precise meaning (*De Fin.* v. 28); speaking of the Stoic philosophers, he says their arguments have a remarkable 'contextus': respondent prima extremis. In this sense it is here used; it had also in Pliny's time acquired a signification nearly equivalent to that of our 'context.'

14. *consulares*—sc. Rufus and Pollio, both counsel for the provincials.

15. *probationes*—sc. 'the evidence and the examination of witnesses.' A post-Augustan sense of the word.

16. *censuit . . . designatus.* It was in accordance with the precedents of republican times for the consul-elect to be the first called on for his vote.

lege repetundarum. For a clear case of 'repetundae' the punishment at this time was 'exsilium.' See Tacit. *Ann.* xiv. 28, where we find a Roman eques so punished for this offence.

Caepio . . . dandos. Caepio's view of the case, though differing widely from that of Macer's in being much more lenient, did not amount to a denial that Bassus was amenable to the law of 'repetundae'; it merely implied that the case might be dealt with by the less formidable process of litis aestimatio, for which 'judices' nominated by the praetor in the usual way would be appointed. This seems evident from Pliny's own explanation. Nor was it in Caepio's judgment even necessary, as it would have been according to the lex Julia de repetundis (B.C. 59), that Bassus, if convicted under this process, should be degraded from the senatorian order; his 'dignitas' as a senator might still be 'salva.' For the phrase 'iudices dandos,' see note 2, A. XI.

17. *legem*—'the law,' generally, with reference of course to the many and various 'leges de repetundis.'

intendere—like our expression 'to strain.' It does not, however, mean more than 'to insist on the law being fully carried out.'

quod solet residentibus—'which is usually done when they resume their seats.'

19. *incongruentem*—sc. 'inconsistent with the public interests.' The word is post-Augustan and is rarely used, as here, absolutely.

20. *cui iudices dederis*—sc. one whose acts have been the subject of a 'litis aestimatio,' in which an unfavourable verdict usually carried with it the loss of a man's rank or office.

legationem renuntiasset—sc. 'had announced the "legatio" and given in a full and official report of its object.' In this all the charges of the provincials against Bassus would be specified. Theophanes was the leading man among the 'legati,' the 'fax accusationis.' His zeal in the prosecution had according to Paullinus drawn him within the meshes of the very 'leges' under which Bassus was accused. We may suppose that in getting up the case there had been an interchange of presents, &c., between him and some of the provincials whom he represented.

A. XV. (ii. 7.)

1. *triumphalis statua*—sc. a statue habited in the dress worn by a general when celebrating a triumph. Tacitus (*Agr.* 40) includes it among the 'triumphalia ornamenta' bestowed on Agricola.

decus istud—' decus' and ' decora' are especially used of military rewards and distinctions.

2. *Bructerum*—see Tacit. *Ger.* 33, where it is said that the Bructeri had been almost wholly destroyed by an irruption of other tribes. At any rate, it may be presumed they were sufficiently weakened to be not very formidable to Spurinna. They were an important and widely-spread tribe, and are frequently mentioned by Tacitus as coming into collision with the Romans.

ostentato bello—' ostentare bellum' is to display on a great scale the actual preparations for a campaign. Comp. Tacit. *Ger.* 13, ipsa plerumque fama bellum profligant.

5. *quo quidem . . . prospectum est*—' by means of this distinction, as far as my judgment goes, regard has been had not only to the memory of the deceased and to the sorrow of a father, but also to public example.'

ad liberos suscipiendos—there is here an allusion to that aversion to marriage and its responsibilities which was so characteristic of the empire, and which some of the emperors sought to overcome by direct encouragements to married life.

consummatissimum—this word implies a rare combination of moral and intellectual qualities. We have no single word by which it can be adequately rendered. It is post-Augustan, 'perfectus' or 'absolutus' being the corresponding expression in Cicero and the writers of his time.

7. *refertur*—' is represented,' ' is recalled to memory.' Comp. Lucan, i. 358: servati civis *referentem* praemia quercum.

A. XVI. (iii. 20.)

2. *in senatu*—where the 'comitia' for the election of magistrates were held from the time of Tiberius. See Tacit. *Ann.* ii. 15, tum primum e campo comitia ad *patres* translata sunt.

omnes—sc. all the senators.

3. *licentiam concionum*—comp. Cicero, *Epp. ad Fam.* ii. 12, where in allusion to the comitia he speaks of 'tumultuosae conciones.' The scenes in the senate, it appears, were even more turbulent than those of the popular assemblies.

4. *in medio*—sc. ' in the middle of the house.' The senators did not remain sitting (non sedendi dignitas custodiebatur), and others as they came in hastily with their clients stood talking on the floor of the house.

5. *ordinem*—' form of procedure.'

suffragatoribus. A 'suffragator' acted as the patron of a candidate, and recommended him, gave him introductions and spoke for him.

6. *natales . . . aut annos*—sc. 'obscurity of birth,' or 'insufficiency of age.'

7. *Quae . . . decucurrerunt*—sc. 'These proceedings having become vitiated by an unrestrained partiality shown to certain candidates, found a remedy in silent voting.'

8. *ex ipso remedio vitia.* Pliny particularises in iv. 25, some of the bad consequences which actually resulted from secret voting. Comp. Cicero, *De Leg.* iii. 15, 'tabella *vitiosum* suffragium occultat.'

9. *beneficio tabellarum*—'thanks to the voting tablets.'

recuperatoriis iudiciis—sc. cases of 'litis aestimatio,' or assessment of damages. The iudices in these cases were termed 'recuperatores;' they were nominated by the praetor almost on the spur of the moment ('repente'), that they might be as impartial as possible.

sinceri—'incorrupt,' inasmuch as there had not been time or opportunity to tamper with them. The remedy applied, as explained, was sudden, and the people whom it affected were 'repente apprehensi.'

12. *quidam*—sc. curae laboresque.

quasi ministrare. The metaphor in 'rivi' is here kept up by a word which denotes 'furnishing a supply of anything.'

A. XVII. (vi. 19.)

1. *Scis tu*—A common interrogative formula.

expressit—sc. gave a somewhat *unwilling* expression to, &c. The senate felt itself obliged to repress the scandal, but did it with some reluctance.

pecunias deponant—sc. 'lodge money in the hands of a third person.' The phrase 'pecuniam deponere' sometimes answers to our 'investment of money.'

2. *hoc tertium*—sc. 'pecuniam deponere.'

3. *Homullus.* He was counsel with Pliny for Julius Bassus. See A. XIV. 15.

sententiae loco—that is, 'by way of a motion.'

4. *solo*—sc. land and all immovable property.

honorem petituros—sc. men intending to become candidates.

stabulo—'stabulum,' here as elsewhere = πανδοχεῖον.

5. *si poenitet te*—'if you are dissatisfied with,' &c.

A. XVIII. (viii. 24.)

2. *veram et meram Graeciam.* Achaia, as distinguished from Macedonia, is so called inasmuch as it contained Athens and Sparta, the two special representatives of Hellenism. With 'veram et meram' we may compare such expressions as 'kith and kin,' 'house and home,' &c.

humanitas. Comp. what Cicero (*Pro Flacco*, 26) says of Athens: 'Adsunt Athenienses unde *humanitas*, doctrina, religio, fruges, iura, leges ortae, atque in omnes terras distributae putantur,' and the opening lines of the sixth book of Lucretius, in which the poet sings the praises of Athens.

o

fruges inventae—alluding to the legend of Demeter and Triptolemus.

ordinandum. The word 'ordinare' (which as here used is post-Augustan) indicates very delicately the functions of government.

liberarum civitatum. The term 'free states' was retained out of a regard to Greek susceptibility of feeling after the reality it expresses had passed away.

homines . . . liberos. They were *men* in the best sense (maxime), because they were highly civilised; they were *free* in the highest degree (maxime) because they had so often fought bravely for freedom.

3. *nomina deorum*—in allusion to cities named after deities, as Athens, Apollonia, Heraclea, &c.

gloriam veterem. Comp. Lucan, v. 52, 'fama *veteres* laudantur Athenae.'

Nihil etiam ex iactatione decerpseris. Comp. Cicero *in Verr.* iv. 56, 'nimium forsitan haec illi (the Greeks of Sicily) mirentur atque efferant,' &c.; a passage which very possibly suggested this part of Pliny's advice.

4. *quae nobis . . . dederit*—alluding to the so-called laws of the Twelve Tables. See Livy iii. 31.

6. *veneratio*—this word denotes the *external* marks of respect and honour; 'reverentia' is the feeling or sentiment of respect, and would therefore be out of place here.

7. *tibi ipsum . . . civitatum*—'to make yourself clearly understand the nature and the importance of the work of governing free states.'

civilius—'more constitutional.' 'Ordinatio' excludes the notion of *despotic* government, and (as we have noted above) hints delicately at the exercise of authority.

8. *eversione*—sc. 'the destruction of all national life.'

tibi certamen est tecum—sc. 'you are your own rival;' your past merits (as the context explains) raise our expectations of your future career.

onerat te—'weighs you down with responsibility.' This is rather a favourite expression with Pliny. Comp. B. II. 5, 'onerabit hoc modestiam nostram;' also comp. Ovid, *Heroid.* xvii. 167, 'fama quoque est *oneri*,' and Quintil. *Decl.* 269, 'me *onerat* maiorum meorum dignitas.'

9. *suburbana.* Compared with so remote and wild a country as Bithynia, Achaia might be thus fairly described. It was, at least, within the limits of the civilised world, and was easily accessible from Rome; and the Romans might well for many reasons regard it as closely connected with themselves.

sorte—the quaestors were chosen by *lot*.

iudicio—sc. the emperor's deliberate choice and approval.

10. *admonentem, non praecipientem*—'in a tone of advice, not of authority.'

quod . . . debet—that is to say, 'my love for you,' which has prompted this letter of advice, or of direction, if you like to call it such.

A. XIX. (ix. 5.)

1. *persevera*—so Cortius reads for (inquiro enim et persevere). He is followed by most modern editors.

humanitate—'sympathy.'

ita a minoribus . . . diligare—sc. to have the affection of inferiors while at the same time you have the esteem of the chief people.

2. *sinisteritatis.* This word (which is found only in one other passage (vi. 17), where it is coupled with 'amentia') denotes a mental rather than a moral quality. It answers to the French 'gaucherie.' We may render the sentence thus, 'they get the credit of a bad head and also of a bad heart.'

similis momenti—this implies that Pliny was rather afraid that his friend might err on the side of kindness and good-nature.

nihil est ipsa acqualitate inaequalius—that is, the equality which arises from a confusion of all distinctions, is itself full of the worst inequalities and anomalies.

A. XX. (x. 96.)

1. *sollenne est mihi*—'it is my regular practice.'

ignorantiam instruere—'To instruct my ignorance.' A post-classical use of 'instruere,' which, in the sense of 'instructing,' is confined by Augustan writers to the phrase 'instruere aliquem.'

quaeri—'to be tried,' 'judicially investigated.'

2. *discrimen aetatum.* It was the practice of the Roman law to make such a distinction. Trajan makes no allusion to it in his answer, leaving it, probably, to Pliny's discretion.

teneri—alluding to tenderness of *age* or of *sex.*

desisse—understand 'Christianos esse.'

flagitia cohaerentia nomini—that is, 'crimes popularly supposed to be involved in the profession of Christianity.' On the subject of this popular belief comp. Tac. *Ann.* xv. 44, and Suet. *Ner.* xvi.

3. *supplicium*—'capital punishment.'

duci—sc. 'ad supplicium.'

4. *similis amentiae*—'under a similar infatuation.'

quia cives Romani erant. Such persons (of whom St. Paul was one) could not lawfully undergo extreme punishment from a provincial governor. Comp. Trajan's letter to Pliny (X. 82).

ipso tractatu . . . crimine—that is, the very act of touching and meddling with such a charge conduced to its wider spread. The accusation would be inevitably vague, and so strike at a great number of persons, as the context explains.

plures species—'many phases (of the alleged crime).'

5. *libellus*—sc. 'a document containing the names of accused persons.'

praeeunte me—'while I dictated the form of words.'

imagini tuae—such honours were not paid to the emperor's statue at Rome. Pliny (*Panegyr.* lii. 5) attributes this to Trajan's own wish in the matter. It was as supposed *political* offenders that the Christians were required to pay these honours.

ergo dimittendos. So Minucius Felix, one of the earliest Christian apologists, speaking of the treatment of Christians in his time, says, ' si quis infirmior, malo pressus, Christianum se negasset, favebamus ei, quasi *eierato* nomine, iam omnia facta sua illa negatione purgasset.'

ante lucem. Tert. *Apol.* 2, speaks of ' coetus antelucani.'

7. *carmen*—either 'a hymn,' or, as often elsewhere, simply 'a form of words.'

quasi Deo. Pliny here seems to give the Christian conception of Christ. The language of the hymn, as described to him, suggested the phrase.

dicere secum invicem—sc. ' they repeated the " carmen " among themselves with alternate recitations;' antiphonally.

sacramento. The word 'sacramentum,' which the Christians themselves used, seems to have suggested to Roman governors the notion of a conspiracy against the state, and perhaps connected itself vaguely in their minds with recollections of the oath administered to Catiline's associates. See Sallust, *Cat.* xxii., where the nature of the oath is described.

promiscuum et innoxium—that is, the common ordinary food of man, as opposed to that which popular belief associated with the ' sacramentum.'

hetaerias—A word borrowed from Greek writers, who used it to denote ' a political club or society.' See Arnold's note (Thucyd. viii. 54) on the word συνωμοσία. Pliny here alludes to a letter he had received from Trajan (X. 43), forbidding him to permit the establishment of a 'collegium fabrorum.' The emperor thought that such a 'collegium' would soon become a 'hetaeria,' and would endanger the order of the province. Bithynia and Asia Minor generally were, it appears from Trajan's letter, often disturbed by these societies, with which the Christian churches were no doubt confounded.

8. *ministrae*—' deaconesses.' The equity of Roman law, which did not suffer slaves or servants to be questioned in a case affecting their master's life, seems in this instance to have been disregarded.

superstitionem—' superstitio ' meant to a Roman any *foreign* kind of worship or religious belief.

B. I. (i. 2.)

1. *librum.* The oration spoken of is possibly that which Pliny delivered before the Centumviri on behalf of Accia Variola. This he describes in vi. 33, and there compares it with the famous oration of Demosthenes *Pro Ctesiphonte.*

ζῆλον—'emulation,' and so, generally, 'effort.'

2. *Calvum*—this was C. Licinius Calvus, of whom Seneca says, 'Diu cum Cicerone litem de principatu habuit.' Pliny's friend had always, it seemed, made Demosthenes his model. Pliny himself had in this instance (nuper) moulded his style on the model of Calvus, himself, according to Seneca, an imitator of the Greek orator.

pauci, quos aequus amavit—'the few who are specially favoured.' The quotation is from Virg. *Aen.* vi. 129.

3. *improbe*—arrogantly.

erat enim . . . dicendi—i.e. the speech was almost wholly occupied with answering the arguments of my opponent.

4. ληκύθους—the ornaments of Cicero's style as opposite to the severe energy of Demosthenes ; ληκύθος is a cup or vase for holding unguents and perfume. Cicero (*Epist. ad Att.* i. 14) uses the phrase of his own orations with the same signification : 'Totum hunc locum, quem ego varie meis orationibus quarum tu Aristarchus es, soleo pingere, de flamma, de ferro (nosti illas ληκύθους) valde graviter pertexuit.'

acres . . . tristes—energetic rather than harsh.

5. *exceptione*—the 'exception' is his occasional imitation of Cicero just mentioned.

intendam limam tuam — 'make your correcting pen more vigorous.'

si modo . . . adieceris—if you give your vote in favour of the resolve, possibly a mistaken one (error) which I have come to, of publishing.' Calculus *albus* is an affirmative as opposed to calculus *ater*, a negative vote.

B. II. (i. 8.)

2. *sermoni*—sermo is *strictly* used of the 'speech of ordinary conversation.' Its use here, however, must not be understood as implying that Pliny's address was not a regular set speech, which in all probability it was, but merely as expressing the very modest estimate which he wished it to be thought he had formed of it.

3. *universitati*—sc. the subject-matter and general character of the style. The word implies rather more than 'argumentum,' which confines itself solely to the *subject-matter.*

5. *Onerabit.* The 'onus' which Pliny feels to be involved in the publication of his speech is, in his view, one to be borne cheerfully, as arising out of a moral obligation rather than one of a painful and degrading necessity. Pliny is fond of the words

'onerare' and 'onerosus' in this sense, and Cicero occasionally
uses 'onus' as simply equivalent to a serious and important duty
without intending to suggest the notion of a tiresome or humiliating burden.

pressus—a word regularly applied to *style* by the Roman writers.
Occasionally it is used of the writer himself; see Tacitus, *Dial.
de Orat.* (of Cicero). 'nec satis *pressus*,' &c. It denotes the style
of an author who sticks close to his subject-matter and confines
himself to what is strictly necessary, eschewing all rhetorical
ornaments and flourishes. Hence it is closely allied to the notions
of brevity and conciseness. Its opposites are 'tumens,' 'inflatus,'
'elatus,' 'luxurians,' 'superfluens,' &c. &c. It may be explained
from the metaphor of pruning a tree, one of the recognised meanings of 'premere.'

demissus—'quiet,' 'unostentatious.' The word *may* and sometimes does imply a fault, a weakness; *here* it stands simply in
contrast to a high-flown and ambitious style.

6. *lenocinatur*—'lenocinari,' in Pliny and his contemporaries,
means 'to set a thing off, to make it attractive,' as in ii. 19, 'potest fieri ut libro isti novitas *lenocinetur*.' Here it is used with a
wider deviation from its proper meaning, and almost signifies 'to
excuse, justify,' &c.

7. *ipse mecum*—'I consider with myself'; 'I ask myself the
question.'

quod pleraque . . . retinent. The meaning is: What is done by
way of preparation for any important business is apt to lose its
value and its power of giving pleasure after the completion of the
business. The question for Pliny to consider was this: Would
the labour of revising his speech with a view to publication be
as usefully bestowed as that of its preparation in the first instance?

8. *munificentiae rationem*—'ratio' here, as often elsewhere, is a
comprehensive word, and denotes the general principle and purpose of Pliny's liberality.

tractatu— tractu is the reading of some editors, who compare
tractus verborum from Cicero and *tractus* belli from Tacitus, in
the sense of 'something drawn out to a great length.' 'Tractatu,'
however, seems here preferable; comp. i. 20, 'plerisque longiore
tractatu vis quaedam et pondus accedit'; also Quintilian, v. 8,
'latiore varioque *tractatu*.' The word in Pliny's time answered
almost exactly to our expression 'an author's *treatment* of his
subject.'

Pliny means to say that we see the beauty of noble sentiments
(honestae cogitationes) all the more thoroughly the longer we
dwell on them and speak of them.

largitionis—'largitio' is 'inconsiderate profusion without any
good object,' and is thus contrasted with 'liberalitas.'

9. *non impetu sed consilio*—'not by a mere impulse but by principle.'

10. *annuos sumptus*—these were defrayed out of the rent-charge of an estate, as explained in D. III.

in alimenta ingenuorum. Trajan first established funds for the maintenance and education of free-born children who were orphans or whose parents were too poor to bring them up. Perhaps Pliny was the first private individual who followed the emperor's example. There is the fragment of a monument at Milan on which his bounty is recorded. In later times such bequests became frequent, and an officer known as ' procurator ad alimenta ' was appointed to administer them.

11. *exquisitis adhortationibus* — sc. encouragements addressed with singular skill and tact. ' Exquisitus' is the opposite of ' commonplace.'

12. *non perinde populare*—sc. not so popular as games or a gladiatorial show.

inducere—this has been explained as equivalent to ' ornare ' or ' commendare,' and to have a metaphorical reference to the laying on of brilliant colours, or to the wrapping-up pills in gold leaf, &c. a meaning of the word which is to be traced in the rhetorical term ' inductio.' But ' inducere ' may be simply equivalent to ' introducere ' or ' instituere munus,' and so Cicero (*pro Sextio*, 64) uses the word.

orbis—the ' orbi ' might be divided into two classes—(1) those who might expect in the course of nature to have children ; (2) those who hoped to attain some day the ' jus liberorum.' The word ' exspectarent ' applies to the first, ' mererentur ' to the second class.

13. *intentionem effectumque* — ' effectus' seems more suitably coupled with ' intentio ' than affectus (read by some editors) which can mean only ' the disposition which prompted the gift,' and would thus be a mere repetition of ' intentio.'

14. *praeterea . . . reputatur*—' Besides I am mindful what a much nobler spirit it shows to place the reward of virtue in the approval of one's conscience than in reputation.'

B. III. (v. 8.)

3. *si qua me*, &c. Virg. *Georg.* iii. 8, ' Tentanda via est qua me quoque possim Tollere humo victorque virum volitare per ora.' The idea was suggested by Ennius's epitaph on himself, ' volito vivu' per ora virum.'

illud—sc. what follows, ' victorque virum,' &c.

quamquam o. Virg. *Aen.* v. 194 (from the description of the rowing match), ' non jam prima peto, Mnestheus, nec vincere certo: Quamquam o,' &c.

sed hoc, &c.—sc. diuturnitas et memoria posteritatis. Like Mnestheus, Pliny does not dare to hope for the highest rank among authors, but he aspires to distinction.

4. *orationi . . . gratia*—' to oratory and poetry little thanks are given,' &c.

delectat. Of course Pliny is not to be understood as meaning
that 'to give pleasure' is the highest function of history: he
merely means that it cannot fail to do this, whatever else it
may fail to do. Comp. Cic. *ad Fam.* v. 12 (a letter in which
Cicero asks Lucceius to record in his history the part he had taken
in public affairs), 'nihil est aptius ad *delectationem* lectoris quam
temporum varietates, fortunaeque vicissitudines.'

nuda—there is an implied reference to the preceding 'eloquentia
summa,' which is said to be indispensable to oratory and poetry.
'Nuda cognitio' denotes the knowledge which is conveyed in a
bald and unadorned narrative.

rescribere—'to revise.' In this sense Suetonius (*Jul. Caes.* lvi.)
couples the word with 'corrigere.'

9. *huic oneri*—sc. 'the difficulty of succeeding as an orator.'

illa . . . haec—the ordinary rule as to the use of these pronouns
would require that by 'haec' we should understand historia, and
by 'illa,' oratio. The sense, however, clearly will not allow this.
It would seem that in some instances, 'hic' refers to that which
is most closely connected with the speaker, and 'ille' to what is
comparatively remote from him. Forensic speaking was Pliny's
speciality; history he had not even attempted. The first would
as a matter of course have to deal with the familiar, and often
petty, incidents of daily life; the second with matters requiring
deep research (recondita) and dignified treatment.

10. *Hanc saepius ossa . . . decent.* By the metaphor 'ossa, musculi, nervi' Pliny wishes to convey the notion of a vigorous conciseness; by 'tori et quasi iubae' that of a style which unites
vigour with a certain fulness and richness. Forensic speeches, he
means, should resemble the spare and muscular frame of an athlete
in training; historical composition should have plenty of flesh
and sinew, and of something which, like the horse or lion's mane,
is at once fine and imposing. Pliny developes his meaning in the
next sentence.

tractu—sc. fulness and copiousness of description. Cicero,
Orat. xx. describes the style suitable for history as 'tracta et
fluens,' as contrasted with a 'contorta et acris oratio.'

sonus—'rhythm.'

11. κτῆμα . . . ἀγώνισμα—Thucyd. i. 22; comp. Quintil. x. i. 31,
'non ad actum rei pugnamque praesentem, sed ad memoriam posteritatis et ingenii famam componitur.' Ἀγώνισμα is a particularly
suitable word for 'forensic speaking,' which is in its nature an
intellectual contest.

ibi . . . hic—'ibi' in writing history, 'hic' in forensic oratory.

meis verbis—sc. 'the form of expression I use in the lawcourts.'

veniam advocandi—a legal phrase expressing the idea of 'a
delay,' 'respite.' 'Advocare' denotes the step taken by the party
to a suit previous to the commencement of the action. The defendant would ask the praetor for a reasonable time, within which
he could decide whether he should defend the action, or yield to

the plaintiff's demand. This time he would employ in consulting with his friends (advocati). Hence the delay itself was sometimes termed 'advocatio.'

12. *parata . . . collatio*—'the means of investigation are ready to your hand, but the work of collecting materials is burdensome.' Gierig explains 'onerosa collatio' to mean 'comparison with other authors is disagreeable.' The sense we have given to 'collatio' is that which it usually bears, and we think it suits the context better.

intacta tempora—'times untouched by history.' Comp. the expression 'intactus honor,' E. X. 8, of one who had been appointed to the aedileship, but who had not actually entered on the office.

B. IV. (vii. 9.)

1. *studere*—this absolute use of studere, answering to our 'to study,' is limited to post-Augustan writers.

2. *multi praecipiunt.* Quintilian among the number (x. 5, 2). Compare also the following passage in Cicero, *de Orat.* i. 34 (it is put into the mouth of Crassus), 'quibus (Graecis orationibus) lectis hoc assequebar ut cum ea quae legerem Graece, Latine redderem, non solum optimis verbis uterer, et tamen usitatis sed etiam exprimerem quaedam verba imitando quae nova nostris essent, dummodo essent idonea.'

proprietas . . . verborum—'proprietas' denotes the selection of the most suitable words, and precision in their use. 'Splendor' implies a certain beauty and dignity of expression, and the rejection of all mean and commonplace words. Compare the phrase 'splendor narrandi.'

vis explicandi—this includes 'forcible argument' and powerful description.

intelligentia et iudicium—this answers to our expression 'good taste.'

3. *Nihil . . . scribere*—'There will be no harm in your writing,' &c.

hactenus—'with so much attention as to,' &c.

quid . . . commodius—'what you, what the author you have been reading, has expressed the most neatly.'

Licebit . . . electis—'Occasionally you may both pick out some very familiar passage and also try to rival what you have selected.' To paraphrase successfully a passage with which we are very well acquainted is, as we know, a peculiarly difficult task. The more familiar are its words and expressions, the harder it is to find genuine equivalents for them.

4. *Audax . . . contentio*—'This is a bold, but, inasmuch as it is done secretly, is not an arrogant kind of rivalry.'

quosque subsequi . . . antecessisse—'satisfied if they could come close they, actually, by keeping a good heart, got before them.'

5. *interscribere*—'insert.'

7. *orandi*—orare = causas agere. Hence 'oratio,' a 'forensic speech.'

recoluntur—'are refreshed, renewed.'

8. *pressus purusque*—'pressus,' as an epithet of style, denotes the total absence of anything superfluous or redundant, and, by consequence, brevity and precision. Comp. stilus *pressus* demississque, B. II. 5. 'Purus' points to a style which is the reverse of ornate and rhetorical, and such as a man of taste and education uses in ordinary conversation. Somewhat similar in its meaning is 'purum argentum,' 'plate without figures embossed on it.'

9. *remitti*—'give yourself relaxation.'

sed hoc . . . distinguit—'but pretty little scraps of poetry, which make an excellent break in any sort of occupations and cares.' Poetry of the epigrammatic and kindred kinds is intended. Argutus, as elsewhere, conveys the notion of something neat and pretty.

ut laus est cerae—'as it is the merit of wax,' &c. Compare a similar passage in Quintilian, x. 5, 9.

iussaque fiat opus. This application of 'iubeo' to inanimate objects is thoroughly poetic. So too pareo, impero, sequi, and cognate words are used by a metaphor.

12. Work and relaxation were not only alternatives but went on together.

13. *in vita*—sc. 'in every phase of life.'

14. *Iuest . . . utilitas*—'These little poetic effusions have too the same advantage as other and larger poems,' &c. The advantage, as he goes on to explain, is that after having experienced the restraint of metre one returns to prose composition with a sense of freedom and relief.

16. *provulgatum*—'so well known' or 'so much discussed.'

B. V. (viii. 19.)

1. *quae . . . feram*—'which make me feel adversity more keenly, but bear it more patiently.'

2. *quod . . . hominum*—sc. 'which I am going to publish.'

intende—this is a late use of the word 'intendere.' Cicero would have added 'te' or 'tuam mentem.'

ut vacuo . . . luctoque—understand 'scriberem.'

proveniunt—the word has here a double sense, as is indicated by the change of construction. 'As a glad mind *arises out* of studies, so are studies *promoted* by cheerfulness.' This last meaning of 'provenire' is not usual in the Augustan writers.

B. VI. (ix. 11.)

1. *eo maximae quod*—sc. 'a letter peculiarly acceptable, because,' &c.

potior alia—'other preferable subject-matter.'

Sunt . . . occurrent—'for in this (subject-matter to which you allude) there are some slight objections; look round and they will occur to you.'

2. *quibus . . . delector*—'which I am delighted to find retain the popularity which they gained at Rome.'

discreta hominum iudicia—'discreta iudicia' is more pointed and forcible than 'discretorum hominum iudicia' would be. The meaning is the same.

B. VII. (vii. 20.)

1. *Librum tuum*—we have no means of knowing what this book was, but it was probably not one of the historian's chief works, which may be attributed to a date later than that of this epistle.

eximenda—'eximere' has here its usual sense of taking away what may be profitably dispensed with.

2. *vices*—'interchange.'

3. *aetate . . . dignitate*—so Keil reads with the best MSS. By 'dignitas' we are to understand the distinctions of office. In age there was really a greater difference between Tacitus and Pliny than would be suggested by the phrase 'propemodum aequales.' It could scarcely be less than ten years. See *Life*.

4. *cum iam . . . floreres*—Pliny must be referring to the year A.D. 88, in which Tacitus was raised by Domitian to the praetorship. See Tacitus, *Hist.* i. 1 and *Ann.* xi. 11.

longo . . . intervallo—from Verg. *Aen.* v. 320. Pliny's modesty suggests the word proximus rather than 'secundus,' which would have implied more. The notion of 'proximus' simply is that of two objects at a considerable distance with nothing intervening. So Horace, *C.* I. xii. 19, uses the word in reference to Jupiter and Pallas, distinguishing it from 'secundus': 'nec viget quidquam simile aut secundum, *Proximos* illi tamen occupavit Pallas honores.' Pliny may possibly have had in his mind a precisely similar passage in Cicero, *Brut.* 47, 'duobus summis Crasso et Antonio L. Philippus *proximus* accedebat, sed longo tamen intervallo proximus.'

maxime . . . imitandus—'most suitable for imitation, most deserving of imitation.'

5. *una nominamur.* See B. X.

sed nihil . . . iungimur—with the punctuation we have adopted, the meaning will be, 'still the fact remains, we *are* spoken of together, I care not in what position relatively to other authors.'

debes adnotasse—'you ought to have noted the following fact.'

suprema hominum indicia—sc. men's judgments as expressed in their wills. Precisely the same phrase, with the same meaning, occurs in Suetonius, *Aug.* 66, 'amicorum *suprema iudicia* morosissime pensitavit.' Iudicium *by itself* was susceptible of this meaning, and is thus used more than once. See Just. XII. xv. 3, 'otsi non voce nuncupatus heres, *iudicio* tamen electus videbatur.'

B. VIII. (viii. 7.)

1. *contra*—sc. 'discipulus.'

in scholam revocas. Comp. Martial, v. 85, 'jam tristis nucibus puer relictis | clamoso *revocatur* a magistro.' The Saturnalia coincided with the month of December, and corresponded to our Christmas holidays.

2. *Num potui . . . facere*—'could I have used a longer parenthesis?' 'Hyperbaton' means, a longer parenthesis than the rules of grammar strictly allow. Quintilian (viii. 6, 65) explains the term. It includes the notion of any awkward or clumsy expression, arising from the transposition of a word or of a clause.

Non modo magister, &c. For this construction of 'non modo' for 'non modo non' comp. Cic. *de Senect.* 16, 'ad quem (agrum bene cultum) fruendum *non modo* retardat, verum etiam invitat atque allectat senectus.'

In quo te ulciscaris—'on which you may take your revenge.'

B. X. (ix. 23.)

2. *cum quodam.* So Cortius reads for 'equitem Romanum,' which is the common reading. The alleged objection to it is that Tacitus, who was a senator, could not well have been sitting by the side of an eques, as distinct places had been assigned to the two orders by Nero. See Tacit. *Ann.* xv. 32. But how should it happen that a senator did not know Tacitus by sight? This seems inconceivable, and we must suppose that Tacitus on this occasion was not sitting among the senators. It appears from a passage in Dion Cassius that a senator, provided he laid aside his distinctive dress, had the privilege of sitting where he pleased.

3. *literis redduntur.* 'Reddere' is to give back something due to a person; hence, the meaning here is that literature has a sort of claim on the names of Tacitus and Pliny, as worthily representing it.

4. *Recumbebat mecum*—'was dining at the same house.'

5. *noscitavit.* 'Noscitare' means 'to recognize.' As is often the case with our word, it implies both the recognition and the gesture or speech which indicates that the recognition has been made. The anecdote is told also by Cicero, *Disput. Tusc.* v. 36.

B. XI. (iii. 5.)

2. *indicis.* 'Index' denoted what we call the 'title' of a book, also the 'table of contents,' and thus answered to the Greek terms εἴθεσις, κατάλογος, ἐπισημείωσις, &c. In its precise modern sense it appears to have been unknown to the Romans.

studiosis—'to students.' 'Studiosus' used absolutely for 'studiosus litterarum' is post-Augustan. It is in this sense equivalent to 'scholasticus.' 'Studere' and 'studiosus' had a special reference to the study of *oratory.*

ac iaculatione equestri. Soldiers who fought in this manner were termed 'equites ferentarii,' 'jaculatores.'

3. *Pomponii Secundi.* He is said to have been a 'scriptor tragoediarum' (vii. 17), in which capacity Quintilian (x. 1, 98) assigns him a high rank. Tacitus (*Ann.* v. 8) describes him as a man 'multa morum elegantia et ingenio illustri.'

4. *bellorum Germaniae.* Comp. Tacit. *Ann.* i. 69, where there is a reference to this work (tradit Plinius, Germanicorum bellorum scriptor, &c.).

latissime victor. Comp. Virg. *Aen.* i. 25, populum *late* regem. Drusus penetrated into Germany as far as the Elbe.

5. *studiosi tres*—'studiosi' (after the analogy of the other titles) is the *genitive.* These were books on the study of oratory, and as such are alluded to by Quintilian (iii. 1, 21) where he classes the elder Pliny among the writers on this subject.

volumina. The work in question was in three 'libri' or divisions, according to the subject-matter, and in six *rolls*, for the sake of convenience. Authors would often make the 'libri' and 'volumina' coincide, but of course, as in this case, there would be exceptions.

dubii sermonis. This was a work on grammar which discussed verbal forms and analysed ambiguous phrases and expressions.

omne studiorum . . . erectius. The allusion is to books of history, biography, politics, &c., which under Nero could not be undertaken with safety. Compare what Tacitus says of the danger of such writing in reference to Domitian's time (*Agr.* 2).

6. *A fine Aufidii Bassi*—Pliny's work was a continuation of the history of Aufidius Bassus, who lived in the reigns of Augustus and Tiberius, and related the events of his time. He is ranked among great historians by Quintilian (x. 1, 103) from whom it appears that he wrote a narrative of the German war. A passage from his works describing the death of Cicero has come down to us. The elder Pliny, in the preface to his *Natural History*, says, 'nos quidem omnes, patrem, te (sc. Vespasianum) fratremque diximus opere justo, temporum nostrorum historiam orsi *a fine Aufidii Bassi.*'

7. *scrupulosa*—'involving difficulty.'

8. *principum*—Vespasian and Titus.

Vulcanalibus. The Vulcanalia or feast of Vulcan fell on August 23, when from the shortening of the days 'lucubratio' (working by candle-light) becomes a necessity for students.

non auspicandi causa—sc. not merely for the sake of making a lucky beginning, &c. Pliny means that his uncle did not begin early rising at a particular time simply for the sake of conforming to the Roman fashion of entering on any serious work on certain important days of the year, but with a view to diligent study.

statim a nocte multa—'Nox multa,' here 'midnight,' the same, in fact, as 'sexta hora.'

somni paratissimi. For this use of 'paratus' comp. E. I. 25, obvius et *paratus* humor occurrit. 'Paratissimus' seems to suggest the notion of an enemy attacking (instantis) him, and quitting (deserentis) him again when resisted.

9. *ad delegatum sibi officium*—sc. 'any business entrusted to him.'

11. *gustabat*—sc. 'he took a light lunch.' The 'gustatio,' also called 'promulsio,' was properly the *first* course of the coena; it also denoted the light meal taken by the Romans between the 'prandium' and 'coena.'

12. *versus*—not 'verses,' but 'lines,' as in A. IV. 16 (speaking of a letter), ego non paginas tantum sed etiam *versus* syllabasque numerabo.

13. *intra primam noctem*—sc. before 7 p.m.

14. *interioribus*. The next sentence seems to show clearly that by 'interiora' we are to understand the period of actual immersion in the bath, not 'studia,' as has been suggested, after the analogy of Cicero's phrase, '*interiores* et reconditae litterae' (Cic. de N. D. iv. 16).

destringitur. The 'strigilis' was used in this process.

15. *notarius*—'a secretary who could write shorthand.' 'Nota' is a mark or symbol used in such writing. Cicero's freedman, Tiro, had the credit of having invented the art. The perfection to which it had been brought is attested by Martial, xiv. 208, 'currant verba licet, *manus* est velocior illis.' Shorthand writers were also called 'actuarii' (Suet. *Jul.* lv.).

17. *hac intentione*—'by this intense industry.'

electorum—passages selected from various writers, with a view to future works. The word finds its explanation in the preceding, nihil legit quod non excerperet.

commentarios—'note-books.'

opisthographos—comp. Juv. i. 6, 'scriptus et in *tergo* necdum finitus Orestes.' Writing materials were costly, and so occasionally, as in the case of these 'commentarii' which were merely books of reference for Pliny's own use, the back or reverse side of the roll was written on. This was done by children in their exercises, as we infer from Martial, iv. 87, '*inversa* pueris arande charta.'

procuraret—'procurare' is used absolutely by later writers, as 'curare' is by Sallust (*Cat.* lix. 3; *Jug.* xlvi. 7). Pliny the elder was one of the emperor's procurators. These officers were appointed by Augustus both for Rome and the provinces, and were responsible for the payment of the revenue into the fiscus.

quadringentis millibus nummum—about 3,200*l*. This would represent the value of the copyright of the work.

instantia—a post-Augustan word, meaning much the same as 'intentio,' used above, only rather stronger.

B. XII. (iii. 7.)

1. *media vitam finivisse*—compare the case of Corellius Rufus (E. VIII.) Cicero's friend Atticus put an end to his life in the same way.

3. *sponte accusarisse*—comp. Tacit. *Hist.* iv. 42, where the notorious Regulus is said (when quite a youth) '*sponte* accusationem subisse.'

industriae—in ironical allusion to his practices as a 'delator,' already hinted at. 'Industria' usually implied 'diligence in *public* business,' which in a Roman citizen was the highest possible merit.

in Vitellii . . . gesserat—comp. Tacit. *Hist.* iii. 65.

laudabili otio—sc. 'his literary occupations,' employment which the Romans often described as 'otium.'

4. *cubiculo semper non ex fortuna frequenti.* We may take these words as a locative ablative, or as an ablative absolute. The meaning is that the chamber of Italicus was crowded with visitors, who came out of respect and friendship for the man, not out of regard to his rank (fortuna), which was no longer what it had been.

7. *usque ad emacitatis reprehensionem*—comp. what Spartianus (life of Hadrian) says of that Emperor, 'venandi usque ad reprehensionem studiosus.' Emacitas is a post-Augustan word.

8. *Vergilii . . . natalem*—October 15th, B.C. 70. See Martial, xii. 68, '*Octobres* Maro consecravit *Idus*.'

ut templum. Statius, *Silvae*, IV. iv. 54, speaks of Vergil's tomb as Maroneum *templum*.

10. *ultimus . . . periit.* He was consul at the time of Nero's death, and he outlived all whom Nero had made consuls.

12. *Pisonis illius.* This was the grandson of the Piso who was suspected of having poisoned Germanicus. He was proconsul of Africa under Vespasian, and there was murdered, A.D. 70. The circumstances are related by Tacitus, *Hist.* iv. 48-50.

10. *tantae multitudinis*—sc. 'such a number of senators,' which since the time of Augustus had been fixed at 600.

Xerxen, &c. See Herod. vii. 45, 46.

14. *tanto magis hoc*—'all the more for this reason.'

materia in aliena manu—that is, the opportunity for great actions was not in one's own power, but rested with the Emperor.

proferamus—'let us lengthen out.'

15. Ἀγαθὴ δ' ἔρις. From Hesiod, *Works and Days*, v. 24, a passage in which the poet speaks of the effects of emulation in increasing wealth.

B. XIII. (iii. 21.)

1. *Acutus*—an epithet especially applicable to a writer of epigrams, whose chief merit is *point*.

et qui . . . minus. This clause explains the particular force and meaning of the preceding epithets; hence the subjunctive 'haberet.' 'Et satis et fellis' is a comprehensive expression to denote smart and pungent wit. For 'candoris' comp. *Panegyr.* 84, where 'candor' is coupled with 'simplicitas' and 'veritas,' and is about equivalent to its English derivative. It seems to have much the same meaning here, along with the notion of clearness and perspicuity of style, which in Martial, Pliny would imply, was the reflection of a frank and straightforward character.

2. *prosecutus . . . secedentem.* Prosequi (originally used of a procession in honour of a person) is a suitable word here, and signifies the paying of a marked compliment. Martial was leaving Rome for Bilbilis, his native place in Spain, where he died. The 'viaticum' was a present in money.

3. *fuit moris antiqui.* So Pompey the Great made Theophanes of Mitylene, by whom his life had been written, a Roman citizen. The poet Archias, too, as we learn from Cicero, had received the same reward in acknowledgment of his literary distinction.

4. *Remitterem te*—' I would refer you,' &c.

5. *adloquitur,* &c.—The epigram here quoted in part is extant, and appears as X. 19.

tempore non tuo—sc. 'at an unfavourable time.' The precise meaning is explained by the context, haec hora est tua, &c.

tetricae Minervae. In reference to the dry and severe character of Pliny's forensic studies. The next line alludes to the court of the centumviri.

Arpinis chartis—sc. the writings of Cicero, who was a native of Arpinum.

B. XIV. (ii. 3.)

1. *graciles.* This epithet conveys the idea of ' neatness,' 'elegance,' ' finish,' &c., and is akin in meaning to ' subtilis.' Quintil. xii. 10, 36, uses it of style ('non possumus esse tam *graciles;* simus fortiores).'

graves . . . erectae—'occasionally impressive and stirring.' Melmoth : 'solemn and majestic.' Elegance was the chief, but not the only merit of these exordiums.

2. *amicitur* —' he arranges his toga.' Comp. A. IV. 3, where it is said of Licinianus, a professed rhetorician, that he rose to speak 'postquam se composuit, circumspexitque habitum suum.' Quintilian (xl. 3, 156) also refers to the same practice, the object of which he thus explains—' ut et *amictus* sit decentior et aliquid spatii ad cogitandum.' Amictus is properly used of an *outer* vestment, such as was the toga or pallium.

multa . . . elucet—that is, ' his extempore speeches show much reading, and much practice in composition.'

3. *colligit fortiter.* 'He sums up forcibly.' Colligere here is ' to recapitulate ' rather than ' to infer.' Collectio and enumeratio are thus used by Cicero, answering to the Greek terms ἀνακεφαλαίωσις, συναγωγή, &c. The notion of 'powerful reasoning ' is implied in the preceding ' pugnat acriter.'

ornat excelse—alluding to metaphors and rhetorical figures.

voinara— sc. ' short striking reflexions,' called by Quintilian (xii. 10, 48) ' sententiae ' and thus defined, ' feriunt animum et uno ictu frequenter impellunt, et ipsa brevitate magis haerent, et delectatione persuadent.'

circumscripti—'concise,' 'condensed.' Comp. B. XIX. 5, where *circumscriptus* is coupled with *pressus* and *adductus*.

effecti — 'perfect,' 'complete,' and consequently 'thoroughly effective.' Cicero would have expressed this by 'absolutus' or 'elaboratus.' Comp. Quintil. xii. 10, 'aures nitidius aliquid atque *effectius* postulantes.'

quod . . . est—'a result which it is a great thing to attain even with the pen.'

5. *scholasticus tantum*—sc. he is simply a rhetorician (declamator) and never applies his eloquence to professional advocacy.

malitiae—'malitia' here as elsewhere means a sort of low unprincipled cleverness, such as the practice of the law is apt to develope.

6. *auditorium*—answering to the 'gymnasia.' Comp. E. XI. 6.

8. *Gaditanum*—'a man from Gades' (Cadiz), which to the Roman mind conveyed a notion of extreme remoteness.

ἀ·διδάκτοι—a word denoting the absence of all taste and cultivation.

9. *acriora. . . legas*—sc. 'what you read is more clearly understood than what you hear.'

B. XV. (v. 5.)

2. *Veritate promptissimus*—veritas here seems to denote an intellectual rather than a moral quality. It signifies the accuracy of an able and clear-headed man.

prosecutus est—understand some such word as 'legatis.' Comp. Suet. *Claud.* iii. legato circa sestertium vicies *prosecutus*.

3. *subtiles*—'finished,' of style.

Latinos—this epithet specially denotes grammatical correctness. The phrase 'Latine loqui' is used in this sense by Cicero *de Orat.* i. 32, iii. 13.

inter sermonem historiamque medios—'sermo' means the style which is adapted to the expression of the ordinary circumstances of daily life. In D. III. 9 the difference in character between 'oratio' and 'historia' is pointed out. We must not associate with sermo the notion of careless, slipshod writing; it merely points to something rather less dignified and stately than historical composition.

4. *acerba*—almost the same as 'immatura.' Comp. E. IX. 6 (of the death of the daughter of Fundanius), 'triste *acerbumque* funus,' and Virgil, *Aen.* vi. 429, 'funere mersit *acerbo*.'

vivendi . . . finiunt—'put an end every day to all motives for living.' Comp. Juv. viii. 84, 'propter vitam *vivendi* perdere causas.'

abrumpat—'abrumpere,' to break off a thing, so that it is never resumed, but remains unfulfilled.

5. *imaginatus est*—'imaginari' is an entirely post-Augustan word. Suetonius, *Jul. Caes.* lxxxi. uses it for 'somniare' ('Calpurnia uxor *imaginata* est collabi fastigium domus').

revolvisse—we should have expected *evolvisse*. The words however seem to be interchanged. So Livy xxxiv. 5, 'tuas adversus te Origines (Cato's work on early Italian history) revolvam.'

B. XVI. (vi. 21.)

1. *lassa et effeta*—comp. Lucr. ii. 1150:
    ' Iamque adeo fracta est aetas, effetaque tellus
     Vix animalia parva creat.'
2. *Vergilium Romanum*—his name occurs only in this passage, from which we gather that he was writing a play on the model of the Aristophanic comedy. He wrote also, as it appears, plays after the style of the new comedy as represented by Menander.
3. *absolutum*—' when thoroughly well done.'
5. *non tanquam inciperet*—' not as if he were now making the attempt for the first time.'
granditas—the Greek equivalent to this word is ὗψος. Cicero expresses the notion of it by the following periphrasis, ' ampla et sententiarum gravitas et maiestas verborum.' He once uses the phrase ' granditas verborum ' (*Brut.* 31).

B. XVII. (ix. 22.)

1. *eoque . . . praecipuus*—' and consequently exceedingly like him (Propertius) in that in which he is pre-eminent,' sc. elegiac poetry.
2. *tersum*—properly, ' wiped clean '; hence ' correct,' ' elegant,' &c.
molle—a word specially applicable to elegiac poetry as appealing to the tender passions.
mobilitas—this implies that, as is explained in the context, Passenus could readily and gracefully pass from the description of one kind of emotion to that of another.
omnia . . . absolvit—' in a word, he does everything to perfection, just as if it was the only thing he attempted.'
3. *pro hoc . . . animo*—sc. ' distressed in mind for such a friend, such a man of genius,' &c.
tandem . . . recepi—sc. ' he is at last restored to me, and I am at last restored to myself.' ' Se recipere,' ' to recover oneself,' is a well-known phrase.

B. XVIII. (viii. 4.)

1. *tam copiosa tam lata*—sc. so rich in strange events, and embracing such varieties of scene.
2. *immissa . . . flumina*—a poetic way of saying ' rivers turned into new channels.' There is a special reference to the river Sargetia, on which stood the palace of the king Decebalus. It was diverted from its course by Trajan, with the view of securing the royal treasures, which, he had understood, were concealed beneath its bed.

novos pontes—referring to Trajan's famous bridge over the Danube.

pulsum etiam vita. Decebalus killed himself when he found that he could not escape capture. His head was brought to Rome. 'Pulsum vita' is a highly poetical expression; it can be justified only as a kind of zeugma in connexion with 'pulsum regia.' Comp. Ovid, *Metam.* ii. 312.

3. *amplissimis operibus increscat*—this answers to our phrase 'rising to the occasion.'

regis ipsius. The name Decebalus would suit hexameter verse. The name, however, appears as Diurpaneus in some writers, a less tractable form, to which perhaps Pliny alludes.

4. *Graecis . . . resultent*—'do not respond to Greek verses,' that is, 'do not suit them.' Martial in ix. 12, 13, 14, complains of the intractability in verse of the name Earinus, and Virgil is said by his biographers to have been deterred from celebrating the Alban kings in consequence of their unpoetical names.

mollia—that is, soft, and easily moulded to the exigences of poetry. We may render it 'plastic,' 'tractable.'

levitatem—'smoothness of expression.' So Quintilian, x. i. 52, 'levitas verborum.'

5. *delicata*—'capricious,' 'affected.' As opposed to 'necessaria' the word here implies a needless and arbitrary licence in changing the forms of words and names.

immitte rudentes, &c. Pliny seems to have imitated a passage in Verg. *Aen.* viii. 707, &c.; comp. also Verg. *Georg.* ii. 41; Ovid, *Fast.* i. 4. The comparison of a poem to a ship was very familiar to the Roman poets.

toto ingenio—sc. 'with the full tide of your genius.'

6. *prima . . . absolveris*—'as soon as you have finished each part of your introduction.'

7. *similia nascentibus*—comp. an expression of Claudian (*De Consulatu Theodori*, 115), 'nascentes libri.' So we speak of a work 'in embryo.'

carptim ut contexta—we should have expected 'carpta,' answering to the following 'inchoata.' Ernesti's explanation that Pliny meant to oppose carptim texta to contexta, and for brevity's sake omitted 'texta,' is far-fetched. There is, however, some justification for the text as it stands in a rather similar construction in Sallust, *Jugurth.* 5, 'cuius in Africa magnum atque late imperium valuit,' where 'latum' would seem more natural. Comp. also Livy xxviii. 25, 'seu carptim partes, seu universi mallent,' where again there is a similarly ungrammatical construction.

B. XIX. (i. 16.)

1. *varium*—'versatile.' Applied to *character* the word has a *bad* meaning, and denotes 'shifty,' 'unsteady,' &c. This is by far the more usual meaning of the word.

multiplex—'many-sided.'

2. *tenet, habet, possidet*—a legal formula to express full and complete possession.

sententiae—answering to our 'general reflections.'

constructio—sc. the structure of the periods.

sonantia—'impressive.'

antiqua—'old' in the sense of simple and unaffected. Pliny does not so much mean to contrast genuine Latin words and phrases with those of new and foreign origin as the simple, natural style of earlier writers with that of some of his contemporaries, which was highly artificial and always straining after effect. More or less this was characteristic of all the Latinity of his time.

omnia . . . retractentur—that is, the compositions of Saturninus give pleasure not only when they are heard, but when they are read and studied. So Quintilian (x. 1, 19) says of *reading* in contrast with mere *hearing*, 'lectio libera est nec actionis impetu transcurrit,' meaning that what one *reads* can be judged of more fairly and dispassionately than what one *hears* under the influences of excitement.

4. *concionibus*—'concio,' properly 'a popular assembly,' then 'a popular harangue,' here means a speech which a historian after the manner of Thucydides or Livy introduces into his narrative. 'Oratio' is a 'forensic speech.'

5. *pressior, circumscriptior, adductior*—these words all denote conciseness, terseness, and compression under somewhat different aspects. For 'pressus' see note on word, B. II. 5. The notion of 'adductus' (a word which Tacitus often uses in its metaphorical sense) is derived from the phrase 'adducere habenas.' The later writers regularly use it of a condensed style.

amaritudinis—'pungency.' In allusion to the character of his wit.

data opera—'designedly.'

7. *cum remittor*—comp. B. IV. 9, 'fas est carmine remitti.'

hortor et moneo—'hortari' is 'to appeal to the *feelings*,' 'monere' 'to appeal to the reason.'

8. *gratia*—sc. his power of pleasing.

B. XX. (iii. 11.)

2. *philosophi ab urbe submoti*—this was done by the order of Domitian, A.D. 93. See Suet. *Domit.* x.; Tacit. *Agr.* 2 and 45. Pliny also alludes to it, *Panegyr.* 47, by way of pointing a contrast between Trajan and Domitian.

3. *gratuitam*—sc. 'without the payment of interest.' Comp. Suet. *Jul. Caes.* xxvii. '*gratuito* aut levi fenore obstricti.'

fulminibus quasi ambustus—this metaphor recurs *Panegyr.* 90 (of Domitian), 'utrumque nostrum . . . in proximum iacto *fulmine* adflaverat.' Comp. Livy xxii. 35, 'Aemilius Paullus damnatione collegae et sua prope *ambustus*; Juvenal viii. 92, 'quam *fulmine* iusto et Capito et Numitor ruerint,' &c. The phrase points to some very heavy calamity, such as exile or death.

5. *proximum simillimumque sapienti*—this is added by way of qualification, inasmuch as the wise man of the Stoics existed only in idea.

intelligere—not 'to understand his philosophical teaching,' but 'to see and recognise his worth and ability.'

7. *adsectatoribus*—sc. suitors of the daughter of Artemidorus. The word frequently means 'hearers,' 'pupils'; but this meaning is out of place here, as it can hardly be supposed that all the philosopher's pupils solicited the hand of his daughter.

B. XXI. (i. 10.)

2. *in Syria*—it was in Syria that Pliny also made the acquaintance of the philosopher Artemidorus; see B. XX. Syria was a general term for the district properly so called, and the adjoining countries of Palestine, Mesopotamia, &c.

militarem—sc. serving as a military tribune.

obvius et expositus—that is, Euphrates was something more than 'easily accessible'; he would himself make the first advances towards friendship. 'Expositus' means 'one who throws himself open to you without reserve.' Quintilian (ii. 5, 19) speaks of a person as 'candidissimum et maxime expositum.' Statius (*Silvae*, V. ii. 246) has the expression 'expositi mores' in the sense of openness and candour.

3. *quia magis intelligo*—'because I better appreciate them.'

5. *latitudo*—this word, for which Cicero uses 'amplitudo,' implies a fulness and richness in the development of a writer's ideas and arguments. This was specially characteristic of Plato. It seems out of place to suppose that there is a play in 'latitudo' on the connection of Plato's name with πλάτος. It is much more likely that the word is suggested by a Greek expression πλατότης -ῆς ἑρμηνείας which is found in Diogenes Laërtius, iii. 4. In Ep. i. 20, we have the phrase 'lata oratio,' where 'lata' is coupled with 'magnifica' and 'excelsa'; and would seem to denote 'full,' 'luxuriant,' and thus be opposed to 'pressa,' 'adstricta,' epithets which exclude rhetorical ornament.

7. *Nullus . . . cultu*—sc. no affected negligence in his dress and appearance.

tristitia . . . severitatis—severitas would represent the good side, tristitia the bad side of Stoicism. The first conveys the notion of a genuine and noble earnestness; the latter that of an affected gloom and austerity.

reformides—the special idea of 'reformidare' appears to be the kind of fear which can give no distinct account of itself, but which arises from vague and undefined presentiments of something disagreeable or dangerous. Perhaps our word 'shrink' is its nearest equivalent.

pendens—comp. Ovid, *Heroid.* i. 30, 'narrantis coniux *pendet* ab ore viri.'

persuades . . . cupias—the meaning is, 'you wish to hear further arguments from him even when you are already convinced;' his eloquence is so attractive and delightful.

8. *altissimas conditiones*—'conditio' was technically used in legal phraseology to denote a 'betrothal' or 'marriage contract.' This, no doubt, is its meaning here, so that by 'altissimae conditiones' we are to understand 'the highest and most illustrious matches.'

9. *officio.* It was only in the time of the Empire that 'officium' was used to mean 'a public office' or employment, which previously had been expressed by 'honos,' 'magistratus,' 'munus publicum,' &c. Pliny is here alluding to the 'praefectura aerarii,' which he held for two years with Cornutus Tertullus for his colleague. Ep. v. 15.

subnoto libellos—'libellus' here has a comprehensive meaning, and may stand for accounts of receipt and expenditure, and for various petitions and applications which would come before the praefectus aerarii. Subnoto means, 'I write my name at the bottom' (as a voucher of the accuracy of the accounts), or, 'I write my opinion on the matter submitted to me under the petition.'

illiteratissimae literae—comp. the similar expressions 'concordia discors,' Hor. *Epist.* I. xii. 19; 'insaniens sapientia,' Hor. *C.* i. 14; 'innumeri numeri,' Lucret. ii. 1052.

cognoscere—sc. 'to hear causes.'

ipsi—sc. philosophers.

B. XXII. (i. 13.)

1. *proventum*—provenire and proventus are especially used by Pliny and his contemporaries to denote intellectual activity and progress. Comp. B. V. 2, 'studia hilaritate *proveniunt.*'

mense Aprili—July and August were the months during which these recitations were most frequent, legal business being for the time suspended. The poets it appears were too impatient to wait beyond April.

nullus fere dies—so Martial (x. 70), 'auditur toto saepe poeta die.'

2. *stationibus*—the 'stationes' were lounging places chiefly in the neighbourhood of the Forum, where people met and chatted together in the intervals of business. They were under the shelter of porticoes, and were provided with seats, and to a certain extent answered to our taverns. Pliny says of himself when canvassing for a friend (Ep. ii. 9), 'domos *stationesque* circumeo.' Comp. Juv. *Sat.* xi. 4, 'convictus, thermae, *stationes*, omne theatrum,' &c. Statio in this sense is post-Augustan, and answers to the Greek λέσχη.

audiendi fabulis—'the time which should have been spent in listening to the recitation was frittered away in gossip.' By 'fabula' Pliny means what in Ep. viii. 18, he calls 'fabulae urbis,' town gossip.

3. *Nonianum* — Servilius Nonianus is mentioned by Tacitus, *Ann.* xiv. 19, *Dial. de Orat.* 23; and by Quintilian, x. 1, 102. He

wns, it appears, distinguished both as a pleader and as a historian. Quintilian says that he admired his speeches, but thought his style too rhetorical for history. The poet Persius had a high esteem for him, and regarded him almost as a father.

4. *quia non perdiderit*—Gierig would read 'perdidit,' so as to attribute the sentiment to Pliny, as at first sight appears reasonable. By the subjunctive, however, Pliny may well mean to hint at the debased tone of the man who would complain that he felt he had *wasted* a day just because he had not wasted it in idle gossip.

B. XXIII. (vi. 15.)

1. *excepit*—Pliny means that when he came to town every one met him with the anecdote.

splendidus—as applied to an *eques*, generally means a man of distinguished birth.

Prisce iubes. These were, in all probability, the opening words of the first line. It would have been an act of excessive rudeness in Priscus if, as some suppose, the words had been addressed to him and he had met them with such an answer. The anecdote has been made the subject of much controversy. Priscus was an eminent lawyer, some of whose legal wisdom is still preserved in the Pandects; and it has excited much surprise, not to say indignation, that the phrase *dubiae sanitatis* should have been applied to him. We may suppose it to mean nothing more than excessive absence of mind. His friendship with the poet had brought him to assist at a proceeding which we may suppose not to have been very much to his taste. Deep in thought about other matters he is roused by hearing his own name, and in the forgetfulness of the moment makes the ludicrous remark or answer which forms the subject of the anecdote.

3. *ius respondet*—the phrase 'ius respondere' or 'de iure respondere' was the technical definition of the functions of the jurist. It occurs in Cicero, *De Leg.* i. 4 ; ii. 12 ; and in Hor. *Epist.* I. iii. 23, where we have 'Civica iura Respondere paras.'

aliquantum frigoris attulit—as we should say, 'it threw a damp over the whole affair.' Frigus denotes either the chilled feelings of the audience or the cold and languid manner in which Paullus gave his reading, in consequence of the interruption of Javolenus. Pliny uses the word in this latter sense in A. XIV. 11 : 'erat periculum ne reliqua actio mea *frigus* ut deposita pateretur.' It has something like this meaning in Horace, *Sat.* II. i. 62, 'maiorum ne quis amicus *Frigore* te feriat.'

B. XXIV. (viii. 12.)

1. *praemium.* This seems to be hardly a suitable word, and Schaefer accordingly prefers to read 'gremium,' which Cicero (*pro Caelio*, 24) couples with 'sinus.' Pliny, however, especially in such passages as this, is not always over-scrupulous in his choice of words. The following expression, 'omnium exemplum,' is

somewhat tame and out of place, after such phrases as 'portus,' 'sinus,' &c.

reformator—a word resting solely on the authority of this passage; 'reformare' is a good word, although it is post-Augustan. Pliny uses it in *Paneg.* 53.

2. *domum . . . praebet*—comp. Juvenal vii. 40, 'Maculosas commodat aedes.' If an author had not a room suitable for a reading in his own house, he would either hire one, or ask a rich patron to lend him the use of one.

mihi . . . nunquam—sc. 'he has never failed to be present at one of my readings if only he was in Rome.'

3. *obeunti vadimonia mea.* We have also the phrases ad vadimonia venire, currere, decurrere, descendere, &c. 'Vadimonium' denotes not merely the security given, but also the day on which the person undertaking to furnish it had to appear in court.

tanta . . . possum—sc. 'to one who often takes such pains to do a thing, of which I will not say that it is the only thing which can lay me under an obligation, but which certainly can do so in the very highest degree.'

4. *honestate materiae.* 'The excellence of the subject-matter (of his reading).'

B. XXV. (viii. 21.)

2. *in triclinio*—sc. at dinner-time. Pliny, as we know, liked an intellectual accompaniment on such occasions.

Iulio mense. July and August were vacation time at Rome, and ordinary law suits were suspended. We see however from this letter that legal business might be occasionally transacted.

lites interquiescunt—comp. Statius, *Silv.* IV. iv. 39,

 'Certe iam Latiae non miscent iurgia leges,
  Et pacem piger annus habet, messesque reversae
  Dimisêre forum.'

cathedris—sc. writing-desks. Comp. for this use of the word Propert. IV. v. 37, 'posita tu scribe cathedra Quidlibet,' &c. and E. 1. 21 (of a 'zotheca') 'duas *cathedras* capit.' It is implied that Pliny's friends would from time to time put their thoughts into writing as the reading proceeded.

3. *praeloquendi*—sc. 'of offering an apology,' which Pliny would do before the reading began.

advocationem. 'Advocatio' was a kind of legal assistance or advice, and did not necessarily imply 'pleading a client's cause in court.' But in this case we must suppose that Pliny had not only to advise a client, but to say something in his behalf before a court, although he would not have to make the regular speech of a counsel.

ut irreverentem operis—sc. 'as though I slighted the work of reading aloud.'

quod . . . abstinuissem—'because when about to read aloud, though simply to a small circle of friends, I yet had not kept myself clear of other friends and of law-business.'

4. *opusculis variis et metris*—sc. on various subjects and in various metres.

imputantque quod transeunt—'make a merit of omitting them.'

electa recitantibus—'those who read (to their friends), only select passages from their works.'

illud—sc. the practice of reading select passages. 'Illud,' which usually means 'the former,' here happens to denote 'the latter,' on the principle that the writer is speaking of something done by others, not by himself.

5. *reverentius*—'more respectful.'

hoc—sc. this my own practice.

simplicius et amantius—'more artless and loving.'

amat . . . pertimescat — 'for a person really loves you who thinks that you love him so much that he is not afraid of tiring you.'

quid praestant sodales—'what good do friends do you?' The meaning is that an author gets no useful hint from his friends if they come to hear him only for their own amusement.

delicatus—that is, one who is so fond of his own amusement as to give himself no trouble for the sake of a friend, one who, as we might say, will not let himself be bored. It is clear from the context that the idea of fastidious criticism, or indeed of anything implying serious intellectual effort, is quite absent from the word. Quintilian's 'delicatae aures' (iii. 1, 3) is meant to express this notion.

6. *musteum.* A post-Augustan word used in a similar sense by Sidonius Apollinaris (viii. 3), Pliny's imitator.

longiore mora—sc. 'the delay of excessive revision.'

C. I. (ii. 14.)

2. *pauci . . . dicere*—'there are few with whom it is any pleasure to act as counsel.'

expresse. 'Exprimere rem' is 'to represent a thing clearly and vividly'; hence 'expresse dicere' means to use a striking or picturesque expression.

ut ab Homero in scholis. Homer in a Roman school was regarded as the foundation of all learning and culture; he was studied both for style and for subject-matter. Next to Homer, Hesiod and Menander appear to have taken their place in the course of study.

hic quoque . . . est—sc. in the lawcourts as in the schools that which is the most important is the first thing to be studied and practised. Just as the greatest of authors is the first to be read in schools, so in the forum the actual practice of the law precedes the declamatory exercises which were always supposed to be a necessary preparation for it.

4. *conducti et redempti.* There were, it appears, people at Rome exactly like the 'claqueurs' in the Paris theatres. The worst speaker could for a consideration secure applause, and the context shows plainly that the business was reduced to an organised system. These hired claqueurs were rewarded with a dinner or with ready money, as it appears, to the amount of almost three denarii, or approximately 2*s*. 8*d*.

manceps convenitur—'an agreement is made with a contractor.' By 'manceps' is meant the person who undertakes to hire and arrange the claqueurs.

in media, &c.—this is the beginning of a new sentence. It was the fact that these sportulae were distributed as openly in a place where the courts were sitting, as by long-recognised custom they were given at the entertainments of the rich, which Pliny considered so disgraceful. The 'basilica' referred to would be the Basilica Julia, in which it was usual for four courts (quadruplex iudicium, as Pliny calls them, Ep. i. 18) to sit at the same time. The punctuation we have adopted is not that of the older editions, except that of Cortius; it is, however, that of recent editions, and seems, as we have explained, to bring out the meaning more forcibly. The gist of the sentence lies in the contrast between 'basilica' and 'triclinium.' By 'sportulae' Pliny means 'presents in *money*' (as in *Epp. ad Traj.* 118) which were habitually accepted without any sense of degradation by the clients of the rich, and even by men of genius, such as Martial.

5. Σο εκλὶc—sc. persons among the audience who continually applauded the speaker with the exclamation σοφῶς. Laudicoeni (an incorrectly-formed compound, perhaps after the analogy of tibicen, fidicen, &c.)—'persons who praise to get a dinner.'

6. *Nomenclatores*—such slaves would be youths who had been carefully trained and educated. They were brought up in the paedagogium, as it was called. See E. XIV. 13.

habent, &c.—this age was fifteen.

tanti ... *disertissimus*—'so much does it cost to be very distinguished for eloquence.'

9. *Largius Licinus*—he is mentioned in B. V. 17 as having offered a great sum of money to the elder Pliny for a portion of his works. It appears from the context that he did not go so far as to hire an audience, but only begged people to be present while he was speaking in court.

10. *assectabar*, &c.—'I used to go to hear.'

Domitium Afrum. See Tacit. *Ann.* iv. 52, 66; xiv. 19; and *Dial. de Orat.* 13, 15, whence it appears that he turned his great oratorical powers to base purposes, and sought the favour of Tiberius by accusing persons obnoxious to the Emperor. Quintilian pronounces him to have been in his time at the head of the Roman bar. He lived into the reign of Nero.

12. *hoc artificium*—sc. 'this art of forensic eloquence.'

quod alioqui, &c. — 'indeed generally it was beginning,' &c. Alioqui means, that apart from the incident just mentioned, there were other circumstances which tended to the decay of the 'artificium' above named.

fracta pronuntiatione — 'fracta' is equivalent to 'mollis' or 'effeminata,' and conveys the notion of affectation. Comp. *fracti soni,* Tacit. *Ann.* xiv. 20. It is used of a feeble, nerveless style ; also of soft, voluptuous music. Tener in *teneris* clamoribus has the same meaning. Our word 'sing-song' fairly represents both these epithets.

13. *cymbala* . . . *tympana*—these instruments were used in the worship of Cybele and of Bacchus, as being suitable to rites of a soft and effeminate character. Consequently Pliny suggests that they would be a very suitable accompaniment to the effeminate eloquence of these youthful orators. Quintilian (v. 13, 17) has the phrase '*tympana* eloquentiae' for a soft, nerveless rhetoric.

illis canticis—by 'cantica' are meant the speeches which were spoken like songs. To this practice, as stupid and offensive, Quintilian alludes (xi. 3, 57), 'quodcumque vitium magis tulerim quam quo nunc maxime laboratur in caussis omnibus scholisque, *cantandi*.' So that it would appear that both in pleadings at the bar, and in rhetorical declamations, a kind of sing-song delivery had become fashionable.

ululatus—the same as 'teneri clamores.'

14. *ratio aetatis*—'my age,' Pliny means to say, 'is not yet sufficiently advanced to excuse me from such legal practice.' The expression 'ratio aetatis' occurs E. XV. 11.

C. II. (iv. 24.)

1. *in quadruplici iudicio*—this is wanting in several MSS. It is quite possible that either these or the preceding words 'apud centumviros' may have been added by a copyist by way of explanation. The court of the 'centumviri' was known as the 'quadruplex iudicium.' They sat in the Basilica Julia. Occasionally (in what cases we do not know) they sat as four distinct courts, each of which by itself heard causes; this may perhaps explain what otherwise would be a mere repetition, and Pliny's exact meaning will be, 'one of the four courts into which the "centumviri" are divided.' Comp. Quintil. xii. 5, 6.

4. *studiis . . . processimus.* Three periods are glanced at : (1) the beginning of Domitian's reign ; (2) its latter years, so dangerous to virtue and distinction ; (3) Nerva and Trajan's reign. By 'studia' he means as elsewhere 'forensic eloquence.'

6. *nihil . . . fidere*—some word like 'oportere' seems to have dropped out. As the sentence stands, it can only be rendered, 'this may be taken as a proof that we despair of nothing,' &c. For the meaning 'this may warn us not to despair,' &c., we should have, 'ne quid desperemus,' &c.

C. III. (vi. 2.)

1. *nonnunquam*—'pretty often,' interdum = occasionally.

quaerere . . . desiderare — Pliny means to say that he *missed* (quaerere) Regulus, so zealous had he been in his profession, but remembering his odious character could not regret him (desiderare). Comp. A. VIII. 7, where desiderandus is used to complete the sense of quaerendus.

2. *habebat . . . scribebat*—he thought so much of his work that he was exceedingly anxious about his success (timebat); he applied himself intensely to his labour (pallebat—comp. Pers. i. 124); and even took the trouble of writing out his speeches (scribebat). This is a favourite practice of painstaking extemporary speakers.

ediscere—'though he could not learn by heart.' This is what Keil substitutes for the common reading which puts a full stop at *scribebat*, and has dediscere, connecting it with the following clause, ' He never could unlearn the habit.'

circumlinebat—this can scarcely mean, as some think, that he imitated the dark rings round the eyes which betoken excessive study. It would have been eminently absurd to paint one eye only. Most probably it signifies that he put some pigment round the eye which might give it more expression, applying it to the eye that bore on his antagonist. Compare, however, for the first signification Pers. iii. 44:

> ' Saepe oculos, memini, tingebam parvus olivo
> Grandia si nollem morituri verba Catonis
> Discere.'

At the best the matter is somewhat unintelligible.

splenium—properly a medical term for the bandage on a wound. We gather from Martial that the wearing of these was not an unusual practice with fops and dandies. See Epig. ii. 29, in which he ridicules a certain Rufus, and hints that if you were to strip off the ' splenia ' from his face you would find out that he was a branded runaway slave. Regulus possibly wore his ' splenium ' to add height to the forehead.

auspices consulebat—Regulus, as appears from E. XVII. 4, did this on other occasions.

3. *illa*—sc. the two practices mentioned in the next clause, ' quod . . . petebat ; quod . . . corrogabat.'

una dicentibus—' to those who were engaged as counsel in the same case.'

libera tempora—sc. an indefinite time for speaking. The time, as we learn from this letter, was subsequently limited by the clepsydra ; the influence of Regulus secured his freedom from any such limitation.

quod . . . corrogabat—' because he got together an audience.' This practice of getting an audience by entreaty or even by coarser methods is alluded to in C. I. 4, ' sequuntur auditores actoribus similes, conducti et redempti.' It appears to have been by no means rare with Roman advocates of Pliny's time.

sub alterius invidia—by ' invidia ' is meant the odium which the practices above mentioned would be sure to bring on an advocate. But as Regulus set the example of them, this ' odium ' would fall upon him rather than upon those who, being engaged as counsel in causes in which he was concerned, merely did what he did. Consequently such persons might claim the privilege of speaking as long as they pleased (liberum tempus) at the expense of Regulus.

in alieno . . . deprehensum—alienum auditorium is 'an audience collected by another' (Regulus in this case got the audience together). The notion of 'deprehensus' is that of a man who suddenly finds himself in circumstances on which he did not in the least calculate. An advocate had thus two advantages—(1) he could speak as long as he pleased on the strength of Regulus' example; (2) he could exhibit his eloquence before an audience which he found collected for him without any trouble on his part.

commode dicere—sc. to speak at your convenience, without any interruption and without any anxiety as to time.

poterat—comp. the use of *ei* with the imperfect to express contingencies no longer possible.

dimidia—the Augustan writers used 'dimidius' with 'pars' only.

periculorum—'periculum' specially denotes a danger arising out of judicial proceedings, just as studium here and elsewhere has a correspondingly restricted meaning. Cicero, *Pro Archia*, ii. couples together the words iudicia and pericula in one signification.

comperendinationes—comperendinatio (from 'perendie,' 'the day after to-morrow') is the adjournment of a cause to the third day. It is said in a similar passage in Tacit. *Dial. 38*, that 'liberae comperendinationes' (adjournments without any limit), were very common in the old days of the republic and tended to promote eloquence.

7. *O Regule . . . praestant*—'O Regulus, you who by your pertinacious vanity got from all our judges a privilege which only a very few grant to sincere conscientiousness.' Ambitio and tiles are words for which it is hardly possible to find English equivalents. The first denotes a kind of restless self-display, the love of speaking merely to show off one's eloquence; the second, a conscientious anxiety to do full justice to the cause on trial.

aquae—sc. as much time measured by the water-clock as was demanded.

8. *primam*—sc. his very best.

religioni—the word is to be understood as including both the oath itself taken by the judge and the scrupulous regard which he ought to feel for it.

etiam—'just so' = *vai*.

9. *amore communium*—this must mean either 'love for the general interests of the state,' or love of things in which Pliny and the friend to whom he was writing, took a common interest. The first view seems preferable. 'Communia' may very well imply 'things in which all people take an interest'—sc. the state and its welfare. There is, it would appear, a contrast between communia and 'domos nostras' in the next sentence. Both Gierig

and Schaefer acquiesce in this reading, which is that of the MSS. and is consequently retained by Keil.

C. IV. (vi. 29.)

1. *probavit*—'esteemed.'

praecipere solitum—sc. Thrasea.

destitutas—'causes which were either so difficult or so dangerous that no advocate would undertake them.'

ad exemplum pertinentes—'such causes as would establish a precedent.' Pliny explains his meaning a little further on.

2. *quia . . . induceretur*—'because it was of vast importance whether a good or a bad precedent was introduced.' We have the subjunctive 'referret' because Thrasea's opinion is being quoted, and the sentence is consequently in the oblique narration.

5. *commode . . . minus commode*—Quintilian, x. 3, 10, has a very similar passage : 'cito scribendo non fit ut bene scribatur ; bene scribendo fit ut cito.'

6. *mollitie frontis*—we speak of a person as being 'brazen-faced' ; mollitics frontis denotes exactly the opposite character. Mollitics naturae is used by Cicero (*Att.* i. 17) to imply what we should call 'delicacy of feeling,' 'sensitiveness.' Cicero (*De Orat.* ii. 3) says of Isocrates, 'Ipse pater eloquentiae de se Isocrates scripsit : pudore a dicendo et timiditate ingenua quadam refugisti.'

7. *temperamentum* —understand by this word the 'principle which had guided Pliny as an advocate in his choice of cases.' Its idea is, choosing some things and rejecting others. It is seldom found but in writers of the silver age.

8. *quaesitum . . . inquisitio* —'the question was asked (in the senate) whether a judicial inquiry ought to be granted.'

9. *utebatur . . . legis*—the meaning is that Marius begged to be tried before a commission of iudices, as he might have been in an ordinary case of 'res repetundae,' rather than to be impeached before the senate. He thus threw himself on the mercy of the law.

10. *iudicibus acceptis*—Bassus, as we learn from A. XIV. 9, was allowed to have his cause tried before an inferior court. This is expressed by iudices accipere.

11. *postulante . . . liceret*—Varenus proconsul of Bithynia when accused by the provincials, asked to be allowed to summon in his defence witnesses from the province. See Ep. v. 20.

C. V. (vi. 31.)

1. *hoc loco nomen.* We may suppose that the place had recently received its name, Centum Cellae.

2. *ubi haec maxime recludyntur*—'where they, sc. iustitia, &c.,

are preeminently revealed.' Comp. Tacit. *Ann.* vi. 6, si *recludantur* tyrannorum mentes.

3. *innoxie popularis*—his popularity had no ill effects; no one was the worse for it. Cicero (*De Off.* i. 25) opposes to the 'popularis' the man 'studiosus optimi cuiusque.'

delator immissus—' an accuser was hounded on.'

5. *excussis probationibus*—'having thoroughly sifted the evidence.' Probatio in this sense is confined to the silver age.

exauctoravit—' cashiered.' The word, however, originally does not mean 'dismissal with disgrace.' It means merely release from the military oath (sacramentum). Those who were so released were called 'veterani,' and as such had to serve again under special circumstances. In this sense the word is used by Tacitus, *Ann.* i. 36, '*exauctorari* qui sena dena fecissent ac retineri sub vexillo ceterorum immunes nisi propulsandi hostis.'

contentus—the participle of 'contineo.' Its construction with the infinitive appears to be confined to *poets* of the Augustan age and to later writers.

6. *Iuliae legis poenis.* These penalties were (1) forfeiture of half the woman's dower and of a third of her property; (2) the kind of exile known as relegatio in insulam.

Caesar . . . videretur. The meaning is, that the emperor, in passing sentence marked the case as an exceptional one, naming the particular centurion and dwelling on the importance of maintaining military discipline. He did not wish it to be thought that he intended to try all similar cases.

8. *substituebantur crimini*—' were brought under the charge.' Subjicere is used in the same sense.

procurator. He was, as was often the case with freedmen under the emperors, employed in the administration of the fiscus, and probably, too, in that of the emperor's private property. In this latter capacity he would answer to our 'steward.'

9. *Polycletus.* Mentioned by Tacitus, *Ann.* xiv. 39; *Hist.* i. 37, ii. 95, from which passages we gather that he was a favourite freedman of Nero, and used his opportunities for amassing enormous wealth. Trajan of course meant that his freedman Eurythmus never had such opportunities.

10. *cum detulissent omnes*—'since all had made the charge.' The full phrase, as it appears in the Augustan writers, is 'deferre nomen,' i.e. 'to give in the name of the accused person to the praetor with a view to trial.' Later writers, as Pliny, Tacitus, &c., simply use deferre in the sense of 'to accuse.'

11. *isti*—sc. Senecio and Eurythmus.

12. *isti enim . . . accusare.* Trajan's meaning is, that it rested with these persons originally whether or no they would bring forward their accusation; that having done so, and being under an obligation to follow it up, they ought to think themselves fortunate in being allowed to drop it.

aut singuli . . . agendi—' or that they should one by one give satisfactory reasons for not pursuing the action,' &c.

alioqui . . . pronuntiaturum—the plaintiffs (the heredes) were to understand that they must either go on with the action or give good reasons for dropping it, or else the emperor would at least pronounce them guilty of 'calumnia,' a legal term which denoted the crime of one who from corrupt motives brought a false or vexatious accusation against another.

13. *acroamata*—the word acroama had become naturalised in the Latin language. Cicero uses it several times. It might be a piece of music, or a play, or something more intellectual in the shape of a reading or recitation of prose or poetry.

14. *xenia*—these presents were also called apophoreta, 'things which the guests were to carry away with them.' We learn from Suetonius that Augustus, and even the parsimonious Vespasian, were in the habit of making presents on such occasions as the Saturnalia. Suet. *Aug.* 74; *Vesp.* 19.

simplicitas convictus—'the perfect freedom of our social intercourse.' Comp. Tacit. *Ann.* vi. 5, 'convivalium fabularum simplicitas.'

15. *cum maxime*—this implies that the harbour coincided exactly with the 'sinus' or 'bend in the shore.'

16. *elaboratur*—'is in process of completion.'

insula—this artificial island was to serve as a breakwater.

arte visenda—'by a process well worth seeing.'

contra—this word seems to have little meaning, whether joined with 'provehit' or with the following haec. If it is retained, it must be taken to mean, 'facing the harbour seawards.'

17. *saxeum dorsum*—sc. the 'insula' above mentioned.

pilae—'piers,' which projected from the breakwater and gave it additional strength. Virgil, in his description of the harbour of Baiae, uses the word in this sense:

> 'Talis in Euboico Baiarum littore quondam
> Saxea *pila* cadit.' *Aen.* ix. 710.

D. I. (iv. 8.)

3. *in hoc . . . possit*—sc. 'all that fortune can do is to bestow this honour; she cannot take it away.

Iulio Frontino—comp. D. XI., where Frontinus is spoken of as 'spectatissimus'; A. X., where he is said to have forbidden the erection of a monument to his memory. He was an able soldier, as we gather from Tacitus, *Agr.* 17 (vir magnus quantum licebat), and was Agricola's predecessor in the government of Britain. He was the author of a military work, which has come down to us.

principi viro—comp. Horace, *Epp.* I. xvii. 35, 'principibus viris.'

per hos continuos annos—the pronoun denotes recent time. Comp. A. XIV. 1, caussam per *hos* dies dixit Julius Bassus.

tanquam cooptaret —' with the intention of electing me into his place.'

6. *quae sunt . . . hominum.* Referring to such distinctions as the consulate, &c., which, it is implied, were within the reach of a fair amount of energy and industry.

illud—sc. the genius of Cicero.

D. II. (iv. 13.)

2. *in fine.* This is Cortius's emendation of the common reading 'in finem,' which cannot be defended. It is now generally accepted.

ne . . . pereat — sc. ' that my impatience may lose nothing. Festinatio here denotes ' an impatient eagerness ' in a good sense. It is almost equivalent to 'alacritas.'

3. *praecursoria.* A post-Augustan and very rare word, for the use of which Pliny apologises.

praetextatus. This implies that the youth was under 17.

studes?—' do you go to school ?' This *absolute* use of studere (to be a student) is confined to post-Augustan writers.

Mediolani—Mediolanum (now Milan) was, in Pliny's time, the chief city of northern Italy, and had a specially great literary reputation. Cellarius quotes an inscription in which it is described as ' Novae Athenae.'

5. *quantulum est*—' what a trifling matter it would be!'

viatica. Like the Greek ἐφόδια, this denoted money for travelling expenses, and was used as here in reference to the expenses of a student away from home.

mercedibus—sc. the fees or salaries of professors and masters. This is a by no means uncommon meaning of ' merces.' Comp. Cic. *Acad.* ii. 30, ' *merces* dialecticorum.'

6. *ambitu corrumperetur* — ' be spoilt by jobbery.' The best masters, Pliny was afraid, would not be chosen unless the townspeople themselves bore a fair share of the expense, and were under a direct motive to see that their money was usefully spent.

7. *ius conducendi*—the right of engaging masters.

religio recte iudicandi—' conscientiousness in making a right choice.'

10. *haec . . . repetenda*—that is, ' I thought it best to tell you the whole story from the beginning, so that you might know my reasons for making this request of you.'

ne cui . . . obstringam—sc. ' that I do not pledge my word to anyone.' As is explained in the next sentence, the choice of teachers is to rest with the parents, not with Pliny.

12. *eat illuc . . . ferat*—' let him go to Comum on condition that he takes with him no other certainty but confidence in himself.' The meaning is, that if a teacher thinks fit to go and offer his services, he must not count on being a successful candidate ; if he fails, he must lay the blame on himself for having over-estimated his qualifications for the position.

Q

D. III. (vii. 18.)

1. *Deliberas mecum*—'you consult me.'

post te—'after your death.'

numeres . . . summam—'would you pay over to the "municipium" (Comum) the entire capital?'

ne dilabatur. As we should say, 'that it will be frittered away.'

agros—farms.

2. *agrum . . . daturus*—'I made a fictitious transfer to the public agent of one of my landed estates, which was worth considerably more (than 500,000 sesterces); this same estate I had re-conveyed back to me with a rent-charge upon it, on condition that I was to pay 300,000 sesterces.' The 'actor publicus' was an officer who stood in a similar relation to the state that a steward or agent stands in to a private individual. Purchases or sales of property, and all the business arising out of them, would pass through his hands. He would have to keep accounts of such transactions and hand them in to the aerarium. His office was probably subordinate to that of the 'procuratores aerarii.' We hear of him only under the empire. On two occasions during the reign of Tiberius the slaves of a suspected and accused man were sold to the 'actor publicus' with a view to their being examined by torture as to their master's guilt. See the account in Tacitus, *Ann.* ii. 30; iii. 67, of the trials of Libo Drusus and Silanus.

3. *sors*—'the principal.'

reditus—'the interest,' as opposed to the principal. In this case it coincided with the 'vectigal,' or the rent-charge.

quod . . . inveniet — 'because it greatly exceeds in value the rent-charge, it will always find a tenant to cultivate it.' Pliny explains in this sentence the effect of the precaution he had taken. The capital was safe, being invested in an estate; the interest was secured, as Pliny intended, to the benefit of the town, since it was permanently charged as a vectigal on the estate, to be paid over yearly by the occupying tenant.

D. IV. (iv. 19.)

1. *Fratrem optimum*—Calpurnia's father.

amitae affectum—affectus in the sense of 'fondness,' 'affection,' is post-Augustan. Comp. Suet. (*Titus*, 8), 'parentis affectum.' In Cicero and his contemporaries it rather denotes 'a mental state' or 'condition' generally.

repraesentes. Repraesentare in its strict and original meaning signified 'the doing something without a moment's delay, on the spot.' It is used, however, by such writers as Cicero and Horace much as it is here.

2. *quod . . . indicium est.* Pliny's meaning is explained by the context; 'Non aetatem meam aut corpus,' &c.—His wife's love

was chaste, because it was attracted by what was noble and enduring in her husband.

3. *cum videor acturus*—'when she thinks I am going to plead a cause.'

clamores—equivalent to 'plausus.'

4. *formatque cithara*—'sets them to the lyre.' 'Modulari' is the more technical word in this sense.

6. *contubernio*—contubernium, properly a military term, was used by the post-Augustan writers to denote specially 'the society and friendship of a teacher.'

D. V. (vi. 4.)

1. *in Campaniam*—probably to the warm baths of Baiae.

e vestigio subsequi—to follow immediately.

2. *corpusculo*—a diminutive of affection.

inoffensa. Pliny expresses a hope that his wife had traversed these luxurious and pleasure-seeking regions without meeting anything to harm her.

3. *fortem*=bene valentem. Comp. D. XIV. 7.

D. VI. (vi. 7.)

1. *vestigio*—the place where I was wont to sit, to recline, &c.

2. *his fomentis adquiescis*—'that you find rest in these consolations.'

D. VII. (vii. 5.)

1. *similis excluso*—Pliny borrows the common language of lovers.

D. VIII. (iv. 1.)

2. *vestri*—sc. Fabatus and his daughter.

atque adeo . . . alligamus—'and indeed we are actually packing up.'

3. *itineris ratio*—'the plan of our route.'

in Tuscos—'to my Tuscan estate.'

4. *Tiferni Tiberini.* Two towns of Umbria bore the name Tifernum. They were distinguished as 'Tiberinum' and 'Metaurense,' the latter epithet being derived from the river Metaurus.

patronum. Towns were accustomed to choose a patron or protector, who, among other duties, would act as what we call 'a standing counsel.' Comp. Suet. *Aug.* 17; *Tiber.* 6. Cicero (*Div. in Caecilium,* 16) speaks of the 'patronus' of a state or province as the 'defensor sui juris: ultor injuriarum.' It would seem, from the present passage, that the custom of selecting a patronus had become a mere formality. *Adoptare* patronum is the usual expression.

studio—'kindly feeling.'

6. *epulo celebrare.* The 'epulum' would naturally follow the

'sacrificium,' which was an essential part of the ceremony of a 'dedicatio.'

viam ipsam corripiemus. A poetical expression. Comp. Verg. *Aen.* i. 418, 'corripuere viam interea.' Comp. also the common phrase, 'corripere gradum.' It means 'to hurry over.' Somewhat similarly we say, 'to devour the way.'

D. IX. (i. 6.)

1. *et quidem.* Writers of the Augustan age would have generally said, 'et eos,' in this connection.

inertia mea et quiete. By this expression Pliny modestly describes his literary pursuits. So Sallust (*Jug.* 4) says that he supposes that some persons will give the name of 'inertia' to his historical labours. A Roman was naturally inclined to think meanly of any work or occupation which was not connected with politics, or was not of a thoroughly practical character; and spoke of it by the term 'otium.' This word had special reference to the life and employments of a man of letters, and thus answered to our 'learned leisure.' 'Inertia' seems to be here used deliberately by Pliny, as a word of less dignity and importance than 'otium.' In E. XXI. 8, he speaks of himself, when in the retirement of the country, and busy with his books, as 'otiosus.'

3. *pugillares*—answering to our note or memorandum books. What was written in them could be easily and quickly effaced. (The process of erasure was described by the phrase 'stilum vertere.') The term is derived from 'pugillus,' and means something which may be conveniently held in the hand.

ceras—sc. 'pugillares,' which were made of wax.

lagunculam—'a wine-flask.'

D. X. (ix. 10.)

2. *delicate*—'lazily,' in a dilettanti fashion. Suetonius (*Calig.* 43) couples the word with 'segniter.'

ut in secessu, &c.—'as is to be expected in retirement,' &c.

in via—sc. 'when out walking or riding.' Pliny's uncle under the same circumstances could give his mind to serious study. See B. XI. 15.

ea . . . seruntur—'in the chatty fashion in which conversation is carried on in a carriage.' 'Serere sermones' is a familiar phrase. Comp. Virg. *Aen.* vi. 160: 'Multa inter sese vario sermone serebat.' 'Serere' and 'sermo' are cognate words.

extendi. In allusion to the diffuseness of style which arises from lazy and careless writing. Its meaning is explained by the preceding 'garrulitas.'

3. *inamoenum.* This is a rare word, and found elsewhere only in poets. Properly it has reference to gloomy, dismal scenery: here it may be rendered 'repulsive.'

D. XI. (ix. 36.)

1. *diem disponam*—comp. Tacit. *Ger.* 30 : ' disponere diem,' ' to portion out the day.'

2. *non oculos . . . sequor.* The meaning is, that instead of allowing his eyes to determine the direction of his thoughts, he took care that his thoughts should control his eyes.

si quid in manibus. As we should say, ' if I have any work in hand.'

cogito . . . emendanti. Pliny means that he not merely pursued a certain train of thought, but that he also put his thoughts into words, just as if he were actually writing, and was careful at the time to choose the best words. Comp. Quintil. x. 7, 25, where this mental exercise is spoken of as ' exercitatio totas materias vel silentio (dum tamen quasi dicat intra se ipsum) persequendi ' (following out whole trains of thought in silence, provided, however, one does it as if one was talking to oneself).

ut vel . . . potuerunt—according as (my thoughts) have admitted of being put together and retained with ease or with difficulty.

notarius. See note, D. XI. 15.

die admisso—sc. ' having opened the windows.'

quae formaveram—' what I had put into shape.' ' Formare ' implies that the words and phrases had been provided as well as the thoughts—the *form* as well as the *matter*. ' Componere ' would not necessarily have meant so much as this.

3. *ut dies suasit*—sc. according to the weather : ' dies ' is often almost equivalent to ' caelum ' in the post-Augustan writers.

durat intentio—sc. ' my mental exertion is still continued.'

stomachi—sc. ' digestion.' Celsus the medical writer says (i. 8), ' si quis *stomacho* laborat, legere clare debet.'

4. *cum meis . . . eruditi.* Gierig understands by ' meis ' Pliny's slaves, among whom, as we know, were some highly educated youths. He is probably right.

dies cito conditur. For the phrase ' condere diem ' (to see the day go down), comp. Verg. *Ecl.* ix. 52 :

> ' saepe ego longos
> Cantando puerum memini me *condere* soles.'

Hor. *Carm.* iv. 5, 29 :

> ' *Condit* quisque diem collibus in suis.'

Lucr. iii. 1090 :

> ' Vivendo *condere* saecla.'

The expression is imitated from Callimachus (*Ep.* ii. 3) :

> ἤλιον ἐν λέσχῃ κατεδύσαμεν.

6. *non sine pugillaribus.* Comp. D. VIII. 3 (a letter to Tacitus on this subject).

colonis—' to my tenants.'

quorum . . . querellae. In ix. 15, Pliny alludes to the annoyance he experienced from letters of complaint addressed to him by his tenants, when he was at his Tuscan villa. (Tam multis undique rusticorum libellis, et tam querulis inquietor.)

haec urbana opera. 'These city occupations.' It may be hence inferred that the present letter was written from Rome.

commendant—'make more delightful.'

D. XII. (v. 1.)

1. *cur amplissimo gratius.* This repetition, though wanting in some MSS., is thoroughly characteristic of Pliny's style.

2. *praeiudicio.* 'Praeiudicium,' though *usually* denoting an 'unfavourable judgment,' is really a 'vox media,' and may, as here, mean the opposite. Of course, if Pliny gave up his share of the property to Curianus, it would imply that he thought the man had been wrongfully disinherited, and it would be an example or precedent which the other legatees would be likely to follow.

3. *non esse . . . orbo.* The meaning is that it would have a bad and suspicious appearance to make a handsome present to a rich man who had no children.

non profuturum . . . cessissem. If Pliny handed over his legacy as a present to Curianus, he would be treating him as an object of pity, which would do Curianus no good; if he waived his claim to it, he would get for Curianus the credit of having been unfairly disinherited.

liqueret—a legal term, which Pliny uses deliberately, as implying the certainty arising from clear evidence.

4. *minorem*—sc. 'of less honour, uprightness,' &c. Pliny's meaning is: 'If *you* think me equal to giving a fair and upright decision, there is no reason why I should think myself unequal (minorem) to doing so.'

constantium—sc. the moral courage which will not shrink from telling a person a disagreeable truth.

6. *sedi.* 'Sedere' was the technical word for 'sitting as a judge.' As such it is here purposely chosen.

pudorem—sc. the virtuous self-respect which would be incapable of a harsh or unjust action.

ex consilii sententia. 'Consilium' here as elsewhere means 'the persons engaged in deliberation,' 'the arbitrators.'

subscripsit centumvirale iudicium—'gave them notice of an action before the court of the Centumviri.' 'Subscribere cum aliquo,' properly, 'to sign one's name to an accusation as plaintiff against a person.' The phrase is an unusual one, and seems to have had its origin in the circumstance that the plaintiff and defendant both had to sign their names to the notice of the action. In this case Curianus was the plaintiff; the legatees, with the exception of Pliny, were the defendants.

7. *metu temporum.* It was in the time of Domitian. Rusticus had been put to death; his wife Gratilla was banished, and people might well be afraid of anything which might seem to imply friendship with them. The legatees were naturally anxious to get the matter settled as quietly as possible, as the context explains.

8. *ne ex centumvirali . . . . exirent.* The Centumviri could not condemn to death, their jurisdiction being civil, not criminal. But a criminal case might arise out of an action tried before their court, and of this the defendants under all the circumstances of the affair, and considering the Emperor's disposition, were afraid. It was quite possible that the property might be claimed by the 'fiscus,' and judicial proceedings might on this ground be instituted against them with a fatal result.

9. *ex parte quarta.* Referring to the lex Falcidia passed in the time of Augustus, which provided that a fourth part of the estate should be secured to the heir at law. It applied to persons who died, as Gratilla did, in exile. Hence the 'quarta pars' is sometimes spoken of as 'legitima et debita portio.'

10. *omnia me usu cepisse.* Possibly these words are due to a transcriber. They describe the consequences of Pliny having been in possession of the property for *two* years, a period which, according to Roman law, conferred a prescriptive right (usucapio) of ownership in the case of land and immovable goods.

12. *honore signavit.* Comp. Ovid, *Fasti*, v. 474, ut celebrem festo *signet honore* diem. 'Honor' has sometimes the special meaning of a 'complimentary legacy'; here, however, perhaps 'honore signare' may be taken as simply equivalent to 'honorare.'

D. XIII. (v. 19.)

1. *tuos*—sc. servos.

2. *indulgentia.* Usually this word has a slightly unfavourable sense. Here it has a good meaning, and denotes 'fair and merciful treatment,' as contrasted with the ordinary harsh and capricious exercise of authority by a Roman master over his slaves. Comp. Tacit. *Agr.* 4, 'in matris sinu *indulgentiaque* educatus.'

πάτηρ, &c. Homer, *Odyss.* ii. 47, 234.

3. *literatus.* The context explains this epithet. Zosimus, like some other slaves, had had an intellectual training which fitted him to be a reader or a secretary to his master. Such slaves very frequently received their freedom. 'Servus literatus' in Plautus is humorously used for 'a branded slave.'

inscriptio—a title describing his various qualifications was attached to the neck of a slave when he was offered for sale. This was called 'inscriptio.' In the case of Zosimus the word 'comoedus' would have been his 'inscriptio.'

acriter—'with distinct articulation.'

sapienter—sc. 'so as to show that he understands what he is reading.'

apte, decenter etiam. 'Decenter' implies more than 'apte,' which hardly goes beyond the idea of correctness and propriety. An actor might be said to represent a character 'apte,' if he exhibited at all adequately its chief features; he would represent it 'decenter' only if he seized all its various points, and skilfully combined them into a harmonious whole.

6. *in Aegyptum*, &c.—The elder Pliny dwells on the good effects of a voyage down the Mediterranean for consumptive people. (See *N. H.* xxxi. 6, 33.) The medical writer Celsus (iii. 22) recommends such people to go from Italy to Alexandria.

nimis imperat voci—'tasks his voice too severely.' Comp. Virg. *Georg.* i. 99, '*imperat arvis*' (he gets as much as he can out of the land). In the same sense we meet with the expression '*imperare vitibus*' (to task vines by making them bear as much fruit as possible).

D. XIV. (iv. 1.)

7. *fortes*—'in good health.' Fortis in this sense is a favourite word with Pliny. It is like our 'hearty.' Comp. D. V. 3.

D. XIV. (viii. 16.)

1. *Infirmitates.* Only post-Augustan writers use this word in the sense of 'an infirmity' or 'indisposition.' Comp. B. V. 1, '*infirmitate* uxoris.'

facilitas manumittendi—'my readiness in granting them freedom.' The construction is changed in the succeeding clause, 'alterum quod,' &c. Comp. Tacit. *Ger.* 43: 'Osos Pannonica lingua coarguit non esse Germanos, *et quod* tributa patiuntur.' Pliny (vii. 32) commends his friend Fabatus for having availed himself of a favourable opportunity to bestow freedom on a number of his slaves.

quasi testamenta facere—sc. 'to make a sort of will.' In the strict sense of the word it would be a 'testamentum.'

2. *quasi civitas*—that is, their 'domus' (the establishment to which they belong) in the case of slaves answers to the 'civitas' of the free born. A slave had no 'civitas,' consequently he was legally debarred from all the acts of a 'civis,' and could neither make a will nor inherit property under a will.

3. *hoc ipsum*—sc. 'the privilege of leaving their property in the manner described.'

eoque . . . videre. Pliny perhaps alludes to the elder Cato, surnamed 'sapiens,' who, it appears from Plutarch, left his cruel treatment of his slaves on record in his *De re rustica.* He would, however, certainly have before his own eyes many similar instances, and the prevalence of Stoic sentiment may have made such insensibility fashionable.

4. *non, solatiis non egere*—'it is not human to be above the need of consolation.'

5. *dolendi voluptas*—comp. Ovid. *Trist.* IV. iii. 37:

'Est quaedam flere voluptas :
Expletur lacrimis, egeriturque dolor.'

E. I. (ii. 17.)

1. *Laurentinum . . . Laurens*—comp. the forms Piceus, Picettinum; Camers, Camertinum, &c.

2. *opportunitatem loci.* In allusion to the near neighbourhood of Rome, Ostia, Laurentum, &c., and to the convenient and pleasant roads leading to these places.

litoris spatium. This has been explained of the distance of Pliny's villa from Rome along the seacoast. It seems, however, much better to understand it as meaning the wide frontage of the villa and its grounds to the sea.

secessit. Pliny compares his villa to a man who has gone into retirement.

salvo . . . die—'salvus dies' is opposed to 'perditus dies;' 'a day on which no duty has been omitted.' 'Compositus dies' is a day on which everything is in its right place, and the duties of which are well arranged. It excludes the idea of hurry and bustle. Pliny means that he could get through all his business with comfort to himself, and then pass the evening at his country house in a tranquil frame of mind.

iunctis—'for carriages.' Comp. E. XVIII. 3, 'mannulos junctos,' 'carriage horses.' Columella (ii. 22) uses 'junctum' for a carriage: '*juncto* advehere non permittitur,' &c. Usually the Roman carriages were drawn by mules.

3. *varia . . . facies*—'on either side the scenery is diversified,' &c.

tepore verno. 'Tepor' is the exact expression for mild spring breezes. Comp. Ovid, *Met.* i. 107, &c.:

'Ver erat aeternum, placidique tepentibus auris
Mulcebant Zephyri natos sine semine flores.'

nitescunt—nitere and nitescere were words regularly used for denoting the sleek condition of well-fed cattle. So Virg. *Aen.* vi. 654: 'quae cura *nitentes* Pascere equos.' Lucretius (ii. 189) has the expression '*nitidae* fruges,' 'smiling crops.'

4. *usibus capax*—that is, 'roomy enough for all sorts of purposes.'

non sumptuosa tutela. This is a *descriptive* ablative. 'Tutela' means what we call 'keeping up a house,' and includes all expenses connected with furniture, repairs, &c. So Columella (vii. 1, 2) speaks of the ass as 'tutelae exiguae animal,' meaning that his keep is not expensive.

atrium . . . sordidum. By the word 'frugi' a contrast is intended between this atrium and the splendidly furnished atria of some great houses, which were crammed with statues and works of art. There was, however, nothing niggardly or shabby (sordidum) about it. The atrium, or entrance hall, was, as we see by the context, distinct from the cavaedium afterwards mentioned.

D litterae. This is probably the right reading, though some have preferred O. In that case, however, Pliny would, as we should suppose, have expressed his meaning differently. D, it may be observed, is the only other letter which includes a space, as these porticoes are said to do.

festiva—sc. 'bright and cheerful.' So Plautus (*Curc.* I. i. 93) has the expression 'aedes *festivissimae.*' Pliny uses this word of a fine statue (E. VI. 1); also of a sprightly and charming girl (E. IX. 1). Very possibly the pavement of the area was of mosaic work.

specularibus—'specularia' were windows made of a 'lapis specularis' which under the empire came into very general use. See Pliny, *N.H.* xxxvi. 22, 45 (Spain and Cappadocia are said to have furnished the best quality of these stones). Commonly the Roman windows were simple apertures in the walls, and rain or bad weather was kept out by wooden shutters, or curtains. In Pliny's time, however, it seems clear that the windows in the better class of houses were furnished with thin transparent plates cut out of this 'lapis specularis,' or with 'vitrum' (something like our modern glass), as appears from discoveries at Herculaneum and Pompeii. Martial (viii. 14) implies that the 'lapis specularis' was sometimes used for greenhouses. See also a passage in Seneca (*Epist.* 90) which speaks of specularia as a comparatively modern discovery in his time.

imminentibus tectis—'by the projecting roof.'

medius—sc. porticus.

5. *cavaedium hilare.* Here the cavaedium would seem to have answered to what elsewhere is called 'impluvium.' 'Hilare' must mean 'light and cheerful,' and is perhaps intended to suggest the presence of sculpture or of frescoes.

fenestras non minores—both 'valvae' and 'fenestrae' were openings in the wall which might be closed with blinds or shutters. 'Fenestrae,' however, were properly small apertures at a considerable height, and were thus usually distinguished from 'valvae,' which would often be almost level with the floor of the room.

6. *huius . . . amplum*—'on the left of this cavaedium,' rather further (from the sea), is a spacious chamber, &c.

admittit . . . retinet—sc. 'it has both the morning and evening sun.' 'Retinet' means that the room has the light till the sun has entirely set, and perhaps suggests that the warmth is felt throughout the night.

7. *longius intuetur.* The meaning is that the prospect of the sea is more distant but is more enjoyable. There seems to be an implied contrast between this room and the 'triclinium,' which, we are told, is sometimes washed by the waves in rough weather.

huius cubiculi . . . accendit—sc. 'The angle formed by the projection of this chamber with the 'triclinium' before mentioned, retains the warmth of the sun at its height, and intensifies it.' The rays of the sun are at this point collected, as it were, into a focus, as though by a concave lens.

serenum . . . eripiunt. That is to say, it is the increasing darkness from the clouds rather than the bad weather and the cold, which at last makes it impossible to use the room.

8. *apsida*—not 'a vaulted roof,' as the older interpreters after the analogy of the expression οὐρανία ἄψις (the vault of heaven) used to explain it, but 'a semicircle.' One end of the room was semicircular in form, answering to our 'bow-window.' The windows at this end were, as it appears, so arranged as to receive alternately the morning and afternoon sun. In ecclesiastical writers 'apsis' denotes the choir or chancel of a church.

in bibliothecae speciem. From the time of Sulla and Lucullus, who brought with them from the East vast collections of books, the Roman villa was commonly furnished with a library. Pliny out of modesty prefers to use the term 'armarium' (book-case) rather than the more dignified word 'bibliotheca.'

9. *membrum*—'room.' So used in the following letter. The metaphysical senses of the word are very widely extended. It is akin to the Greek μῆρος.

suspensus et tubulatus. 'Suspensus' must mean that the 'transitus,' or passage from one part of the house to another, is raised on pillars after the manner of a bridge. 'Tubulatus' is read by most recent editors in place of 'tabulatus,' and it derives confirmation from the 'subulatus' and 'sublatus' of some MSS. It yields also a good sense. The covered passage was 'furnished with pipes' (tubuli), by which the heat was diffused. There is a passage in Seneca (*Epist.* 90) which alludes to an apparatus of this kind, and which by the mention of 'impressi parieti *tubi* per quos circumfunderetur calor qui ima simul et summa foveret aequaliter,' forcibly reminds us of our modern method of heating rooms. The reading 'tabulatus' can mean only 'made of boards,' and is open to the objection of being vague, and far less suitable to the context than 'tubulatus,' which tells us how the heat was received and dispersed. Comp. a passage in the following letter from which we may infer that these pipes for the transmission of heat were connected with the bath-rooms—(cohaeret hypocauston, et si dies nubilus, immisso vapore solis vicem supplet.)

conceptum vaporem. We may take this to mean the heat received by the covered passage, or the heat already engendered in the 'hypocauston.'

plerisque, &c.—this cannot conveniently be referred to 'usibus'; it is better to understand some such word as 'membris' or 'cubiculis,' which may be naturally connected with 'reliqua pars lateris.'

10. *politissimum.* 'Politus' usually implies 'literary culture'; hence the phrases '*polita* oratio,' '*polita* epistola,' &c. Applied as here, to a room, it means 'tastefully and elegantly furnished.' Comp. Phaedr. iv. 5, 6, 'domus *polita*.' Anything like vulgar show is deliberately excluded by the word.

vel cubiculum . . . coenatio. That is, a room large for a sleeping apartment, small for a dining-room. 'Coenatio' is confined to post-Augustan writers.

plurimo mari lucet—the room is bright with the reflection of the sun from a wide extent of sea.

altitudine aestivum. 'Altitudo' has been wrongly explained to mean 'depth under ground.' The coolness of the room and the suitability for summer was due to its *height* and consequent free circulation of air. This seems the obvious explanation. We have no hint of the existence of underground apartments.

munimentis—sc. the protection of trees, buildings, &c.

11. *cella frigidaria.* In addition to this the Roman bath was furnished with a 'cella tepidaria' and 'cella caldaria.' Cold water bathing had become fashionable among the Romans ever since the court physician Antonius Musa had successfully prescribed it to the emperor Augustus.

velut ciecta sinuantur—'ciecta' means that the basins (baptisteria) project from the walls; being a rather bold word, 'velut' is prefixed to it. 'Sinuantur' describes the circular, or at least the curved, form of the basins.

abunde . . . cogites—'more than sufficiently large if you bear in mind the close proximity of the sea.' That is, when you can, if you please, bathe in the sea itself, it seems almost superfluous to have swimming-baths of a very great size within the house.

elegantes—'in good taste.' 'Elegans' of a room means much the same as 'politus.'

12. *sphaeristerium.* Playing at ball was the regular Roman preparation for the bath. See Martial, *Ep.* xiv. 163; also Suetonius (*Vesp.* 20), whence it appears that Vespasian used to strengthen himself by means of this exercise. The 'sphaeristerium' seems to have been a circular hall, and was always to be found in a Roman country house of any pretensions.

turris. Hardly a 'tower' in our sense, but simply a part of the villa which contained one or more stories. Occasionally, as in Horace, *C.* I. iv. 14 (regumque *turres*), it denotes a grand and lofty pile of building.

diaetae—'day-rooms,' from 'dies.' A post-Augustan word. Diaeta would seem sometimes to have denoted a suite of rooms as well as a single spacious apartment. It was quite distinct from the dining-room (coenatio).

13. *apotheca*—answering to our 'wine-cellar'; only the Romans kept their wine at the top of the house. Here at least it would appear to be the same as what is elsewhere called 'cella vinaria.'

15. *interiore circuitu*—that is, the vine plantation is enclosed by the 'gestatio.'

vinea tenera et umbrosa. It is difficult to reconcile these two epithets. If it was a young and newly-formed vineyard (as 'tenera' would seem to imply) the vines could not have been 'umbrosae.' Gierig refers 'tenera' to the character of the ground, and explains it by the context. In this case 'umbrosa' is very awkwardly interposed, and the epithet itself seems superfluous. Perhaps Pliny uses the word rather vaguely, meaning merely to hint at the delicate nature of the plant, and to introduce a sort of ornamental epithet. The 'tenera vitis' had passed into a stock phrase, and as such, very possibly finds a place here.

hac . . . *facie*—'this prospect of the garden, which is no less pleasant than that of the sea.'

cingitur . . . *tergo*—'the back of the "coenatio" is closed in by two day-rooms or parlours.' For 'cingitur' (which does not seem quite a suitable word), Cortius and other editors prefer 'vincitur,' which would mean that the rooms in question are, so to speak, 'bound or linked together.'

hortus . . . *rusticus*—sc. 'a kitchen or vegetable garden,' as opposed to an ornamental or pleasure garden. 'Hortus pingui-' would naturally mean 'a productive garden'; so Virg. *Georg.* iv. 118. Pliny adds 'rusticus' to make his meaning perfectly clear.

16. *cryptoporticus.* This was like our arcade, and would be particularly agreeable in such a climate as that of Italy, on account of its comparative darkness and coolness. The word (which is partly Latin and partly Greek) is found only in Pliny, though no doubt it was a recognised term.

prope publici operis. A descriptive genitive. Comp. Suetonius, *Jul.* 47, 'Fabulas *operis antiqui.*'

utrimque . . . *pauciores.* Were it not for the 'alternis pauciores,' the meaning would be that for every two windows towards the sea there was one in the opposite wall looking on the garden. But the 'alternis pauciores' seems to imply that there was but one such window for every other two windows looking seaward.

serenus . . . *dies*—comp. Tacit. *Hist.* i. 86, where we have exactly the same conjunction of words. 'Immotus' *in prose* is post-Augustan.

17. *xystus.* The Greek xystus (so called from its smooth and polished floor) was an adjunct of the gymnasium; it was in fact a portico or colonnade for the convenience of the athletes in winter or bad weather. Roman writers transferred the term from the portico to an open space immediately adjoining the portico. Our 'terrace' seems very nearly to represent the Roman 'xystus,' but it does not appear that the xystus was *necessarily* a raised walk. It may have been simply like a lawn coming close up, as is often the case, to the windows of a house. Being to some extent sheltered by the portico, it was a pleasant place for a stroll, and this was its special purpose. It was usually adorned with flower beds and statues.

18. *nam ante* . . . *cadit.* The meaning is, 'during the forenoon the "cryptoporticus" throws a cooling shade upon the "xystus," during the afternoon upon the part of the promenade and of the garden close to the "xystus," the shade being greater or less as the day approaches noon or inclines towards evening.'

19. *ad hoc*—'in addition to this' (advantage).

aëre . . . *manente*—'close and stagnant air.'

ingravescit—'becomes oppressive'; 'gravis' in this sense is joined with 'odor,' 'aestas,' 'umbra,' 'coelum,' &c.

20. *in capite xysti*—'at the upper end of the xystus.'

deinceps cryptoporticus. Either parallel to one side of the xystus, or being an extension of it. It is impossible to determine the matter with certainty, as 'deinceps' is a vague word, and, like the Greek ἑξῆς, merely signifies that the 'xystus' and the 'cryptoporticus' closely adjoin each other. Of course this cryptoporticus is distinct from the one previously mentioned.

horti diaeta—this is in apposition with 'cryptoporticus,' which here is in fact a sort of garden-room, or rather, several such rooms.

heliocaminus. This word means a room as much as possible exposed to the sun.

cubiculum, &c.—this room opened on to the 'cryptoporticus,' by 'valvae,' and was thus almost part of it. All these rooms were included in the 'horti diaeta.'

21. *zotheca*—properly 'a cage for live animals.' The word is very rare. It is used by Sidonius Apollinaris, and is found in an inscription at Tibur. It seems to have meant a little room or cabinet especially devoted to statuettes, pictures, and other works of art. Although separated by curtains (as here explained), it was merely part of a larger room. The word 'recedit,' and the expression in the following letter (*zothecula refugit*) indicate that it was of the nature of a recess.

tot facies . . . miscet—that is, 'so many different views can either be seen separately, or blended into one prospect.'

22. *cubiculum . . . somni*—rather a poetic form of expression for the simple 'cubiculum nocturnum.' 'Cubiculum' *alone* (as we see throughout these two letters) would not have this meaning.

tam alti . . . consumit—'the cause of this profound tranquillity is that a passage between the two separates the chamber from the garden, and thus drowns all sound by the intervening vacancy.' 'Andron,' in writers of this period, has a meaning quite distinct from its Greek signification. It denotes either a passage or corridor connecting two rooms in a house, or, as here, a passage between two walls.

23. *applicitum . . . retinet*—'close to this chamber is a tiny stove room, which, by means of a little aperture, lets out or retains the heat from underneath.'

24. *festisque clamoribus.* For this use of 'festus,' which is poetical, and post-Augustan, comp. Tacit. *Ann.* iii 9, 'domus *festa* ornatu'; xii. 69, '*festae* voces'; xiv. 13, '*festus* cultus'; *Ger.* 40, '*festa* loca,' &c. Earlier prose writers used the word in a more restricted sense.

25. *haec utilitas . . . salienti*—'these advantages and charms are partially spoilt by the want of a running stream,' &c. 'Aqua saliens' is the running water of a brook which leaps over rocks and stones, &c.; hence it answers to our 'fresh water.' Comp. Virg. *Ecl.* v. 47.

puteos . . . fontes. 'Puteus' differs from 'fons' in being at a greater depth. Comp. Columella (*de Hortis*, x. 25).

'Aut fons illacrimet *putei* non sede profunda,
Ne gravis hausturis tendentibus ilia rumpat.'

in summo—'on the surface.'

26. *corruptus*—now generally read for 'salsus,' the common
reading. It has good MSS. authority; and it seems more likely
that 'salsus' was a gloss in explanation of 'corruptus' than the
contrary. Pliny was just the writer to choose the less obvious
word.

quem . . . discernit—'between which and my house there is
but one villa.'

balnea meritoria—'baths, for the use of which people paid.'
'Meritorius,' in various applications, was commonly used by the
writers of this period.

27. *continua*—'continuus' denotes that the parts of which a
thing is made up hang together closely; 'perpetuus' altogether
excludes the notion of division into parts. Pliny here means villas
which adjoin each other without being actually connected.

mollit . . . indurat. The water hardens the sand over which it
flows. This, in a tideless sea, happens during rough weather
only. Editors ignorant of this phenomenon have explained the
passage by giving an unusual meaning to 'mollit' and 'indurat:'
'A continuance of fine weather makes it (the shore) pleasant for
walking, but the frequent dashing of the waves upon it more often
renders it disagreeable.' If this is the right interpretation, Pliny
has expressed his meaning obscurely, and in very affected language. 'Mollire,' after the analogy of the phrase 'mollire
clivum' (to make the ascent of a hill easy) may admit of such an
explanation, but 'indurare' seems to be used in a very harsh and
strange manner. 'Contrarius' has probably the twofold meaning
of 'dashing against the shore,' and 'of being hostile to persons
walking on it.'

29. *incolere, inhabitare*—a strong way of marking his attach-
ment to the place, and the care he bestowed on it. Similarly,
Silius Italicus, xiv. 672 (of the gods), templa *incolere atque
habitare.*

nimis urbanus—a sort of play on the word 'urbanus,' which
almost always had a good sense.

dotibus—'charms.' 'Dotes' often stands for good qualities of
both body and mind. It is unusual to apply it to a thing distinct
from either of these, but it is quite in Pliny's manner to do so.

E. II. (v. 6.)

2. *Ora . . . extenditur.* This is not a mere repetition, as 'ora'
and 'litus' are by no means synonyms. The first is what we
term the coast-land generally; the second, the sea-coast or shore
properly so called. 'Ora' embraces much more than 'litus.'
Pliny's meaning consequently is—'that part of the coast-land

which consists of the mere strip of sea-coast, is unhealthy ; my
estate, though situated on the coast-land, is too far up the country
to be affected by its unhealthiness.

hi—se. Tusci mei.

4 *gelidum*—'gelidus' is a stronger word than 'frigidus,' and
implies a degree of cold sufficient to produce frost and ice.

nitidissimam—'nitidus' and 'nitere' are applied to plants
when in their richest bloom. Ovid (*Met.* i. 552) says of a laurel,
'remanet *nitor* unus in illa.'

auras . . . ventos—'aura' specially denotes a gentle sea-breeze.

8. *caeduae . . . descendunt*—'caeduae silvae' are opposed to the
preceding 'procera nemora et antiqua.' The meaning is, that as the
mountain sinks and descends into the plain, the more timber fit
for cutting is found.

terreni colles—these are opposed to the rocky or stony hills in
the neighbourhood.

10. *nono sulco.* Pliny's uncle speaks of rich soils in Italy requiring to be ploughed up five times before they could receive the
seed. It is therefore quite possible that the statement here made
may not have been an exaggeration.

11. *florida et gemmea*—this is a sort of hendiadys. 'Glitter-
ing with flowers' is Pliny's meaning.

12. *summittitur* - 'sinks below its banks.' The middle voice.

13. *formam . . . pictam*—'a landscape painted with a view to
an exceedingly beautiful effect.' Pictures of this kind, as may be
gathered from passages in Pliny's *Natural History*, had long been
familiar to the Romans.

descriptione—'arrangement of objects,' which, it is implied, was
singularly pleasing.

14. *villa . . . summo.* Pliny's meaning is not quite clear, and
it has been suggested that 'imo' and 'summo' should change
places. Gierig ventured on this alteration, contrary, however, to
the MSS., and he is followed by Döring. Their notion is that
'prospicit ex imo' is a sort of intentionally paradoxical expression (such expressions being characteristic of Pliny), implying that
the ascent is so gradual as to be almost imperceptible, and that,
consequently, though the villa itself was on the top of the hill, the
view which it commanded seemed to be from the foot. As good
a meaning may, we think, be got out of the words as they stand.
The villa is at the foot of the hill, the slope of which is so gradual
as to make little perceptible difference in the prospect at various
stages of the ascent. Hence the villa may be said to have almost
as good a view as if it stood on the summit. This explanation,
however, is not quite satisfactory. The following sentence, 'ita
. . . leniter ascendisse,' seems to imply that one must ascend the
hill in order to reach the house. Very possibly by ' villa,' Pliny
may mean both the house and its grounds, the house itself being
at the foot of the hill, and the grounds stretching up the slope to
its top. Thus the villa may be described as possessing the advantage denoted by the words ' prospicit quasi ex summo.'

15. *infractas.* 'In-' has here simply a *strengthening* force. 'Infractus,' in the sense of 'unbroken,' is not found in classical writers.

pro modo longam—long in proportion to its breadth.

membra—rooms.

atrium ex more veterum. This seems to imply that in Pliny's time the atrium, usually a necessary part in every great Roman house, was not generally found in a 'villa.'

16. *Pulvinus*—this word (properly meaning 'a cushion,' as distinguished from 'pulvinar,' a couch) had acquired in Pliny's age a technical meaning in reference to gardens, and denoted a sort of terrace, or raised border, thus differing not very materially from 'xystus.' The 'pulvinus' here spoken of was closely connected with the 'xystus,' and sloped down from it.

liquidus—this is a translation of Theocritus' ὑγρὸς ἄκανθος (i. 55), which Virgil (*Ecl.* iii. 45) renders by 'mollis.' The notion of the word is 'waving in the breeze.' For the acanthus (the acacia), see Pliny, *N. H.* xxii. 34.

17. *rarie tonsis*—cut in various shapes.

viridibus—shrubs; this meaning of 'viridia' is found only in writers of the silver age.

retentas manu—'kept back by the hand pruning.'

gradata—'cut into steps.' Pliny seems to have borrowed this word from his uncle, who uses it in his Natural History (xiii. 4, 7), in reference to the palm-tree.

subtrahit—'withdraws from view.'

18. *superiora illa*—sc. the xystus, pulvinus, &c.

19. *quod prosilit villae*—'the projecting wing of the house.'

20. *subiecta*—sc. loca.

22. *podio tenus*—'as far as the ceiling.' 'Podium,' it would appear, means the projecting part of the wall of the room (corresponding with our cornice), from which the ceiling (lacunar) was built. The word was generally confined to the upper part of the wall which surrounds the arena of the amphitheatre, and was consequently used to denote the first tier of seats.

24. *fenestris servit*—this implies that the special purpose of the pond was to present a pleasant view from the windows.

albescit. So Ovid uses 'recandescere,' *Met.* iv. 530: 'percussa recanduit unda.'

25. *plurimo sole*—the room has several windows to take the sun. This is the force of 'plurimus.'

apodyterium—'the stripping-room,' for which the Latin language supplies no equivalent but 'spoliarium,' which was restricted to a different meaning. For those who began with the warm bath, the 'tepidarium' answered this purpose.

puteus . . . adstringi. A cold bath was often taken by the Romans after a warm one, with the view of counteracting any mischief which might arise from the pores of the skin being too much opened. This is the force of the word 'adstringi,' which implies a bracing and strengthening of the system.

26. *caldariae magis*—sc. 'sol magis praesto est.' 'Caldaria' or 'caldarium' was a room in which a vapour-bath was taken, and was hence also called 'sudatorium,' &c.

descensiones—'places sunk in the floor of the room to various depths, for swimming or plunging baths.'

27. *circulos*—'sets of players.'

28. *jungitur cubiculum*—'another chamber joins on to that just mentioned.'

30. *ambitu*—'aditu' might seem a more appropriate word, and has been suggested as an emendation. All the best MSS., however, have 'ambitu,' by which we must understand the communication to have been a winding staircase.

32. *dispositionem*. In Cicero this word is confined to an 'arrangement' in a rhetorical sense. The meaning it has here is post-Augustan.

medius—sc. 'in the middle of the grounds.'

illae—sc. 'platani.'

33. *rectus . . . faciem*. It was in this form ▔▔▔▔╮

circulis—sc. circular paths or walks, into which the hippodrome was divided. The outermost of these, as it seems, was shaded by trees; the inner ones were left comparatively open to the sun.

34. *umbrarum . . . distinguit*—that is to say, the hippodrome in its different paths combines the variations of cool shade, and of a not unpleasantly warm sun.

multiplici—'containing many winding paths.'

recto limiti redditur—'it returns to its straight course.'

35. *in formas mille descripta*. Martial in allusion to this practice speaks of the 'tonsile buxetum,' iii. 58, 3.

metulae—sc. box-trees cut into pyramidal forms, in imitation of the conical columns in the circus at Rome.

poma—'fruit-trees.' These contributed to give the hippodrome the rural appearance spoken of in the next sentence.

36. *lubricus et flexuosus*. See note on liquidus (16). These epithets suggest a comparison between the acanthus and a serpent.

stibadium—a semi-circular sofa, adapted to what the Romans termed a 'mensa lunata,' which had become fashionable at this time. Martial thus describes a stibadium (xiv. 87):

'Accipe lunata scriptum testudine sigma;
    Octo capit; veniat quisquis amicus erit.'

in capite—'at the head of the hippodrome.'

columellae Carystiae—columns of Carystian marble.' The green marble of Carystus in Euboea was very highly prized by the Romans.

37. *gustatorium, coena*—both these words here stand for parts of the dinner service.

margini—either the margin of the 'stibadium,' or of the marble basin already mentioned.

iunctis hiatibus—'by consecutive apertures.'

e regione . . . cubiculum—'a chamber exactly facing the stibadium.'

40. *subducitur*—se subducit. Comp. 'se subducere colles,'
Virg. *E* ix. 7. 'The fountain rises and disappears.'

argutior—'too chatty.' So Cicero *ad Attic.* vi. 5: 'Obvias
mihi literas quam *argutissimas* de omnibus rebus crebro mittas.'

43. *percolui*—'brought to perfection.'

vel iudicium meum vel errorem—'either my deliberate opinion
or my prejudice.'

si materiae immoratur—'if he lingers on his subject.'

si aliquid . . . attrahit—'if he introduces and drags in anything
irrelevant.' 'Arcessitus' sometimes answers to our expression
'far-fetched.'

43. *quia . . . instituit*—sc. because he does what he purposes to
do, and does not go beyond it.

Aratus. He was the author of two astronomical poems, and
lived in the third century B.C. He is the writer from whom St.
Paul quotes the words, 'we are also his offspring' (Acts xvii. 28).

excursus—'a digression.' This meaning of the word is confined
to post-Augustan writers. 'Excessus' is also used by them in
the same sense. See below, 'in quod *excessi*.'

44. *ut parva magnis*—understand 'componamus.' The reference
is to Virgil, *Ecl.* i. 23: sic magnis componere parva solebam.

inductum—sc. introduced merely for the sake of effect. 'Inducere' often means 'to introduce a topic for discussion.'

45. *pinguius*—'more comfortable, snug.' Comp. E. XX. 3,
pinguis secessus; *pinguis* vita (vii. 26), and Ovid, *Rem. Amor.* 206,
pinguis quies.

nulla necessitas togae—the Romans always associated the 'toga'
with state occasions and matters of business. As the 'vestis
forensis' it suggested to them a number of tiresome duties.
Martial (iii. 46) in allusion to these uses the phrase 'opera
togata.' At home or in the country the 'toga' was exchanged for
the 'tunica'; hence Martial (x. 51) speaks of 'tunicata quies'
(rural retirement), and (x. 41) mentions 'toga rara' as one of the
chief elements in a happy life.

quod ipsum . . . accidit—'which very circumstance (the tranquillity of the place) is just as much an addition to the healthfulness
of the district as is the unusually pure sky and clear air.'

46. *venia sit dicto*—this is said in allusion to the idea of the
Nemesis supposed to threaten excessive prosperity. Comp. Herod.
i. 32, where in the conversation between Solon and Croesus this
belief is brought out. There was an old word 'praefiscine' used
by Plautus with just the same meaning as Pliny's 'venia sit
dicto.' It was connected with the superstitious dread of the evil
eye, to which the words 'fascino,' βασκαίνω point.

(E. III. ix. 7.)

1. *patrocinium*—sc. 'the encouragement of a patronus,' of one
who could set Pliny an example. Rich Romans of this time had

an almost insane passion for building, and created a sort of prejudice against it by the ridiculous lengths to which they sometimes carried it. Hence Pliny felt that he was glad to shelter himself under his friend's example.

Aedifico ratione—' It is with good reason that I am building,' &c.

ut maxime . . . exercent—' while they very much charm me they also find me occupation,' ' call out my ingenuity,' &c.

2. *more Baiano.* The villas at Baiae looked on the bay. See Horace, *Epist.* I. i. 83: ' Nullus in orbe sinus Baiis praelucet amoenis.' Baiae, as a peculiarly choice and favourite place, became as to the style and situation of its houses a model and example.

3. *quasi cothurnis*—the rocks on which the house stood are compared to the ' cothurnus,' or high-heeled buskin of tragedy.

sua utrique amoenitas—' each has its own special charm.'

4. *latius utitur*—sc. enjoys a wider prospect (of the lake).

haec . . . amplectitur—the meaning is that the villa is so built as to follow the bend in the shore of the lake.

duos—sc. ' sinus,' which the ridge (dorsum) separates.

illic . . . inflectitur—that is to say, to the villa furthest from the lake is attached a straight (recto limite) promenade, at some height above the shore, while the other villa had a promenade with a slight bend at one point, which bend had been made into a spacious ' xystus.'

hae mihi . . . supersunt—' such are my reasons for adding to each villa what is wanting to it, in consequence of its many existing advantages.' In other words, ' each villa is so good and attractive that I will make it as perfect as possible.'

5. *quid ego . . . facere*—' why should I speak to you about my reasons for doing this, when I know that with such a person as yourself doing what I do will be reason enough.' Pliny means that any sensible man would at once recognise the utility of what he was doing without further explanation.

E. IV. (viii. 20.)

1. *ut proximorum . . . sectemur.* For a similar sentiment comp. Pindar (*Pyth.* iii. 19, 20), ἀλλά τοι ἤρατο τῶν ἀπεόντων, and Ausonius,

' spernimus in commune omnes praesentia.'

2. *Achaia*—sc. Peloponnesus, Attica, Euboea, and other islands. This was the regularly accepted meaning of the term ' Achaia ' under the Empire. Comp. its use in A. XVIII.

miraculorum . . . commendatrix—sc. a land which not only abounds in wonders, but also procures general belief for them. ' Commendare miracula ' would mean ' to make wonders generally believed,' ' to vouch for their authenticity.'

3. *Amerina.*—Ameria was a town in Umbria, about 56 miles from Rome, near the junction of the Tiber and the Nar. It was

ᴀ 'municipium,' and would appear from Cicero's speech for Sextus Roscius to have been a moderately flourishing country town.

subiacens lacus. The town of Ameria stood on a hill; hence the force of ' subjacens.'

4. *in similitudinem . . . aequalis*—that is, ' perfectly circular.' Were it not for the words ' undique aequalis,' the lake might be supposed to be of an oval form. By ' subiacens rota ' is meant ' a wheel lying on the ground.' Pliny purposely avoids technical language, by which he might have expressed his meaning more concisely.

nullus sinus, obliquitas nulla. ' Sinus ' and ' obliquitas ' denote ' an irregular bend, or winding,' which would have destroyed the circular form of the lake. ' Obliquitas ' is a post-Augustan word.

dimensa—' regular in form,' the curve being of exactly the same kind in all parts of the circumference. Comp. Virg. *Georg.* ii. 284, ' Omnia sint paribus numeris *dimensa* viarum.'

quasi artificiis . . . excisa—this seems to mean that the lake, besides being exactly circular in its outlines, is also hollowed out in such a manner as to form a perfect hemisphere, thus presenting a thoroughly artificial appearance.

pressior. Words which denote colour are generally difficult of interpretation. ' Pressior ' here has been variously explained. It has been understood by some as meaning ' fainter,' ' less distinct ' than the colour denoted by ' coerulus,' by others, as denoting exactly the reverse. As ' pressus ' may mean ' close,' ' concentrated,' as well as ' dark,' ' obscure,' &c., both these explanations are justified, and we have little or nothing to guide us in choosing between them. We have, indeed, one passage in which the word is used of colour in the latter of these senses, being coupled with ' nubilus ' and opposed to ' acutus.' It occurs however in Solinus, a very inferior writer, whose date is quite uncertain. Forcellini explains it to be ' niger, albicanti mixtus ' (a sort of iron-grey) and meaning much the same as ' spadix,' which Virgil uses of a horse.

sapor medicatus—' its flavour has medicinal properties.'

qua fracta solidantur—' by which fractures are healed.'

5. *quaeque alia . . . effert*—' and with whatever other (plants) the surrounding marshy ground, and the edge itself of the lake, produce in greater abundance.'

sua . . . modus—' each island has its peculiar shape and size.'

derasus—' worn away,' so as to present a broken and uneven outline.

altitudo—sc. ' depth in the water.'

par levitas—that is, all these islands move with equal facility.

humili radice—' humilis,' as opposed to ' altus,' implies that the roots or foundations of thei slands reach only to a slight depth under water. Hence their resemblance to a ship's keel. ' Humilis ' means ' low ' in the sense of being on the surface.

6. *haec*—sc. radix.

perspicitur—' is *clearly* seen.'

eademque . . . *mersa*—' both that portion of the " radix " which is above and that which is under water.' The meaning seems to be that on whatever side you view this ' radix,' its keel-like form is distinctly perceivable.

destitutae. Either ' forsaken by the wind' (from the preceding ' ventis '), or else ' quitting their place.' The first rendering seems to be confirmed by a passage in A. II. 6, ' nubes recenti spiritu evecta, dein senescente eo (spiritu) *destituta*,' &c.

tranquillitate—' when there is a calm.'

7. *cursum certamenque.* A hendiadys, meaning, in fact, 'a race,' to which the motion of the islands, relatively to each other, is compared.

desumunt—a word implying choice and voluntary action, and consequently suitable to the context.

qua steterunt, promovent terram—that is, the place which they quit, they restore to the lake; the place which they occupy in turn, they take from it.

8. *non contrahunt.* Of course in one sense the presence of the islands contracts or diminishes the size of the lake. The meaning, however, is that when they occupy the middle of it, its circular form is not broken, and there is no apparent contraction of its dimensions.

quasi illata et imposita—' as if they had been forcibly placed on shipboard.'

descendisse . . . *ascendisse.* Both words are used in their technical sense of ' disembarking ' and ' embarking.' The floating islands are aptly compared to ships.

subduceretur—comp. E. II. 40, ' fons simul nascitur subduciturque ' (withdraws itself from view).

E. V. (viii. 8.)

2. *exprimitur*—' bursts forth.' The weight of the hill, as it were, squeezes the stream out of it, somewhat after the manner of a hydraulic engine.

eluctatus . . . *gurgitem*—' the pool which it forms after having broken loose.' ' Eluctatus ' answers to ' exprimitur,' ' gurges ' is equivalent to ' lacus,' with the notion of the water being rough and agitated with the rapidity of the stream. Both words are picturesque and somewhat poetic, and were, no doubt, carefully selected. Construe the passage as if it stood, ' gurges, quem eluctatus facit, lato gremio,' &c.

3. *iactas stipes*—' little coins thrown in.' It was usual to make such offerings to rivers. Seneca (*Quaest. Nat.* iv. 2) alludes to the custom in connexion with the Nile : ' in haec ora *stipem* sacerdotes iaciunt.'

relucentes calculos—comp. Ausonius (of a similar stream),

' lucetque latetque

Calculus, et viridem distinguit glarea muscum.'

fons . . . flumen—sc. 'It is but a spring (i.e. still close to its source), and already it is a considerable river,' &c.

obvias—'meeting the current.' The stream carries such vessels along with it (transmittit et perfert), though, as afterwards explained, it can be overcome by extreme exertion.

illa—seldom used adverbially, never by the Augustan writers. The usage occurs in Plautus, and is afterwards met with in post-Augustan writers.

4. *per iocum ludumque fluitantibus*—'those who sail about by way of amusement and sport.'

quas perspicuus . . . adnumerat—that is, the reflexion (imago) is as distinct as the actual object : the very number of the trees can be clearly distinguished ; this of course was a mark of the singular transparency of the water.

nec color cedit. 'Nor is the colour inferior to that of snow.' Such water would be described as 'limpidus' or 'liquidus.' Martial (*Epig.* vii. 31, 11) has the phrase '*niveae* undae.'

stat Clitumnus ipse. The chief deity of Umbria was known as Jupiter Clitumnus. Hence the *erect* position of the statue ; this was characteristic of Jupiter and the other celestial deities ; whereas river gods were usually represented in a reclining attitude, resting the head on the elbow.

5. *praesens numen.* The notion of 'propitious' is contained only indirectly in 'praesens,' which is in fact 'cuius vis et potestas in promptu.' 'Powerful and ever ready' represents the idea of the word.

capite discreti—sc. 'taking their rise from different sources.'

6. *navigare . . . natare.* Roman religious feeling was very sensitive on all such points. Tacitus (*Ann.* xiv. 22) tells us that Nero was believed to have been visited by the gods with a severe illness as a punishment for having bathed in the sacred waters of the 'fons Marcius.'

Hispellates. The town of Hispellum (now Spello) in Umbria was more than twelve miles distant from the temple mentioned above. It is described in inscriptions as Colonia Julia Hispelli, and Colonia Urbana Flavia, titles which connect it as a 'colonia' with both Augustus and Vespasian. It would seem in Pliny's time to have been a considerable town, as it is mentioned by several writers, and as its existing ruins are by no means contemptible.

7. *legas . . . inscripta*—'you will be able to read a number of inscriptions written by a number of persons on all the pillars and walls,' &c. Comp. Claudian, *Idyll.* vi. 5 :

> ' Et sit nulla manus cuius non pollice ductae
> Testentur memores prospera vota notae.'

See also Aristophanes, *Achar.* 144, and Küster's note on the passage.

E. VI. (iii. 6.)

1. *festivum et expressum*—'pleasing and life-like.' 'Expressus,' of a *statue*, 'exhibiting a sharp, distinct outline,' as opposed to 'adumbratus'; of *pronunciation*, 'clear,' 'articulate.'

in hac . . . sapio. Cicero speaks of his acquaintance with art in the same depreciatory terms, *Verr.* iv. 2, 3; ii. 36. Such language was considered to be in good taste, as it contrasted with the silly affectation of artistic knowledge which was fashionable in certain sets.

2. *est enim nudum.* Pliny means that it would require a *special* knowledge of the rules of art to judge of the merits of a draped, as opposed to a nude, statue. Anyone, he implies, could tell whether limbs, sinews, &c., were accurately represented.

laudes—'its merits.'

ut spirantis—comp. Virgil's expression '*spirantia* signa,' *Georg.* iii. 34, and '*spirantia* mollius aera,' *Aen.* vi. 847. The Greeks used the similar phrase, τὸ ἔμψυχον, of a good statue.

cedentes—nearly the same as 'rari.' The hair was thin and beginning to fail. Perhaps 'receding from the forehead.'

pendent lacerti. The arms, instead of exhibiting well-knit muscles, hung down loosely and feebly. Comp. Ovid, *Met.* xv. 231: 'fluidos *pendere lacertos.*'

papillae iacent. 'Iacere' conveys the contrary notion to that of fullness and vigour, and so here implies a shrunk and shrivelled state of the frame. It thus means nearly the same as the following 'recessit.'

6. *honores*—'the offices he has held.'

7. *excurrere isto*—'to make an excursion to a given neighbourhood.' 'Isto' as an adverb often occurs in Cicero's letters.

E. VII. (iv. 28.)

2. *iniungo*—a word specially used of imposing something painful or disagreeable, but also, as here, denoting the act by which a serious responsibility is intrusted to anyone.

3. *quam diligentissimum*—'as painstaking as possible.'

ex vero—from the reality: 'from the life.' Gierig, it would seem, rightly explains this by 'ex animali exemplo.'

E. VIII. (i. 12.)

1. *si iactura dicenda est.* Pliny thus corrects himself for using a word which properly denotes the loss of earthly and recoverable possessions. 'Iactura' is said to mean in its original signification the act of throwing overboard part of a ship's cargo in a storm, and it appears to have been quite exceptional to apply the word to a very grievous loss or calamity.

2. *quae non . . . fatalis.* It is by no means clear that we can here distinguish between 'mors ex natura' and 'mors fatalis.' The latter has indeed been explained to mean the death which

results from the accident of shipwreck, fire, murder, &c., and which may be just as unavoidable as death by disease. Whether it can bear this meaning seems questionable; it is at any rate certain that the phrase 'fato concedere' very often simply signifies what we call 'a natural death.' 'Mors fatalis' would thus appear to be substantially the same as 'mors ex natura,' and to differ from it only in introducing the idea of a fixed and appointed destiny.

3. *plurimas vivendi causas.* Comp. Juvenal viii. 84:

'Summum crede nefas animam praeferre pudori,
Et propter vitam vivendi perdere causas.'

pignora—applied specially to *children*, as pledges or tokens of affection. It is however used in a wider sense, and comprehends relations and intimate friends. Comp. Tacit. *Ger.* 7 (of the Germans on the field of battle) in proximo *pignora.*

4. *pretia vivendi*—sc. the various things which make life worth having, as 'conscientia,' 'fama,' &c.

8. *latroni*—sc. Domitian, one of whose special vices was rapacity.

ut iam securus . . . abrupit—'feeling that he could now die in security and freedom, he broke through those numerous but now less forcible attachments to life.'

9. *perseverantem constantia fugit*—'he escaped by a courageous resolution the persistent attacks (of the disease).'

10. *Hispulla*—Pliny's aunt.

Iulius Atticus. His *surname* pointed to his Greek attainments, for which he is praised by Martial, vii. 32, 'Attice, facundae renovas qui nomina gentis.' He was the author of a work on the cultivation of the vine, as we learn from Columella. He is probably referred to by Juvenal, xi. 1, '*Atticus* eximie coenat,' &c.

E. IX. (v. 16.)

3. *nutrices . . . paedagogos.* Both would belong to the *upper* class of slaves. The 'paedagogus' had however nothing to do with what we understand by the *education* of the child; he simply had to take care of its bodily safety and welfare. The distinction implied in the words '*paedagogus* instituit, magister docet' is not sufficiently definite.

6. *acerbum funus.* Comp. Juvenal, xi. 44 (for this use of 'acerbus'), 'non praematuri cineres nec funus *acerbum.*'

8. *altioribus studiis*—sc. such studies as history and philosophy, which imply deep research. The notion of 'altus,' as in the phrase 'altius repetere,' is carrying an inquiry about a thing up to its very first cause and origin.'

9. *pietatis est totus.* A Graecism, answering to ὅλος εἶναι τινος.

11. *clementer admotis adquiescit*—'is lulled by their gentle application.'

E. X. (viii. 23.)

1. *curas*—'business,' with special reference to Pliny's forensic duties.

avocamenta—sc. amusements, which he elsewhere speaks of as 'lusus,' 'solatia.'

4. *semper ita . . . factus*—'he always parted from you with the feeling of having been made better.'

5. *exactissimo*—sc. one so perfect himself that he would have a very high standard of duty and be very difficult to please.

cepit. Either in the sense of 'percepit' ('fully understood and appreciated him') or else equivalent to 'suum fecit,' 'sibi adjunxit' (endeared himself to him). Perhaps this latter is preferable. Comp. for this use of 'capere,' Horace, *A. P.* 362 (ut pictura . . . te *capiat.*)

comes adsectatorque — 'his friend and admirer.' 'Comes' implies the notion of inferiority, and may be defined as 'is qui officii causa maiorem comitatur.' It is thus in sharp contrast with 'commilito.'

modestia—sc. 'respectful bearing towards a superior.'

discursu—'bustling about.' Generally 'discursus' has rather an unfavourable meaning; here it denotes a praiseworthy energy. It is commonly found in post-Augustan writers, as well as the verb 'discursare.'

6. *preces.* Alluding to his canvassings for office.

quem meruit tantum—sc. which he only won by his merit, but never enjoyed.

redit animo. The obvious phrase would have been 'redit in memoriam,' for which Pliny substitutes an expression more exactly answering to the preceding 'obversantur oculis.'

7. *necessitudinum casu*—'the misfortune of his family.' 'Necessitudines' here = 'necessarii.' The word has, at least in post-Augustan writers, a comprehensive meaning.

uxor . . . acceperat—answering to Homer's κουριδίη ἄλοχος.

8. *intactum honorem*—'an honour unenjoyed.'

E. XI. (i. 22.)

1. *attonitus*—this is a very strong word, and denotes a condition of complete mental stupor.

2. *privati juris et publici*—'Ius publicum,' a citizen's rights and duties in relation to the state; 'ius privatum,' in relation to his fellow-citizens.

rerum—sc. *human* affairs. History and its kindred studies are included in 'res.'

exemplorum . . . tenet—comp. Cicero, *de Orat.* i. 5; 'tenenda est oratori omnis *antiquitas exemplorumque* vis.'

3. *quam pressa . . . cunctatio*—Melmoth renders this, 'how humble, yet how graceful his diffidence.' 'Pressa' is not, we think, equivalent to our 'humble,' nor correctly explained by

'modesta,' 'demissa,' &c. The expression 'pressus gradus' (which occurs in Livy xxviii. 14, and denotes 'a firm and measured step' gives the key to its meaning. 'Pressa cunctatio' implies the hesitation which is accompanied by the quiet and subdued manner of one who, along with his caution and reserve, is perfectly conscious of his intellectual strength. Hence, so far from there being a contrast between 'pressa' and 'decora,' the two epithets are appropriately coupled together. The 'cunctatio' of Ariston was marked by a quiet firmness and graceful dignity.

E. XII. (vii. 19.)

1. *Virgini*—sc. the chief of the Vestals.

2. *atrio Vestae.* It was in the forum between the Capitoline and Palatine hills. The 'atrium' was the dwelling-house attached to the temple of the goddess.

3. *spiritus.* The word here approaches our 'soul' or 'spirit,' as it does in Tacitus, *Ann.* xvi. 34, 'dissociatio *spiritus* corporisque.' It has, however, also the particular notion of 'courage and high spirit.'

4. *bis maritum secuta*—Helvidius had been banished by Nero, and recalled by Galba; then again banished, and finally put to death by Vespasian. Comp. Suet. *Vesp.* 15.

5. *quod de vita. . . . composuisset.* Comp. Tacitus, *Agr.* 2, where we are told that Herennius Senecio was put to death by Domitian for having eulogised Helvidius, and that his work was publicly burnt in the forum.

rogatum se—sc. that he had been asked to write the memoir of Helvidius.

Metio Caro—comp. E. XIV. 14 and E. XVI. 3.

commentarios—'notes,' the rough materials out of which the regular and elaborate history was afterwards to be composed.

6. *abolitos*—in allusion to the destruction of Senecio's book in the time of Domitian, Tacit. *Agr.* 2.

7. *quam sic. . . . leguntur.* The meaning is, we admire Fannia while she is yet alive as much as we admire those whom we have never seen but only read about.

8. *ac mihi. . . . videtur.* 'For my part I believe the house itself (the family of Fannia) is now tottering, and will shortly fall, uprooted from its foundations.'

quantis. . . . occiderit. 'For by what merits or by what actions will they attain as a result that not the last (of Roman women) has fallen in Fannia.' So in Tacitus, *Ann.* iv. 34, the expression 'ultimus Romanorum' is said to have been applied to Cassius by Cremutius Cordus.

10. *rescisso vulnere.* 'Rescindere vulnus' is the regular phrase for tearing open a wound which has been sewn up.

non feci. . . paria—sc. what I did for them was not commensurate with their deserts. Properly the phrase is used of money-accounts, and should stand as follows: Non feci paria expensa acceptis. The figure is kept up by the reference to payment in the expression 'solvendi tempora.'

E. XIII. (vi. 25.)

ordinem. Both ordo and ordines are used for the rank of a centurion. Tacitus (*Hist.* iv. 59) has the expression 'alti ordines,' meaning the command of a 'primipili centurio.' Comp. also *Hist.* i. 52, 'redditi plerisque *ordines.*

interceptus. Comp. Tacitus, *Agr.* 43, 'veneno *interceptum.*' The word 'intercipere' does not seem to have definitely acquired this meaning in the Augustan age.

E. XIV. (vii. 27.)

1. *esse phantasmata*—so most modern editors for 'esse *aliquid,*' the common reading. 'Aliquid' may very possibly have crept in from the subsequent 'aliquod.' Casaubon without sufficient reason preferred to read 'phasmata.' All the best MSS. (as Curtius points out) have 'phantasmata.' There is no difference of meaning between the two words. The Mostellaria of Plautus was founded on a play of Menander, entitled 'Phasma' (the ghost) of which word 'monstrum' or the diminutive 'mostellum' is the nearest Latin equivalent. Pliny uses 'monstrum' in this sense in the course of the letter (domus tota illi *monstro* relicta).

propriam figuram—sc. a distinctive form of their own.

numen aliquod—that is, as we might say, a real supernatural existence. Numen=a divine objective reality.

an inania, &c. In indirect questions the *second* half is usually that to which attention is specially drawn. Pliny intimates that he expects that his friend Sura will incline to the sceptical view about ghosts and apparitions.

2. *Curtio Rufo*—comp. Tacit. *Ann.* xi. 21, where there is a brief allusion to this circumstance. It is said to have happened at Hadrumetum, a city on the coast of 'Africa propria.' Whether this Curtius Rufus was the author of the life of Alexander which has come down to us, or whether he was a person glanced at by Suetonius in a book about rhetoricians, or whether the two were one and the same is a question we have no means of deciding.

tenuis . . . . haeserat—'while il a person of slight importance and little known, he had attached himself as companion to the then governor of Africa.'

humana grandior—a somewhat poetic expression and very suitable to a description of something supernatural. Tacitus, (*Ann.* xi. 21) describes the apparition thus: 'oblata ei species ultra modum humanum.' Suetonius (*Claud.* i.) says that a similar phantom presented itself to Drusus in Germany (species barbarae mulieris humana amplior) and warned him against carrying the Roman arms beyond the limit of the northern ocean.

cum summo imperio. This phrase must be distinguished from 'cum imperio,' which implies merely *military* command. It denotes the possession of supreme military and civil power in a province.

3. *implicitus morbo*—comp. an expression in E. XII. 3 (of Fannia) *discrimine implicita.* Seneca (*de Tranq.* 9) has *explicitus morbo* in the opposite sense.

5. *pestilens*—generally 'unhealthy,' as opposite to 'salubris.' Cicero (*de Off.* iii. 13) applies the word to a house. Here it has even a stronger meaning, and almost answers to 'deadly.'

idolon. The Latin equivalent 'spectrum' was not as yet a word recognised by good writers. Cicero (*ad Fam.* xv. 16) ridicules the expression.

6. *oculis inerrabat.* A Graecism rarely found except in the later writers. 'Inhaerebat' has been suggested but unnecessarily.

damnata solitudine—sc. 'condemned and passed by because of its deserted condition.'

7. *titulum.* The 'titulus' merely announced that a particular house was to be let or to be sold; it did not necessarily notify the price.

sterni sibi. The phrase usually points to arrangements for dinner or for sleeping, not, as here, for *study.*

8. *obfirmare . . . praetendere.* This is no doubt the right reading, though there is some little difficulty in the construction. Cortius compares Sallust, *Cat.* 58, timor animi auribus officit, which however does not quite explain the present passage. 'Animum auribus praetendere' must mean 'he makes his presence of mind serve as a guard or a protection to his ears,'—that is, 'he screws up his courage so as to disregard the noises.' 'Praetendere' often has the notion of 'screening a thing from danger.' Sometimes we find it in the military sense of guarding a frontier, as in Tacit. *Hist.* ii. 6, quidquid castrorum Armeniis *praetenditur*; and in Claudian, *de Bello Getico,* 416, extremis legio *praetenta* Britannis.

12. *rite conditis manibus caruit*—'was no longer haunted by the spirit now duly laid to rest.' For the phrase 'condere manes,' comp. Virg. *Aen.* iii. 67, 'animamque sepulcro *Condimus,*' and Ovid, *Fasti,* v. 451, Romulus et tumulo fraternas *condidit* umbras. According to the old Roman religious belief, the spirit of the dead person who had been duly interred rested in the tomb; hence the appropriateness of the expression 'condere manes,' &c. Comp. Hor. I. *C.* i. 28 (the prayer of the unburied Archytas).

13. *priori fidem dedit*—'gave credit to the previous occurrence.'

14. *Caro.* Carus Metius, one of the worst 'delatores' of Domitian's time. He is mentioned in E. XII. and XVI., and by Tacitus, *Agr.* 45.

submittere capillum. Letting the hair grow long was a chief feature of the 'squalor' which persons in affliction assumed.

E. XV. (iii. 1.)

2. *vita disposita*—sc. a well-ordered and arranged life, in which every thing is done in the right time and the right place. In A. XI. 17 we have 'dispositus' applied to a speaker who arranges his topics skilfully. Cicero (*de Off.* i. 40) defines the virtue here praised by Pliny as 'scientia earum rerum quae agentur aut dicentur, loco suo collocandarum. Εὐταξία is the Greek equivalent.

3. *industria. . . . ambitio.* 'Industria' to a Roman meant the activity of a lawyer or politician; it was concerned exclusively with *public* life. Ambitio (in which there was always a shade of unfavourable meaning) here denotes 'a restless pursuit of office,' which would be peculiarly unbecoming in an old man.

parva. . . . circumagit—'these trifling matters, trifling, that is to say, if they are not done every day, he repeats in a certain order and in a kind of cycle.' The meaning is, that repetition of the easiest and most trifling things day after day demands a degree of thought and vigilance which raises them into dignity and importance.

4. *honestissimi sermones explicantur.* 'Explicare' suggests something intricate and complex; consequently the 'sermones' in question were, it may be presumed, of an intellectual character.

7. *praecipere*—sc. 'to be laying down the law.'

scribit. . . . doctissima. Four odes under the name of Vestricius Spurinna, which Barth in 1613 said he found in a MS. at Merseburg and had printed, have come down to us, but they are probably not genuine, though possibly they may be early fabrications based to some extent on existing fragments of Spurinna's poetry. At any rate, they by no means justify the description which Pliny here gives of Spurinna's merits as a poet.

8. *in sole. . . . nudus.* This was supposed to be a particularly healthy exercise. A Roman usually anointed himself by way of preparation for it; hence the singular expression 'unctus sol' (Cic. *ad Att.* xii. 6).

pugnat cum senectute. Comp. Cic. *de Senect.* 11, pugnandum tanquam contra morbum sic contra senectutem.

9. *argento puro et antiquo.* 'Argentum purum' also termed leve (smooth) Juv. xiv. 62, and 'grave' (Seneca, *de Tranq.* 1) in allusion to its solidity as contrasted with mere beauty, was plate without any embossed work or bas-relief figures. Plate so ornamented was described as caelatum, asperum, &c. The epithet 'antiquum' is best explained by the passage of Seneca above referred to; argentum grave, *rustici patris*, &c.

afficitur. The word denotes any sort of mental agitation. Spurinna was a contrast to the man pointed at by Horace, *Sat.* i. 4, 28, hunc capit argenti splendor, &c.

et aestate—'even in summer.' 'Et' for 'etiam' is post-Augustan.

11. *solaque ex senectute prudentia*—that is, he has got experience from old age without any of its accompanying discomforts.

receptui canere—'to sound a retreat,' sc. withdraw from my public occupation.

obiit officia Alluding specially to Spurinna's *forensic* labours.

12. *idque. . . . subsigno*—sc. to this I pledge myself with you, &c. 'Subsignare' and 'subscribere' both signify in later writers 'to give a solemn assurance.'

in ius voces. Pliny playfully says that his friend must call him to account, and bring an action grounded on an appeal to this very letter in the event of his transgressing the limit which he here prescribes for himself.

E. XVI. (i. 5.)

2. *Rustici Aruleni periculum*—comp. Tacit. *Agr.* 2, where we are told that he was put to death by Domitian for having written a laudatory memoir of Paetus Thrasea. See also Tacit. *Ann.* xvi. 26 (where he is spoken of as a youth of high spirit), and *Hist.* iii. 80 (referred to in the following note).

3. *Vitelliana cicatrice stigmosum.* From Tacit. *Hist.* iii. 80 it appears that in the war between Vitellius and Vespasian, Arulenus, who was a Vitellianist, was wounded. He with other envoys from the senate was endeavouring to arrange terms of peace, but his sacred character as ambassador did not save him from violence at the hands of the enemy's soldiery. The 'Vitelliana cicatrix' alludes to the wound received by him on this occasion, and the word 'stigmosus' (applied by him to Regulus) suggests that the scar, so far from being an honourable one, was a mark of disgrace, like the brand (stigma) on a runaway slave. 'Stigmosus' is an incorrectly formed word, having a Greek root and a Latin termination, and Regulus showed ignorance in using it.

meis mortuis—'my dead men,' sc. the men who owed their death to my informations. There is a studied brutality about the expression.

Crasso. Crassus was a brother of Piso, whom Galba adopted, and had been put to death by Nero. See Tacit. *Hist.* i. 48.

Camerino. Sulpicius Camerinus (see Tacit. *Ann.* xiii. 52) was accused under Nero of extortions committed during his proconsulate of Africa. He was acquitted. Both he and his son, as it appears from Dion, were afterwards put to death on a frivolous charge, of which we may infer from this passage Regulus was the author.

4. *quam capitaliter*—'with what deadly purpose.' 'Capitaliter' in a way to affect the life (caput). The adverb is rarely used.

5. *aderam Arrionillae*—'I was counsel to Arionilla.' A well-known use of 'adesse,' common in the best writers.

nitebamur. . . . Modesti—'in one branch of our case we relied on the opinion of Metius Modestus.' Of Modestus we know nothing but from this passage, from which it may be inferred that he was an eminent 'jurisconsult.'

ecce tibi Regulus. Rather a colloquial use of the pronoun, as we might say, 'Here is a pretty fellow for you.'

6. *de pietate*—'concerning the loyalty of Modestus.' 'Pietas' might well have this meaning in the time of the empire. So 'impietas' denoted an offence against the person of the emperor. See A. V. 7, and note on passage.

7. *pronunciatum est*—'Pronuntiare' in its legal sense is 'to pronounce a verdict.'

8. *conscientia exterritus*—comp. for a like use of 'conscientia' Tacit. *Agr.* 2 and 39. The word is almost equivalent to our 'conscience' in the later writers.

Caecilium Celerem. Probably from his name a kinsman of Pliny.

9. *Spurinna.* Vestricius Spurinna, the subject of the preceding letter.

10. *Mauricum*—the brother of Arulenus Rusticus. See A. VII., Tacit. *Hist.* iv. 40, *Agr.* 45.

11. *in praetoris officio*—'Officium' here has been taken to mean 'the praetor's court,' a meaning which it may possibly have acquired in post-Augustan writers, and which is certainly supported by the analogy of 'iudicium,' which denoted both the 'bench of judges' and 'the court in which they sat.' Of this however we have no other instance, and it is perhaps better to take the expression as signifying 'a ceremonial visit' paid by Pliny to a newly elected praetor. This is a well-known and familiar sense of 'officium.'

Satrius Rufus. See A. VI. 17, where he is mentioned as one of the senators who took part in the proceedings against Publicius Certus. He would seem to have been an advocate.

eloquentia saeculi nostri. Comp. Seneca's complaint (*Ep.* 40), Romana eloquentia a Nerone exsiluerat.

15. *nequissimus.* The special notion of 'nequam' seems to be that particular sort of wickedness which is connected with roguery and which hates honest industry. The word was thus peculiarly applicable to a man who had grown rich as a 'delator.' Cicero (*pro Fonteio*, 13) contrasts it with 'frugi.'

15. *curatur a multis*—sc. 'his interests are anxiously considered by many'; that is, those who possibly might be involved in his ruin.

16. *mihi. . . . constabit.* The meaning is, 'I shall have with the aid of his advice a settled principle to guide me in taking action or in remaining quiet.' 'Mihi constat' here, as elsewhere, is nearly equivalent to 'mihi certum est.' 'Ratio constat' is rather a favourite phrase with Pliny (comp. E. XXI. 1). It may be sometimes explained as a metaphor borrowed from money accounts, the primary meaning of 'ratio' being a 'reckoning, a calculation.' Here it is hardly necessary to give this meaning to the word, which stands simply for 'plan,' 'system,' &c.

E. XVII. (ii. 20.)

1. *assem para*, &c. Pliny, by way of a joke, compares himself to persons who picked up a little money by telling amusing stories, and who were known as 'circulatores,' a word which soon came to mean much the same as our 'quack.'

auream—'fine, beautiful, first-rate,' &c., a meaning which 'aureus' often has in the poets, and in the later prose writers.

2. *Verania Pisonis*—'Verania, Piso's wife.' A common formula, to be explained as an ordinary possessive. Verania is mentioned by Tacitus (*Hist.* i. 47). She purchased the head of her murdered husband from his assassins. Galba's adoption of Piso is related by Tacitus (*Hist.* i. 14-16).

3. *esto, si venit tantum*—that is, 'granted that he was an impudent fellow if he only paid her a visit.'

agitat digitos—sc. he counts on his fingers.

4. *climactericum tempus*—'a critical period.' 'Climactericus, from κλῖμαξ, κλιμακτήρ, 'the step of a ladder'; hence associated with the notion of danger.

6. *qui . . . peierâsset*. This is explained by the context. It was not unusual to pray that the evil effects of a perjury might fall upon a son, as the dearest object. Regulus's guilt was all the more atrocious, both because he was knowingly perjuring himself, and because he invoked the consequences of his perjury not on himself but on his son.

7. *Velleius Blaesus*. Blaesus was a well-known name under the empire. The one here referred to does not appear elsewhere. Very possibly he was the son of the Junius Blaesus, the governor of Gallia Lugdunensis under Vitellius, the circumstances of whose death are described in detail by Tacitus, *Hist.* ii. 38, 39.

8. *vertit allocutionem*—'reverses his exhortations.'

9. *scholastica lege*—'according to the rule which obtains in rhetoric.' Three was regarded as a complete and perfect number. Hence the Greek 'trilogy.'

10. *ornata*. An epithet denoting a combination of high moral and intellectual qualities. Its full meaning is, 'excellent and accomplished.'

12. ἀλλά -ι ἐιαττίνομαι. ('Why do I distress myself by giving vent to my indignation?' or 'why do I continue to dwell on these matters?')

13. *exta duplicia*. Pliny the Elder (xi. 37, 73) speaks of a similar phenomenon as having presented itself to Augustus when, on the first day of his imperial power, he was sacrificing at Spoletum. It was told him, on the same occasion, that he would *double* the empire.

14. *genus falsi*. 'Falsum' specially denoted the crime of tampering in any way with a person's will. It was a very common offence at Rome, and was the subject of a lex Cornelia, one of Sulla's 'leges.' Regulus was not actually guilty of the *legal*

S

crime, though, as Pliny implies, in using an improper influence over people making their wills, he was guilty of something far worse.

E. XVIII. (iv. 2.)

1. *hoc uno malo indignus.* This is said sarcastically. To such a man as Regulus the death of his son, under the circumstances here explained, was a piece of good fortune of which, Pliny says, he was unworthy. The bitter tone of the letter does not allow these words to be taken as an expression of pity.

2. *emancipavit.* The legal process 'emancipatio,' by extinguishing the 'patria potestas,' gave the son the full rights of a Roman citizen. Only in this manner could he legally inherit and acquire property.

mancipatum. This word (for which we might have expected 'emancipatum') implies that the boy, though legally released from his father's power, was really as much as ever under his control through the corrupting influences brought to bear upon him. Consequently, people who knew the character of Regulus spoke jestingly of the lad as 'mancipatum,' i.e. 'handed over to his father,' meaning that the 'emancipatio' was a farce.

3. *mannulos.* These were little Gaulish horses remarkable for swiftness. They were often used by Romans of rank when they rode from Rome into the country, and by ladies and youths for pleasure. Comp. Horace, *C.* iii. 27, 7; *Epod.* iv. 14; *Epp.* i. 7, 77.

omnes . . . . trucidavit. By this absurd piece of affectation Regulus sought to imitate the funeral customs of the heroic age. See Homer's description of the funeral of Patroclus (*Il.* xxiii. 166), where we find various animals slaughtered over the hero's tomb.

5. *statuis suis*—'statues of himself.'

6. *vexat . . . . tempore.* The time referred to as 'insaluberrimum' would be the period of the excessive heats of summer or autumn. Regulus showed his want of consideration for his friends by obliging them to pay visits of condolence on him at Rome during this unhealthy season, and Pliny adds that he took a pleasure in so doing.

7. *immaturum*—sc. too soon after his son's death.

E. XIX. (iv. 7.)

1. *vim*—'energy, enterprise.'

quam efficiat. This use of 'quam' (which is commonly joined with adjectives) is rare in Cicero and the best writers.

2. *auditorio.* Rarely used, as here, of 'the audience.' The Greek 'acroasis' is used by Cicero (*Epp. ad Att.* xv. 17) for 'a learned audience.'

scripsit publice—sc. he wrote letters addressed to the various states and 'municipia.'

3. ἀμαθία .... φίρυ. From Pericles' funeral oration, Thucyd. ii. 40.

4. *os confusum*. This is not to be understood of Regulus' countenance, which he was no doubt perfectly able to command, but of his articulation, which, it would seem, was defective and indistinct. In *Ep.* vi. 11 Pliny uses the phrase 'os planum' with precisely an opposite meaning.

inventio. This was a technical term in rhetoric, and is defined by Cicero (*Tusc.* i. 25) as the vis (faculty) quae investigat occulta, and by the Auctor ad Herennium (i. 2) as the excogitatio rerum verarum aut verisimilium quae causam probabilem reddant. It was clearly essential to success as an advocate.

5. *Catonis illud.* Cato's definition of an orator is quoted by Quintilian (xii. 12, 1), Vir bonus, dicendo peritus.

6. *Demosthenes*, &c. The passage here referred to is in the Speech for the Crown. Aeschines is reproached for announcing a public calamity in a loud and jubilant tone, and Pliny here suggests that very possibly Regulus' book about his son may have been read out in a similar manner.

E. XX. (i. 3.)

1. *meae deliciae.* It must be remembered that Pliny had several villas on the lake of Como.

platanon. Platanetum is the proper Latin equivalent of the Greek πλατανών. Martial (iii. 19, 2) has the Greek form of the word. Pliny is rather fond of introducing Greek words and forms in describing villas, gardens, &c.

Euripus .... gemmeus. By Euripus, properly the narrowest part of the strait which separates the island Euboea from the mainland, is here meant 'a canal' or 'aqueduct' connected with the lake. The word seems to have been thus used by certain writers in Cicero's time, though he rather sneers at it (*De Leg.* ii. 1), ductus aquarum quos isti Nilos et Euripos vocant, &c.). The epithets 'viridis,' 'gemmeus,' refer to the banks. 'Gemmeus' (bright with flowers) is applied to 'prata' (E. II. 11). In this sense it is a rather poetic word.

subiectus et serviens lacus — 'subiectus.' 'close at hand'; serviens, 'receiving the waters of the canal, and so acting as a servant to it.' Comp. the expression 'piscina fenestris servit' (E. II. 15), 'the pool is serviceable to, gives a pleasant prospect to, the windows.'

mollis .... gestatio. 'Mollis' suggests that the 'gestatio' was a walk or promenade on turf.

plurimus sol—that is, 'as much sun as the room could possibly get.' This would be the most approved kind of bath-room, receiving, as Seneca (*Ep.* ii. 88) says, totius diei solem amplissimis fenestris. Comp. also E. I. 8, cubiculum quod ambitum solis omnibus fenestris sequitur.

2. *intentione rei familiaris obeundae*—'by close application to the management of his property.' ' Intentio' is almost equivalent to 'intentus animus.' It is implied that Caninius looked after his estates himself, and dispensed as much as possible with the employment of bailiffs.

3. *unus ex multis*—'you are only an ordinary mortal.' The Greeks had a proverb, οὗτος ἐστὶν ἐν πολλοῖς.

pingui secessu—' snug, comfortable retirement.' For this use of ' pinguis' comp. *pinguis* vita (*Ep.* vii. 26) and *pingue* otium (*Ep.* ix. 3). It would seem to be a post-Augustan use of the word.

reponatur—' be reserved.'

4. *effinge . . . et excude.* ' Excudere' denotes a higher form of art than ' effingere,' the notion of which is simply moulding a piece of wax or clay into a particular shape. Hence it appropriately follows the less forcible word.

nam reliqua . . . sortientur. A similar sentiment occurs in Horace, *Epp.* ii. 2, 171–174.

E. XXI. (i. 9.)

1. *quam singulis . . . constet.* ' Ratio constat' is a phrase *properly* used of money accounts, the full expression being ' ratio accepti et expensi constat' (' the accounts balance'). Pliny here means, that if he reckons up *each* day what he has done, he finds, so to speak, his accounts correct, and that he has reason to be satisfied with his performances, but that, if he looks back upon many days taken collectively (pluribus cunctisque), he observes that there is, as it were, an error in his accounts—that is, he might in that period of time have accomplished more satisfactory results than are actually forthcoming. See E. XVI. 16, mihi . . . . *ratio constabit,* and note.

2. *officio togae virilis*—sc. all the ceremonies connected with the assumption of the ' toga virilis,' for which the Roman youth exchanged the 'toga praetexta' in his fifteenth or sixteenth year. The day was termed ' dies tirocinii,' and was a great occasion, on which friends paid congratulatory visits and brought presents, &c.

advocationem. ' Advocatio' denotes both the professional services of a counsel and the attendance of influential friends, whose presence might be supposed to impress the ' iudices' in favour of the plaintiff or defendant. *Here* probably it has the latter meaning. Comp. Livy, iii. 47, ' Virginius filiam cum ingenti *advocatione* in forum deducit.'

3. *frigidis rebus*—frigidus here = inanis. Comp. the Greek ψυχρός.

8. *satius est . . . agere*—' it is better to have nothing to do than to be doing nothing.' Scipio the Elder (as appears from Cicero, *de O.* iii. 1) used to say, ' se nunquam minus otiosum esse quam cum otiosus sit.' By ' otium ' a Roman meant not absolute idle-

ness, but freedom from public business. Hence the word was often applied to literary pursuits. See D. VIII. 1 (inertia mea), and note.

E. XXII. (i. 15.)

1. *dicetur ius*—sc. 'my legal demand on you shall be as follows,' &c.

2. *lactucae singulae*—'a lettuce for each guest.' It was supposed to stimulate the appetite, and so was a suitable beginning.

olivae—these were eaten both at the beginning and the end of the repast.

3. *Gaditanas*—'dancing girls from Gades in Spain.' These are contrasted with 'comoedi,' 'lector,' &c. 'Gaditana' also denoted songs of a loose and voluptuous character. See Juv. xi. 162.

4. *nisi postea . . . excusareris*—that is, 'if ever afterwards you will not by *preference* decline the invitations of others, always decline mine.'

E. XXIII. (ii. 6.)

1. *diligentem.* 'Diligens,' properly 'one who gathers up,' opposed to 'negligens'; hence 'frugal,' 'economical.' 'Diligentia' is defined by Auctor ad Herennium (iv. 25) as 'accurata conservatio suorum'; hence it was the special virtue of the head of a household.

3. *ad coenam non ad notam invito.* The antithesis between 'coena' and 'nota' is more pointed if we suppose Pliny is dwelling on the derivation of coena from κοινός. 'Nota' denotes something which distinguishes, separates, &c.; possibly there is an allusion to the 'nota censoria.' 'I ask my friends to a dinner in which they are all on the same footing, not one in which distinctions are drawn,' is Pliny's meaning, though its expression is rather strained and artificial.

5. *illa*—sc. gula.

in ordinem redigenda. The phrase 'redigere, cogere in ordinem' implies restraint and even some sort of degradation. It was *strictly* used of bringing a man who held public office down to the level of a 'privatus.'

6. *aliena contumelia*—sc. treating others with contempt by making a distinction (nota) between your guests.

E. XXIV. (iii. 12.)

1. *expedita*—'free and easy.'

2. *officia antelucana*—'officia' here seems to mean 'visits of ceremony' or possibly 'the persons paying such visits.' Comp. the expression 'in praetoris officio' (E. XVI. 11), and see note. Such visits were generally made by the Romans in the early morning.

C. Caesar . . . laudet. This was probably in his work termed Anti-Cato, written in reply to Cicero's eulogy of Cato.

3. *potuitne . . . erat*—comp. Seneca *de Tranq.* 15, who alludes to this weakness of Cato : 'Facilius efficiet quisquis obiecerit, hoc crimen honestum quam Catonem turpem.'

E. XXV. (viii. 22.)

2. *lenitas*—sc. the temper of mind which makes allowance for others' faults. Comp. Horace, *Sat.* i. 3, 43, &c., where we have a good definition of 'lenitas.'

emendatissimum—' most faultless.'

3. *qui vitia . . . odit.* Comp. a somewhat similar sentiment in Seneca (*de Tranq.* 15): in hoc quoque flectendi sumus ut omnia vulgi vitia non invisa nobis sed ridicula videantur et Democritum potius imitemur quam Heraclitum, &c.

quaeris . . . scribam—'perhaps you ask who has provoked me to write in this strain.'

4. *qualiscunque*—a contemptuous word.

quem insignire . . . refert—'to expose whom is no good as an example, while to spare him is exceedingly good in the interests of leniency.' Pliny means that the man is so contemptible that the exposure of his fault would go for nothing in the way of example. Observe that this construction of 'refert' with the genitive, except in such a phrase as 'magni refert,' is post-Augustan.

E. XXVI. (ix. 6.)

1. *Circenses*—called also ludi Romani, magni. See Livy, i. 35. At this time the chariot race seems to have been their most conspicuous feature.

2. *traherentur.* 'Trahi,' as denoting a passionate interest in anything, is a stronger word than 'duci,' 'teneri,' &c.

panno. Pliny no doubt intentionally uses a word of disparagement. The allusion of course is to the different colours by which the factions of the circus were distinguished.

studium favorque—'enthusiasm and popularity.'

gratia—' attractiveness.'

3. *mitto apud vulgus*—'I say nothing of its having influence with the common people,' &c.

frigida—' tame,' 'uninteresting.' Comp. E. XXI. 3, quot dies quam *frigidis* rebus absumsi.

E. XXVII. (ix. 33.)

1. *laetissimo*—'laetus' of a *tree* means 'fruitful,' 'luxuriant'; hence applied to 'ingenium' it suggests the notion of richness, variety, &c., and so would come very close to our phrase 'an exuberant imagination.'

poetico. See E. XVIII., where Pliny dwells on the poetical skill of his friend Caninius.

super coenam—'over the dinner table.'

magna auctoris fides. It is somewhat singular that Pliny does not quote the authority of his uncle, who (*N.H.* ix. 8, 8) mentions similar phenomena.

quid poetae cum fide?—'what have poets to do with credibility?'

2. *stagnum.* A word used indifferently of both salt and fresh water. Virg. *Aen.* i. 126, imis *stagna* refusa vadis. The pool in question could have been navigable only at high water.

aestuarium. Livy (x. 2) explains the precise meaning of this word by the periphrasis 'stagna irrigua aestibus maritimis.' In this case the creek or estuary opened out into the above-mentioned pool.

prout aestus, &c.—that is, ' at low or high tide.'

3. *his gloria et virtus*—' with these (the boys) it is a fine and manly achievement,' &c. A somewhat poetic form of expression.

ulteriora—sc. 'further seawards than the others.'

4. *subire*—'takes him on his back.'

5. *obsident litus*—'they throng the shore.'

si quid est mari simile. Referring to the estuary and the pool.

variosque . . . expeditque—that is, the dolphin perpetually makes a series of circular movements and retraces those movements. The word 'implicitat' (frequentative of 'implico,' found only in this passage) conveys the notion of the intricacy of the creature's movements, which from their peculiarity bear a certain resemblance to the process of twining and untwining. In Virgil's well-known description of the equestrian show with its complicated manœuvres we meet with the expression alternos orbibus orbes Impediunt (*Aen.* v. 584), of which what we have here, though not the same in meaning, reminds us.

9. *educto*—sc. delphino.

superfudisse unguentum—this was apparently done with a view of averting any possible evil consequences which such a prodigy might be supposed to portend. It would in fact be a part of the process denoted by the term 'procuratio.'

10. *mora*—'prolonged stay.'

modica respublica—sc. 'a state with rather a small revenue.'

secretum. Often used as a noun by the writers of the silver age to denote anything either entirely hidden or partially withdrawn from view.

E. XXVIII. (viii. 17.)

1. *istic*—'in your neighbourhood.'

2. *demissioribus ripis*—sc. the left bank of the Tiber, on which Rome was situated. Comp. Horace's description of the inundation of the Tiber (*C.* i. 2, 13–16), in which, in accordance with the popular notion, he represents the river as violently driven back

from its Etruscan shore, and consequently overflowing its left or lower bank.

quae solet flumina accipere. Referring to such streams as the Tinnia, Clanis, Nar, and Anio.

devehere—' to carry down to the sea.'

relut obvius sistere coyit—' as it were, meeting (these streams), it compels them to halt in their course.' Under ordinary circumstances the streams in question flowed into and met the Tiber; *now* this was reversed, and the Tiber, so to speak, advanced to meet them. The effect, as here explained, was to drive back these streams on lands which the Tiber itself could not reach.

3. *delicatissimus amnium*—' most delightful of rivers.' 'Delicatus' suggests the idea of rich and beautiful rather than grand scenery. It points to what would be congenial to highly luxurious tastes. Comp. for this use of the word, Phaedus, iv. 4, 26, domum politam et *delicatos* hortulos. So too Curtius (v. 2, 9) uses the expression, ' delicatam aquam ' of the river Choaspes.

relut invitatus retentusque. Here we have a sort of poetical hypallage. The country houses on its banks are said by a very natural figure of speech to attract and detain the stream. Its sudden and destructive fury is thus brought into stronger contrast with its usual gentleness.

4. *eiecit atque extulit.* Of the Nile Lucan says (vi. 471), Nilum non *extulit* aestas. ' Eiecit ' points to the *sudden* violence of the inundation ; ' extulit ' to its continuance for a considerable time.

gravem supellectilem—sc. all the more valuable articles of furniture. Comp. the phrase ' *grave* pretium.'

rectores. Here = aratores.

5. *opera . . . cinguntur*—sc. hedges, fences, enclosures, &c., such as would be required on valuable farms.

monimenta—' public buildings.' Comp. Horace, *C.* i. 2, 15 : ire deiectum *monimenta* regum, &c.

debilitati—' maimed.' 'Debilis,' ' debilitatus,' mean one who has a broken or paralysed limb.

aucta luctibus damna—sc. to losses of property has been added the mourning consequent on deaths.

pro mensura periculi—' on a scale commensurate with the danger.' If (Pliny means to say) we have had such disastrous floods in the neighbourhood of Rome, how have you, Macrinus, fared, living, as you do, in a part still more exposed to such perils ? Macrinus, it appears, had estates in the neighbourhood of the lake of Como.

E. XXIX. (x. 4.)

1. *indulgentia.* The word usually has an *unfavourable* sense, and denotes the culpable weakness which cannot refuse a request. Under the emperors it seems to have become a regular complimentary expression, answering to our ' grace,' ' bounty,' &c.

2. *amplissimum ordinem.* A phrase restricted to the rank of senator. ' Amplus ' and its derivatives had special reference to

the highest officers of the state. Voconius, it must be remembered, had hitherto been simply an 'eques.'

quadringenties—about 340,000*l.*, a sum enormously in excess of the amount at which Augustus, according to Suetonius (*Aug.* 41), fixed the minimum of the property required for admission into the senate. (This is set down at duodecies sestertii, about 5,000*l.*) If therefore we have the right reading (which critics have questioned), we must suppose that there had been a prodigious increase of private wealth during the empire, and that, as a natural consequence, it had become necessary for a senator to be immensely rich. 'Quadringenties' is the reading of all the best MSS.

3. *nondum satis legitime*—sc. without having as yet completed all the necessary legal forms.

fundos emancipavit—'she made over certain estates to her son.' She surrendered by the legal process of 'mancipatio' all her proprietary rights in these estates in favour of Voconius. See note on word, E. XVIII. 2.

4. *subsigno . . . . fidem*—sc. 'I vouch for,' &c. ' Fidem interponere ' was the more usual phrase. 'Subsignare' seems to have been a more solemn and technical expression, and would have nearly answered to our formula, 'I deliver this as my act and deed.'

statim. From this it would appear that there was something exceptional in the disposition of Voconius' father's property. Roman law gave the son his full inheritance immediately upon the father's death, the widow having no claim to a life-interest in it.

5. *quibus singulis . . . credo.* Pliny's meaning is that the distinction which he wishes the emperor to bestow on Voconius will be universally approved, and so will enhance the lustre derived from his birth and from his splendid inheritance. Ex meis precibus—sc. from my request being granted.

iudiciis tuis—sc. your choice of persons for promotion.

E. XXX. (x. 39.)

1. *plus.* For this, which can hardly be the right reading, though found in all the MSS., Döring suggests 'prius.' Pliny's meaning would seem to be that the accounts had not previously been thoroughly examined, and that he could only speak of the matter from hearsay. The only possible explanation of 'plus' is that the accounts have not been examined further than simply to show that more than 1,000,000 sesterces had been expended.

2. *descendit.* ' Discedit ' has been suggested as a more appropriate word. But ' descendit ' may fairly be retained, indicating, as it does, the sinking of the soil.

fulturae—' buttresses,' as contrasted with underground supports (substructiones).

quibus subinde suscipitur—' by means of which it is from time to

time kept up. 'Suscipere' is 'to catch up something falling';
hence it is here a well-chosen word.

3. *basilicae*—sc. spacious corridors with lofty marble columns.
These were a usual adjunct of the Roman theatre in the time of
the empire.

4. *cessante . . . est*—'from the stoppage of the work which must
first be completed.'

numerosius—'on a more extensive scale,' sc. with more rooms
and more places for exercise. 'Numerus' sometimes means 'a
part' or 'section' of anything; so, with reference to the army, it
occasionally stands for 'cohortes' in Tacitus, Suetonius, &c. This
seems to be the key to the right explanation of this passage.

incompositum . . . est—'it is an ill-arranged and scattered building.' 'Sparsum' implies want of compactness and the inconve-
nience consequent on it.

sane aemulus, &c. This is a sneer at the architect, whose opinion,
it is suggested, was not quite to be depended on. 'Sane' often
introduces a sarcastic insinuation.

caemento—'coarse rubble.' If we have the right reading, this
must be the meaning of 'caementum,' which ordinarily denotes 'a
large unhewn block of stone from the quarry' (as in Hor. C. iii. 1,
34, *caementa* demittit redempta) such as would serve for the
foundation of a building. Walls filled in with rubble would require a covering of tiles (testaceum opus) as a protection from
wet, &c.

5. *buleutae*—'the members of the town council,' elsewhere
called 'decuriones.' Persons specially chosen by the emperor into
this body had usually to pay a fixed sum into the imperial trea-
sury. The words 'additi beneficio tuo' suggest that in the present
case this payment was remitted. Buleutae for decuriones is naturally used in the case of a Greek town.

ob introitum—'for their admission into the council.'

6. *illic*—sc. in the case of the theatre.

munus tuum—that is, 'your bounty to the "buleutae,"' as explained above, which had enabled the bath to be constructed.

E. XXXI. (x. 40.)

1. *in re praesenti*—'on the spot.'

a privatis exigi opera—sc. that contracts for works be entered
into with private persons.

2. *Graeculi*. Even under the empire, with its relaxed morality
and luxurious tone, the Romans continued to apply this contemptuous designation to the people to whom they owed what taste
for art and culture they possessed. The gymnasium, to which
Trajan says the Greeks were so passionately addicted, had dege-
nerated from its original purpose of promoting strength and en-
durance, and was now chiefly devoted to useless feats of mere
agility and sports practised for the mere sake of pleasure.

3. *circa balineum*—'with regard to the bath.' A post-Augustan use of 'circa.'

E. XXXII. (x. 71.)

1. θρεπτούς. The meaning of this term is explained in Trajan's reply. From another point of view, such children were called ἐκθέ-οι, which word has been substituted in this passage for θρεπτούς, but without sufficient authority. Parents throughout the entire ancient world had the right to expose their children and leave them to their fate. Hence would sometimes arise the question whether such a child, if found and brought up by another, was entitled to his freedom, whether also the person thus adopting him must grant him his freedom without repayment for the cost of maintenance. The first was a question 'de conditione,' the second 'de alimentis.' θρεπτός might stand for a slave born and brought up in the master's house, answering to the Latin 'verna.'

2. *nihil . . . ferretur*—'nothing either special or general which might be applied as a precedent to the Bithynians.'

exemplo—sc. the precedent established by former emperors. Gierig understands by 'exemplum' actual copies of the imperial edicts, which had become much corrupted in the process of distribution through the provinces. Pliny, however, merely means that in cases requiring, as he thought, Trajan's decision, he must not depend on general precedent, which might indeed, as he goes on to say, be gathered from doubtful and unrevised documents.

3. *non certae fidei*—'of doubtful authenticity.'

scriniis—sc. the imperial archives, in which the original documents of all decrees and edicts which had been issued were deposited.

E. XXXIII. (x. 72.)

1. *expositi*. Like ἐκτιθέναι, exponere was the regular word for the exposure of a child.

sublati. Tollere filium was 'to acknowledge a child, and to indicate one's intention of bringing it up.'

2. *adsertionem*. Adserere, like 'vindicare,' has a twofold meaning. It may mean 'to claim a thing for oneself' or 'to prefer a just claim as against a wrongful one.' Hence, of a person, it is either 'to bring him into slavery,' or 'to rescue him from it.' Here obviously it has the latter meaning.

pretio alimentorum. This decision of Trajan, the effect of which would be that persons would be slow to adopt an abandoned child which, when brought up, its unnatural parents could claim back without any compensation for its nurture, seems harsh, and we find that it was disregarded by the later emperors in their legal decisions on the subject.

INDEX NOMINUM.

ACHILLES, E. ii. 43
Acutius Nerva, A. xii. 2
Aeneas, E. ii. 43
Aeschines, B. xiv. 10
Afer, Domitius, C. i. 10, 12
Albinus, A. ix.
Albinus, Lucceius, A. xiii. 7 ; A. xiv. 13
Ammius Flaccus, A. vi. 13
Annius Severus, E. vi.
Auteia, A. vi. 4 seq.
Apollinaris, Domitius, E. ii. ; A. vi. 13
Aratus, E. ii. 43
Aristo, Titus, E. xi. 1
Ariston, Claudius, C. v. 3
Armenius Brocchus, E. xxxii. 3
Arria, B. xx. 3 ; A. i. 2 seq. ; A. vi. 3 seq.
Arrianus, B. i. ; A. xi. ; A. xii. ; B. xxiv. ; C. iii.
Arrianus Maturus, D. i.
Arrionilla, E. xvi. 5
Artemidorus, B. xx. 1
Arulenus Rusticus, E. xvi. 2, 5
Asudius Curianus, D. xii. 1
Athenodorus, E. xiv. 7
Atticus, Iulius, E. viii. 10
Attilius Crescens, C. i. 2
Attilius Scaurus, E. xiii.
Attius Clemens, B. xxi. ; E. xviii.
Aufidius Bassus, B. xi. 6
Augustus, E. v. 6
Aurelia, E. xvii. 10, 11
Avidius Nigrinus, E. xxxii. 3
Avidius Quietus, C. iv. 1 ; A. vi. 15
Avitus, E. xxiii.
Avitus, Iunius, E. x. 1
Avitus, Octavius, E. xxvii. 9

BAEBIUS MACER, B. xi. ; A. xiv. 16
Baebius Massa, A. v. 4 ; C. iv. 8
Baebius Probus, A. xiii. 12
Bassus, Aufidius, B. xi. 6
Bassus, Iulius, A. xiv. 1 ; C. iv. 10
Blaesus, Velleius, E. xvii. 7, 8
Brocchus, Armenius : v. Armenius

CAECILIUS CELER, E. xvi. 8
Caecilius Classicus, C. iv. 8
Caecina Paetus, A. i. 3
Caepio Hispo, A. xiv. 16
Caesar, C. Iulius, E. xxiv. 2
Calestrius Tiro, E. viii.
Calpurnia, D. iv. ; v. ; vi. ; vii.
Calvisius, E. viii. 12 ; xv ; xvii. ; xxvi.
Calvus, C., B. i. 2 ; xix. 5
Camerinus, E. xvi. 3
Caninius, Rufus, B. xii. ; xvi. ; xviii. ; D. iii. ; E. xxvii.
Capito, Titinius, B. iii. ; xxv. 1
Carus, Metius, E. xii. 5 ; xiv. 14 ; xvi. 3
Catilius Severus, E. xi. ; xxiv.
Catius Fronto, A. xi. 2
Catius Lepidus, E. xix.
Catius, Titus, E. vii. 1
Cato, B. xiii. 5 ; E. xix. 5 ; xxiv. 3
Catullus, B. xix. 5
Catullus Messalinus, A. vii. 5
Celer, A. iv. 10
Celer, Caecilius : v. Caecilius
Cerialis, Tuccius, A. xi. 9
Cicero, M. Tullius, B. i. 4 ; D. i. 4 ; E. xvi. 12
Clarus, Septicius, E. xxii.
Claudius Ariston, C. v. 3
Claudius Caesar, A. i. 7, 9 ; B. xxii. 3

INDEX

WORDS AND PHRASES REFERRED TO AND EXPLAINED IN THE NOTES.

———◦⋄◦———

ACERBUS = premature, B. xv. 4 ; E.
ix. 6
Achaia, province of, A. xviii. 2 ;
E. iv. 2
acroama, C. v. 13
actor publicus, D. iii. 2
adductus, of style, B. xix. 5
adsertio, twofold meaning of, E.
xxviii. 2
advocatio, various meanings of, A.
xi. 19 ; B. iii. 11 ; B. xxiv. 2 ;
E. xxi. 2
aestuarium, exact meaning of, E.
xxvii. 2
Africa, province of, A. xi. 2
Albana villa, A. iv. 6
altus, used metaphorically, E. ix. 8
amaritudo, a rhetorical term, B.
xix. 5
amictus, proper meaning of, B.
xiv. 2
apodyterium, E. ii. 25
apotheca, E. i. 13
apsis, E. i. 8
argentum purum, antiquum, grave,
etc., E. xv. 9
armarium, E. i. 8
Arpinae chartae, B. xiii. 5
arripere, legal sense of, A. iv. 11
auditorium, B. xiv. 6
aureus, metaphorical use of, E.
xvii. 1

BASILICA, E. xxx. 3
bibliotheca, E. i. 8
buleuta, E. xxx. 5

CAEMENTUM, E. xxx. 4
caldaria, E. ii. 26
caligo = vapour, A. ii. 19

canticum, peculiar meaning of, C.
i. 13
cathedra, B. xxiv. 2
cavaedium, E. i. 5
centumviri, their legal powers, D.
xii. 8
Circenses (ludi), E. xxvi. 1
circulator = quack, E. xvii. 1
circumscriptus, a rhetorical term,
B. xiv. 3 ; B. xix. 5
citra, post-Augustan use of, A.
viii. 3
climactericus = critical, E. xvii. 4
coenatio, E. i. 10
cognoscere, cognitio, legal terms,
A. vii. 1
collectio, rhetorical meaning of, B.
xiv. 3
commentarius, B. xi. 17 ; E.
xii. 5
commodus, unusual meaning of, A.
i. 4
comperendinatio, legal term, C.
iii. 6
concio, proper meaning of, B. xix.
4
conditorium, A. ix. 5
conscientia, post-Augustan use of,
E. xvi. 8
consilium, legal sense of, D. xii. 6
constans, constantia, A. vi. 4 ;
xii. 4
consummatus, A. xv. 5
contextus, A. xiv. 13
contubernium, peculiar meaning
of, D. iv. 6
corrigere, distinguished from
'emendare,' C. iii. 9
cumulus, proper meaning of, A
viii. 6
cryptoporticus, E. i. 16

T

PRINTED BY
SPOTTISWOODE AND CO., NEW-STREET SQUARE
LONDON

www.ingramcontent.com/pod-product-compliance
Lightning Source LLC
Chambersburg PA
CBHW020507270326
41926CB00008B/771